AMERICAN MILITARY GOVERNMENT

AMERICAN MILITARY GOVERNMENT

Its Organization and Policies

By HAJO HOLBORN

GREENWOOD PRESS, PUBLISHERS
WESTPORT, CONNECTICUT

Library of Congress Cataloging in Publication Data

Holborn, Hajo, 1902-1969.
    American military government, its organization
and policies.

    Reprint of the 1947 ed. published by Infantry
Journal Press, Washington.
    Includes bibliographical references and index.
    1. Allied military government. 2. United
States--Foreign relations--1945-1953. 3. World
War, 1939-1945--Occupied territories. I. Title.
D802.A2H6 1977   940.53'38   77-23165
ISBN 0-8371-9450-4

940.5338
H723

Originally published in 1947 by Infantry Journal Press,
Washington

Reprinted in 1977 by Greenwood Press, Inc.

Library of Congress catalog card number 77-23165

ISBN 0-8371-9450-4

Printed in the United States of America

TO CONYERS READ
IN FRIENDSHIP AND GRATITUDE

By the same author

GERMANY AND TURKEY: 1878-90 (1925)

HUTTEN AND THE GERMAN REFORMATION (1936)

MOLTKE AND SCHLIEFFEN in MAKERS OF MODERN STRATEGY,
EDITED BY EDWARD MEAD EARLE (1943)

CONTENTS

FOREWORD

EVER SINCE American armed forces invaded foreign countries, liberated Allied nations from Axis domination, and assumed control of enemy countries during and after hostilities, American military government has played an important part in American foreign relations. It is now the foremost practical instrument with which we can hope to mold the present and future conditions of the occupied nations. Thus it constitutes a significant effort toward the achievement of a secure foundation of peace. American military government everywhere is exercised on behalf of the United Nations, and it has in most places taken the form of a combined Allied operation. It has therefore been a unique test of American ability for constructive leadership in international administration and in the formulation of policies designed to continue the cooperation of the Allies in the period of peace.

American military government has aroused great interest among the American people who instinctively felt that the actual policies and conduct of American foreign administration would largely determine the future attitude of foreign nations toward the United States. The American public has been unusually vocal in criticizing, condemning, *and* praising the way in which the Government and American civil affairs officers have discharged their responsibilities. Undoubtedly there has been some good advice even in some of the more violent attacks against military government. On the other hand, its critics have rarely shown a clear understanding of the organization of American military government and its general political aims within the wider framework of the over-all interests of the United States.

The overseas operations of American military government were always open to inspection by the press. But wartime conditions made it impossible to unveil its political motives and objectives to the extent necessary to appraise its individual features and actions as links in a larger chain of events. Although the curtain was lifted after the advent of VE- and VJ-days, the public has remained confused with regard to the national sources of authority and the international implications of the American administration of the occupied areas. The author hopes that his book will be found helpful by all those who want to inform themselves about the management of American military government and its general policies during and since the War. The book does not pretend to be a history of American military government during World War II. The time to write such a history has not yet arrived. It would require a detailed analysis of all military government activities in the various theaters in the light of the changing military and political conditions. It would also call for a fuller study of American foreign policy and inter-Allied relations during the War than is possible on the basis of the presently available sources. Moreover, American military government is a continuing task. It is still far from having achieved all of its aims. It is therefore still wise to reserve judgment on a good many aspects of the American administration of foreign territories.

But the story of the growth of the American military government organization and of the considerations that underlay the formulation of its policies can now be told, and its telling should contribute to a better understanding of the difficult problems with which the American administration of occupied areas has been and still is burdened. I was favored by holding a front seat from which I could watch the evolution of this great national enterprise. I also had the advantage of exchanging ideas with the directors of American military government policies since 1943 and of benefitting from discussing the operations with dozens of civil affairs officers, at the same time having access to official and unofficial reports from the occupied territories. Though I am under a great obligation to the authorities for their assistance in my historical study, the opinions expressed in the book are my own, and they should not be construed as representing the views of any Government agency.

I am most grateful to the Assistant Secretary of State, Major General John H. Hilldring, who headed the Civil Affairs Division from April 1943 to April 1946, and its present director, Major General Echols, for their active interest in my research. I appreciate particularly their permission to publish some of the key documents of American military government for the first time in this book. Many members of their staffs kindly helped me by their criticism and suggestions.

The book is dedicated to Dr. Conyers Read with whom I had the pleasure of working during the War at the Office of Strategic Services. His friendship and wise counsel have been a never failing source of strength.

Yale University   HAJO HOLBORN
New Haven, Connecticut

10 October 1946

INTRODUCTION

DURING WORLD WAR II Military Government assumed a practical role and acquired a political significance unheard of in centuries past. If in addition to military government all civil affairs, *i.e.*, army operations concerned with civilian populations overseas, are taken into consideration, it may be said that the lives of more than 300 million people in various parts of the globe were vitally affected by the civil affairs operations of the American Army. Even now, a year after VE- and VJ-days more than 150 million people live under the control of American military government or, in other words, a population much larger than that of the United States. With the early landings of combat troops civil affairs officers came ashore or even parachuted down, while civilian supplies were carried together with military supplies to the landing beaches. From 1942 to the end of 1945 the United States Army moved more than 12 million tons of supplies to liberated countries, employing three hundred seagoing vessels at the height of this movement.

The nature of modern war and politics produced civil affairs operations of the Army of such scale. It has been one of the most cruel aspects in the development of modern war that it tended to wipe out the distinction between combatants and civilians which had been built up laboriously through many centuries. At least some comfort can be derived from the observation that civilian relief and civil administration have never before loomed so large in the planning and execution of military operations as during the recent war. To be sure these civil affairs activities were undertaken to enhance the successful accomplishment of military campaigns, but they were no less motivated by the earnest desire to conduct a civilized war from which it was felt an easier path would lead to an enduring peace.

During the combat period civil affairs and military government activities assisted in winning the war, in the post-hostilities period military government plays a crucial role in securing American peace aims. Total war has changed the old pattern of peacemaking. As war today is in no way exclusively a matter of soldiers so is peacemaking not merely the concern of diplomatists. Peacemaking proceeds on a much broader front a strategic section of which is held by those who in foreign countries grapple from day to day with the problems of reconverting national societies organized for war to peaceful purposes and of sustaining ordered life amidst the unprecedented devastation and dislocation wrought by the war. Neither the problems of Germany and Austria nor of Japan and Korea could have been solved diplomatically. In all these cases not only military occupation but military government was needed to prepare the countries for an internal order which would guarantee their future stability in a peaceful international society. Foreign administration in all these countries is laying the foundation without which diplomats could not build the house of peace.

This does not mean that the technical problems of foreign administration have replaced all political and diplomatic considerations. On the contrary, the results of foreign administration have to be critically appraised chiefly in political terms. American military government should be judged in the first place by its success or failure in achieving the political objectives of the United States. This is easily forgotten by American officers in the field who wrestle with the tiresome practical problems of lower administration. But it has also often been overlooked by the Government in Washington when it failed or delayed to formulate national occupation policies, thus making it impossible for the administrators to act with determination. Public criticism of our overseas administration, though often justified and constructive, has manifested considerable disregard of the necessity to maintain a consistent line of national policy in these matters. Such unity is needed not only to insure effective operations of American administrators overseas but also to present a clear American policy in the inter-Allied councils.

American military government everywhere is exercised on behalf of the United Nations of which the United States, Great Britain, the Soviet Union, and France are the chief representatives in Europe, while in the Far East China takes the place of the fourth big power. Only in Japan are the actual operations of military government the exclusive responsibility of an American commander. In Italy the responsibility was carried by a combined Anglo-American command, in Korea by an American and Russian army which have failed so far to evolve a combined policy and organization. In Germany and Austria a quadripartite system of military administration has been adopted. American military government is, therefore, burdened with extremely heavy tasks in the development of inter-Allied relations. American military government policies have to be harmonized with those of the other powers and the application of these policies in the field has to take into account the attitudes of the officers from Allied nations.

The history of Allied military government during World War II has seen cases where the coordination of the various national policies on the highest level failed but where Allied officers working together on the solution of practical problems overseas arrived just the same at a common answer. On the other hand, there are examples of the

breakdown of policies agreed to by the statesmen, due to the divergent
national approach of those who were supposed to apply them to the
concrete issues of overseas administration. Allied military government is an unusual school of international relations requiring not only
a continuous effort to reconcile divergent political programs and
philosophies but also calling, irrespective of diversity of principles,
for practical cooperation in a common administrative enterprise. Allied
military government is the greatest test of the ability of the major
nations to find not only a *modus vivendi* but to work together as an
active team on the improvement of world conditions. Even the future
of the United Nations is largely written in the annals of the policies
and operations of Allied military government.

American overseas administration had to be created at short notice
by a country which was ill-prepared to undertake such tasks. American
democratic traditions had not favored the growth of an extensive
civil service and its strength was found almost exclusively in its attention to the administration of domestic affairs. Nothing comparable
to the colonial service of Britain and France existed in the United
States. Suddenly the Government had to select and train a large group
of American foreign administrators. No less important was the development of the machinery within the Government for the formulation of a national policy in this novel field and of offices capable of
giving steady support to the overseas operations from home. On these
arrangements the efficiency of United States overseas administration
has depended. They were made under the strain of war conditions
and have since been further developed to conform to the changing
situation. It is desirable that they should be understood and discussed
by all those who wish to see American military government succeed in
its mission.

AMERICAN MILITARY GOVERNMENT

Chapter 1
Early Preparations for
American Civil Affairs Operations

AFTER GERMANY had conquered most of the European continent and Japan had extended her rule over major regions of the Asiatic mainland and the Pacific islands, it became apparent that all military campaigns of the Allies would have to be fought in territories where friendly administrations would have to be rebuilt by the invading forces. The countries were likely to be found in helpless condition, partly as a result of a long period of occupation by a ruthless enemy, partly in consequence of battle destruction. And, for example, nobody could foretell whether or not the Nazis would choose to repeat their cruel stratagem of 1940 when they used panic-stricken French civilians to clog the roads of France. At the very least, many thousands of people could be expected to be deprived of their homes and to float in the communication zone of the armies, and beyond this special group which would have to be extensively cared for, millions of other people would depend for their subsistence upon the food resources of the invading armies.

As for the Axis states themselves, it could be safely predicted as early as 1941 that they would not surrender before they were bled completely white. It was also doubtful whether the Italian and Japanese monarchies would be capable of surviving the breakdown of the war regimes of their countries, and whether they could be used by the Allies to maintain the structure of an indigenous administration. At all events, we had to be prepared to establish military government at least in certain provinces of Italy and Japan, as we did in Sicily and Okinawa and would have done in Kyushu if Japan had surrendered three months later than it did. With regard to Germany, it was always academic to discuss anything other than complete Allied administration, since it was improbable that any government in Germany supplanting the Nazis would command the support of the Germans on a national scale. Temporarily the militarists could have seized power from the Nazis, but the Allies could not have supported such a regime for a moment.

The War Department early recognized that the solution of the problems of *civilian* administration was an essential contributory prerequisite for the successful conduct of military operations overseas and that under conditions of modern mass warfare their solution called for special planning and preparation. It was also realized that the

1

Army would thus acquire a great political responsibility for executing the foreign policy of the Nation in its relation with the Allies and the enemy countries. Our political intentions in the postwar world would be judged by these nations largely in accordance with the attitude shown by American armies entering foreign countries.

The civil affairs problems of the United States Army comprised urgent military tasks and delicate issues of American foreign policy. Immediately after our forces landed on a beachhead they would need native labor to unload supplies and assist in repairing ports and lines of communication. Almost simultaneously steps would have to be taken for the maintenance of public health, nutrition, security and general administration. How many combat divisions could be carried on invasion fleets, how many combat soldiers could be kept free for combat duties after the landing, would largely depend upon the skill of American civil affairs officers in organizing these services with the help of personnel of the invaded country. A handful of these officers and a minimum of civilian supplies could make the shipment of regiments of military police unnecessary, and would also avoid strong-handed methods in dealing with civilian populations. And this big job had to be done in such a manner as not to compromise the relations of the United States and her Allies or place the peace aims of the United Nations in jeopardy.

The American Army had been acquiring experience in military government for a century.[1] * Since 1846, when the Army introduced democratic government in New Mexico, it had frequently administered control of civilian populations. Occasionally, as in 1848 in Mexico, the treatment of civilian problems contributed materially to the achievement of the military aims of the campaign. More often, however, American military government followed in the wake of military operations and had a political rather than military mission. This happened after the Civil and Spanish-American Wars and World War I. In 1918 American troops were exercising control over parts of Siberia, Dalmatia,[2] and the Rhinelands. But all these earlier experiences of the U.S. Army were dwarfed by the gigantic and enormously complex tasks posed by World War II.

The occupation of the Rhinelands had been the largest of the American military occupations of the past.[3] But in 1918 the American forces occupied but a small section of the Rhinelands, a section which had been completely untouched by war and which had experienced only mild political and social convulsions as a consequence of the collapse of monarchical institutions in Germany. German administrative

---

*Footnotes are at the end of each chapter.

services were still functioning when our occupation began, and continued to operate mainly under orders from the central German government. The American officers merely supervised the local administration of the United States zone in the light of what they conceived to be the security of the occupying forces. Without any preparations made by the Army prior to the armistice and without clear policy instructions from the American Government thereafter, the army of occupation could hardly have done more. The officers displayed considerable ingenuity in discharging their duties in a situation in which the other occupying powers, France, Belgium and Britain, followed different policies of their own, while the United States had practically no official policy. With the refusal of the United States to sign the Versailles Treaty and the Covenant, and with the split of the Anglo-French entente the American troops were left to shift for themselves. The withdrawal of the American forces from Germany in 1923 was the Dunkirk of America's European policy in the period of World War I.

The heads of the American Army in 1941 were aware of the significant role which military government operations were bound to assume in conditions of total war, both for winning the battles and the final peace. They saw that it called for a special personnel procurement and training program. Obviously the necessary personnel could not be obtained merely by commissioning American civilians who were experts in foreign administration. There were too few of them, particularly since many of those best qualified for foreign assignments were already serving in other war agencies. In consequence it was decided to select chiefly men with experience in American public administration and men technically skilled and send these men to a school of military government where they could be trained in military organization and methods, and in the political and social institutions of foreign countries. The Secretary of War approved the plan to train officers for civil affairs and liaison in December 1941 and in May 1942 the School of Military Government began operating in Charlottesville, Virginia.

Its students were men of some accomplishment in such public service as local and state government, judicial work or law enforcement, public health, transportation, education. The School of Military Government aimed at equipping these men with the knowledge that would enable them to use their special skill effectively as members of a military team in foreign countries. The curriculum of the School was designed to acquaint its students with the general and staff organization of the Army, military law and liaison and equip them with knowledge of foreign regions. The program was greatly expanded in 1943 when a number of supplementary civil affairs training schools were established in American universities.[4]

The School of Military Government at Charlottesville and the ensuing civil affairs training program was sometimes called unofficially the school for American *Gauleiters*. This label was entirely misleading. It is unnecessary to point out that the Army never contemplated the imitation of Nazi methods, and that the School did not even propose to turn out political leaders. The direction of military government was rightly judged a responsibility of the military commander in the field to be carried out in conformity with the instructions of the Commander in Chief. The School of Military Government endeavored to produce versatile military administrators who would be competent to rebuild vital services in foreign countries and to translate future policies of the United States into workable plans of administration. It was not forgotten that at a later date, presumably when fighting drew to a close, this group of technicians would have to be strengthened by the use of highly experienced specialists from U.S. Government departments as well as from trade, industry, and the professions, many of them serving during the War in the armed forces in positions of greater urgency.

The civil affairs training program was thus distinctly limited to the more immediate practical tasks. The people of the United States have no idea even yet how difficult and tedious these assignments were and how much practical sense combined with theoretical knowledge they required. Considering the brief span of training time available, it may nevertheless be said that this new venture in the history of American education achieved good results. The enthusiasm with which students and instructors set to work created for the first time a large and well disciplined corps of United States foreign administrators, men who could be relied upon to execute American policies abroad with a fair amount of effective competence even under most trying conditions.

The scheme for the training of civil affairs officers could have gained by greater emphasis upon political education. Though it was certainly wise to discourage the belief that civil affairs officers would have to decide policies, it would have been theoretically desirable to acquaint them with the American policies likely to be accepted. However, the dearth of policy thinking in 1942, or even 1943, made such instruction impossible. Not even the grand strategy of the War was settled. Was the North African expedition to be followed by a general attack against the "soft underbelly of Europe," *i.e.*, Sicily, Italy, the Balkans and the Danube region? Or to take examples from the Far East, would southeastern Asia or perhaps Formosa become areas of American operations? Not even the Joint Chiefs of Staff knew the answers to these questions, since their final decisions depended on circumstances which were not clearly foreseeable. Would the Russian front hold, would China cease to be a major factor in the war, would American war production and mobilization meet the goals originally set? These were only a few of the grave uncertainties which beset the planners of American strategy after Pearl Harbor. The United States did not hold the strategic initiative for a long time. It was, therefore, impossible to concentrate the military preparations, including civil affairs training, exclusively on those regions to which American troops were finally committed.

While the fog of war naturally impeded the planners of Allied strategy, Allied peace policies were shrouded in political cloud banks. The greatest single question was the future of the relations between the Western powers and Russia. In 1941 the strongest tie between them was their common determination to defeat Hitler. There was no positive program about future peace and cooperation. Whether understanding would grow and lead to joint political action hinged upon the speed and effectiveness of our military operations against Germany. A long-range program of American-Russian cooperation could only be framed once it became clear to what extent the isolationism of either country or both would melt under the impact of the war. Only time could tell whether both countries would turn toward international cooperation or to a nationalist policy of worldwide intervention.

In 1942 or even in 1943 it was too early to expect the formulation of concrete American and Allied peace policies. They had to be evolved step by step as the fighting on all fronts, first slowly, then at a faster rate, merged into the concentric final campaigns against the Axis powers, and as popular sentiment in the Allied countries displayed a firmer direction. The directors of the civil affairs training could hardly be criticized for passing over the major American policy issues in their program of instruction. They could only hope that at the proper moment American military government would receive adequate guidance and the support of both a unified government and public.

FOOTNOTES, CHAPTER 1

[1]The experience has been summarized by R. H. Gabriel in his valuable articles "American Experiences with Military Government," *American Political Science Review*, Vol. XXXVII (1943), pp. 417-438 and "American Experience with Military Government," *American Historical Review*, Vol. XLIX (1944), pp. 630-644. Cf. also the suggestive article by A. Vagts, "Military Command and Military Government," *Political Science Quarterly*, Vol. LIX, (1944), pp. 248-263. However, the last section of the article dealing with the existing organization of civil affairs in the American Army was already outdated at the time of publication.

[2]See W. S. Graves, *America's Siberian Adventure*, New York, 1931. A. C. Davidonis, "American Naval Missions in the Adriatic, 1918-21," *U. S. Naval Institute Proceedings*, January 1945.

[3]The chief source for the American administration is the so-called "Hunt Report": American Military Government of Occupied Germany, 1918-20, (Report of the Officer in Charge of Civil Affairs, Third Army and American Forces in Germany), mimeographed edition in 4 vols., Coblenz, 1920; the first volume printed, Washington, 1943. A good critical monograph by E. Fraenkel, *Military Occupation and the Rule of Law*, (Occupation Government in the Rhinelands, 1918-1923), New York, 1944, contains a full bibliography.

[4]See C. S. Hyneman, "The Army's Civil Affairs Training Program," *American Political Science Review*, Vol. XXXVIII (1944), pp. 342ff. The U. S. Navy established its School of Military Government at Columbia University in 1942 and maintained in 1943/44 a regional training school at Princeton University. Cf. S. C. Wallace, "The Naval School of Military Government and Administration," *Annals of the American Academy of Political and Social Science*, Vol. CCXXXI (1944), pp. 29ff.

Chapter 2
The Organization of
Civil Affairs Operations and Policies

WHEN, in November 1942, American and British troops landed in French North Africa it was hoped that the French would be able to carry the burden of civilian administration. This hope was realized, though it finally entailed recognition of Admiral Darlan. Although the Allied policy of liberation thus got off to a bad start, it remains true that any French regime was preferable to an imposed foreign government. Besides, the Allies were militarily weak and ill-prepared to establish a large-scale administrative system.

Even with the French running the internal affairs of North Africa, General Eisenhower was faced with a host of civilian problems. The North African territories, already suffering from scarcities as a consequence of the German occupation of France, were suddenly cut off from all supplies while serving as a base for large masses of troops. They needed Allied assistance which the Army by itself was not equipped to administer. Both British and American civilian agencies were asked to provide help. But it became apparent that practically all these agencies followed a departmental rather than well integrated national line of policy. In the economic field, the Lend-Lease Administration approached the problems differently from the Board of Economic Warfare and, again, from the Office of Foreign Relief and Rehabilitation Operations. The military commander who was preparing the Tunisian and Sicilian campaigns was forced to turn much of his energy toward unifying the aims of the civilian agencies and harmonizing them with the interests of the Allied Expeditionary Force. This proved a heavy burden on General Eisenhower, and the results of all his efforts were not gratifying since a full integration of many policies could have been achieved only in Washington and London and was beyond the reach of the theater of operations. The difficult North African experiences actually demanded a better organization both within the central Government at home and in the theater.

The first step in this direction was taken by the establishment of the Civil Affairs Division of the War Department. Up to that time the only higher military agency concerned exclusively with civil affairs had been the Military Government Division of the Office of the Provost Marshal General, who in turn was under the Commanding General of the Services of Supply or as they were called after March 13, 1943,

Army Service Forces. The Military Government Division was administering the training and procurement program of civil affairs personnel. But this agency was not equipped or placed to represent the War Department in the negotiations with other departments of the Government about common policies of foreign administration nor to coordinate these policies with the military strategy of the war. These were clearly functions of the Chief of Staff and of the Secretary of War. The Secretary's order of March 1, 1943 established a Civil Affairs Division with "primary function to inform and advise the Secretary of War in regard to all matters within the purview of the War Department, other than those of a strictly military nature, in areas occupied as a result of military operations." Thus civil affairs received representation on the highest staff and War Department level. Now the Army could plan its civil affairs in consultation with military and civilian agencies.

Major General John H. Hilldring assumed his duties as the director of the Civil Affairs Division on April 17, 1943 and remained in this position for three years until April 18, 1946, when he was appointed Assistant Secretary of State, in charge of American occupation policies. When he undertook the organization of the Civil Affairs Division D-day of Operation Husky was imminent. In the few remaining weeks before the invasion of Sicily the foundations had to be laid for well integrated civil affairs and military government procedures. The Joint Chiefs of Staff designated the Civil Affairs Division of the War Department as the agency to plan the handling of civil affairs in almost all territories about to be occupied and to coordinate the activities of civilian agencies in the United States in the administration of occupied territories. But it was anticipated that naval forces would occupy small areas in which civil affairs would be of minor significance. In such cases civil affairs would be handled by the Navy. Assuming, however, that military occupation would be as a rule by joint forces, and that the Navy had a special interest in certain aspects of civil administration, close cooperation and consultation between the Civil Affairs Division and the Navy were recommended. The Navy established for this purpose the office for Occupied Areas in the Office of the Chief of Naval Operations which, after the first island occupations, was renamed Military Government Section. The Army and Navy offices worked closely together in all general operations, the Navy being in charge of military government in the Pacific islands. But even in such places as Italy, Germany and Japan, the Navy would assist in military government in various ways, such as control of ports, waterways, merchant shipping, fishing, etc., under the authority of the Supreme Allied Commander.

The joint action of the United States Army and Navy, however, was only a first move. From June 1943 to June 1945 all civil affairs operations were conducted not by American, but by Anglo-American armies, supported by smaller inter-Allied forces. To achieve coordination of British and American policies, the Combined Civil Affairs Committee (CCAC) was established under the Combined Chiefs of Staff. This committee, which was convened in Washington, consisted of members from the British Staff Mission and Embassy and the War, Navy and State Departments. All major civil affairs plans for theaters under combined command were first formulated in this committee. The military government in Italy, the management of civil affairs in France, Belgium, the Netherlands, Denmark, and Norway, as well as the preparations for the military government of Germany and Austria in the period of hostilities, were handled on the combined level. With the dissolution of Eisenhower's Supreme Headquarters (SHAEF) at the end of June 1945, and with military government operations in the Mediterranean Theater subsiding, the Combined Civil Affairs Committee lost its significance. Coordination of Allied policies in military government matters proceeds nowadays chiefly through other inter-Allied agencies.

The Combined Civil Affairs Committee was a coordinating committee for American and British policies. On the American side it was the responsibility of the Civil Affairs Division of the War Department to develop these policies in consultation with the proper Departments of the Government and translate them into plans suitable to the military conditions of the theaters of operations. General policies would usually be worked out by the War, Navy and State Departments and often by the Treasury also. The President, constantly kept informed, made many of the major decisions himself. He took up those matters with the Prime Minister on which the Combined Civil Affairs Committee failed to reach an agreement. The second Quebec Conference of September 1944 was particularly important for the discussion of military government plans between President Roosevelt and Prime Minister Churchill. For matters of more technical nature, special *ad hoc* committees were formed under the auspices of the War Department. In this manner a full integration of departmental policies into a single national policy with regard to civil affairs operations was finally achieved and then, through the Combined Civil Affairs Committee, harmonized with British policies. The commander in the field received clear ideas about the national or Allied policies which he was supposed to execute and he knew what agencies he could turn to for further advice if a new situation arose.

While high political issues were settled through this machinery, the War Department performed a large variety of other duties in support of civil affairs and military government operations overseas. The Civil Affairs Division was charged with the procurement and training of civil affairs personnel. It had to assume the responsibility for planning programs of supplies for the civilian populations of occupied areas, about which more will be said in the next chapter. Another important function was to assist the theater commander by the transmission of intelligence relevant to civil affairs operations. Information on the political, economic, and social conditions of countries to be invaded could not be collected in the field nor evaluated there with a view to post-hostilities policies. The Research and Analysis Branch of the Office of Strategic Services served as the major intelligence agency in the civil affairs field, but other offices, especially the Foreign Economic Administration, made important contributions. An Editorial Committee on Civil Affairs Studies was created by the Secretary of War in November 1943 to provide political guidance and integrate the research with the planning of future operations and with the practical needs of civil affairs staffs in the field.

In the Mediterranean Theater General Eisenhower created his Military Government Section for the Sicilian operation, which proved so successful that it became soon a full-fledged general staff division (G-5). The chief of the military government staff was in charge of all civil affairs operations and military government activities in the theater and was therefore under the commander responsible for planning. The theater commander was bound by the basic directives received from Washington which were mandatory.* But these were confined to basic policies and left the theater commander great discretionary power to evolve his civil affairs operations in conformity with his general military plans. The Military Government Section, later the G-5 division, was also the staff section which coordinated the workings of civilian agencies in the theater of operations. Where, as in the Mediterranean and northwestern European theaters, the armies were combined Anglo-American forces, the G-5 division, like all other staff divisions of the Supreme Commander, were comprised of both British and American officers.

---

*Appendix I.

Chapter 3
The Relations of
Military and Civilian Agencies

WHILE THE ORGANIZATION of civil affairs and military government within the Army soon reached its general form, the scope of its operations remained in doubt. It was never questioned that in the period of actual hostilities full authority had to be vested in the Army commanders. Civil affairs officers had to be attached to division, corps and army headquarters. But once the front had advanced far enough and had left whole provinces or even larger areas behind, the operational military set-up could be changed to a regional pattern. This happened first in Sicily where, after the full occupation of the island, the Allied Military Government of Occupied Territories (AMGOT) in Palermo began to rule directly under the authority of a military governor appointed by the Supreme Commander.[5] Was it not preferable to have this stage of military government presided over by civilians? Or at least to have the economic and social administration turned over to civilians?

The Army was quite anxious to free itself at the earliest possible moment of its responsibilities in foreign civilian administration and loyally supported President Roosevelt's program to form a central office of foreign economic administration composed of all government agencies concerned with foreign operations. A letter from the President to the Secretary of State of June 3, 1943[6] directed the establishment of the Office for Economic Coordination (OFEC). This agency, under the direction of the Department of State and in cooperation with the War, Navy and Treasury Departments, was to bring together representatives of the Board of Economic Warfare, the Lend-Lease Administration, and the Office of Foreign Relief and Rehabilitation Operations for the purpose of developing over-all and area programs for American foreign economic policies.

Once policies and plans had been agreed upon, it was felt that a single representative of all agencies combined could direct the operations in the field. The letter of the President to Secretary Hull suggested the appointment of an OFEC director in each liberated area. The assumption was that in future the theater commander would deal with the civilian agencies only through this area director and that this director with his civilian staff would soon be able to supplant the military administration.

The scheme did not produce the expected results. The Office of

Foreign Relief and Rehabilitation Operations was in fact merely a temporary planning staff to prepare the establishment of the United Nations Relief and Rehabilitation Administration (UNRRA). It would therefore soon cease to be a U.S. organization.[7] Moreover, those who had assumed that UNRRA would not carry out services for enemy countries were, at least for the time being, proved to be correct. The UNRRA Conference at Atlantic City in November 1943 decided that its funds should be used exclusively for the relief of countries which were victims of Axis aggression. In this situation OFRRO was not equal to the other United States members of OFEC as a working partner.

But even more serious were the lack of a clear distinction between policy planning and operations and the lack of a staff of executive officers overseas. The Office of Foreign Economic Coordination was officially a part of the Department of State, but the function of the State Department is one of policy making, not of administration. Secretary Hull rightly felt that it would be unwise to clutter up the Department by building up a large administrative branch for foreign economic operations, nor would it have been possible to draft the additional personnel under the prevailing wartime conditions. The Office of Foreign Economic Coordination was dissolved by Executive Order of September 25, 1943[8] without having contributed materially to a better direction of foreign administration.

The same executive order merged the Board of Economic Warfare, the Lend-Lease Administration, and (temporarily) the Office of Foreign Relief and Rehabilitation Operations into the Office of Foreign Economic Administration (FEA) which was now charged with all civilian economic overseas operations under the policy guidance of the State Department. This consolidation of civilian agencies concerned with overseas administration helped to clarify the Washington scene. From then on American civil affairs and military government policies emerged from the cooperation of the State, War and Navy Departments. Eventually, the State-War-Navy Coordinating Committee (called SWNCC)[9] became the meeting place for this cooperation, although President Roosevelt authorized in 1945 for special purposes an Informal Policy Committee on Germany on which the Treasury and the Foreign Economic Administration were represented in addition to the other three Departments.

In spite of these developments it seemed impossible to have civilian agencies take over from the Army the administration of occupied territories at an early moment. The experiences of the year 1943 showed that such operations simply had to be planned well ahead as an integral part of an invasion campaign. Moreover, supplies for civilians were short. They were under the control of Combined Boards, which gave the Allied armed forces absolute priority. The same was true of war shipping. The Army was in a better position than the special agencies to plan civilian supplies. Since these estimates and time schedules had to be included in the plans for military operations, military security made it inadvisable to have civilian agencies execute civilian supply programs. The President, in a letter to the Secretary of War dated November 10, 1943, declared the planning of civilian relief in liberated areas and its administration for the first six months a responsibility of the War Department.

This decision of the President was the logical result of the practical experience in the course of 1943. The decision had to be made at this juncture, since the preparations for the greatest military operation of the War, the invasion of northwestern Europe, were reaching their final stage. The ruling by which the Army became officially the chief operating agency of the Government in all fields of overseas administration, both in the theaters of war and among the Departments in Washington, facilitated the planning of civil affairs, but it also added to the burdens carried by the War Department. The period of six months extended civil affairs operations further beyond combat into the post-hostilities period than had been expected earlier in 1943. However, the Army was soon to discover that the responsibility for civilian administration might in many cases remain with the Army even longer than six months, since no United States civilian agency was in a position to take over these responsibilities.

The UNRRA charter of November 9, 1943 not only excluded this United Nations organization from relief work in enemy countries but made its operations dependent on a special request from the Allied commanders in the field, and in addition, a full agreement with the rightful governments. The six months' rule made the governments of France and western Europe little inclined to request extensive assistance from UNRRA. They felt that by six months after liberation they would be able to manage their major rehabilitation problems themselves and preferred to arrange for their immediate relief needs with the Combined military authorities. They were, however, persuaded to accept the proposal that UNRRA personnel would be used by the Allied armies to assist in caring for the millions of displaced United Nations nationals in Germany and to take charge of their repatriation after hostilities ceased. The UNRRA teams were to work, however, under the Supreme Commander and the Army also retained the supply responsibilities for DPs in Germany.

But the United States Army after carrying the full burden of operating military government in Italy without civilian assistance for over a year, felt strongly that at least civilian relief activities should be taken over by a civilian agency. Against strong opposition the United States delegation induced the second UNRRA Conference at Montreal in November 1944 to authorize a limited relief program of 50 million dollars to bring food and medical supplies to Italian children and nursing mothers. In March 1945 the first UNRRA shipments arrived in Italy. It was the first modest step in turning over military government responsibilities to an Allied civilian agency.

In Greece no American troops were to participate in the occupation. Greece, to be occupied by British forces, was in extreme need of civilian supplies most of which came from the United States. Therefore, it was decided to attach a group of American officers to the British staffs, but entrust the relief operations to UNRRA. By this method relief operations in Greece could be started in the military period of the occupation.

Important as the tasks were which UNRRA pledged to undertake, they were small compared to the many different problems for which the Army itself was responsible. And these agreements with UNRRA, which were confined to certain areas or to certain functions, did not contain any promise that Allied military government administration could easily be turned over to a civilian group soon after the period of hostilities. The Foreign Economic Administration proved of great service to the Army by acting as its purchasing agent for civilian supplies. The Army began in 1944, first in Italy and then in the preparations for the American groups of the future Allied Control Councils in Berlin and Vienna, to select a growing number of civilian experts and attach them to the G-5 sections and other military government bodies overseas. Although these experts received temporary Army commissions and thus became soldiers, a greater participation of the civilian element in foreign administration was achieved. It was hoped that these men would form the nucleus of a future civilian administration that could take over from the Army without having to start from scratch.

What form such a civilian organization might take was still undefined. At least. in Italy it became clear that military administration would not be superseded by an Allied civilian administration but by the rebuilding of an indigenous Italian government and administration. But this process was slow and took much more than six months. Still, it became possible to withdraw large numbers of officers and men and to use them in other countries. But as yet Italy could hardly be considered a clear precedent for future operations. Even after in addition to southern Italy the central part of the country with Rome and Florence had been liberated in the summer of 1944, the Allied Armies continued to fight a hard and bitter war in the north. And many people, particularly among our Allies, doubted whether the new democratic government of Italy, once the Allied military government was abolished, would be able to avoid chaos and to master the turbulent situation which was likely to develop in northern Italy after the collapse of the Nazi army and its fascist puppets.

In any event, there did not emerge in 1944 an American program for the development of a civilian organization capable of taking over the responsibilities of foreign administration from the Army at a reasonably early date after the cessation of hostilities.

FOOTNOTES, CHAPTER 3

[5]See Lord Rennel of Rodd's article "Allied Military Government in Occupied Territory" in *International Affairs*, Vol. XX (1944), pp. 307-316.

[6]Text of the letter in the Department of State, *Bulletin*, Vol. VIII (1943), pp. 575ff, or *Documents on American Foreign Relations*, ed. by L. M. Goodrich and M. J. Carroll, Vol. V, pp. 675-80.

[7]For the early history of OFRRO and its part in the North African operations cf. *Documents on American Foreign Relations*, Vol. V, pp. 263-285.

[8]For the executive order 9380 see Department of State, *Bulletin*, Vol. IX, p. 205; also in *Documents on American Foreign Relations*, Vol. VI, pp. 98ff.

[9]See the NBC network broadcasts from the State, War, and Navy Departments, October 6, 1945, Department of State, *Bulletin*, Vol. XIII (1945), pp. 538-39, and the article by H. Moseley, C. McCarthy, A. F. Richardson "The State-War-Navy Coordinating Committee," Department of State, *Bulletin*, Vol. XIII (1945), pp. 745ff.

Chapter 4
Tripartite Consultation on
Italian Military Government

BEFORE OCTOBER 1943 the United States, Great Britain and the Soviet Union had not officially agreed on any concrete peace aims nor even on joint arrangements for the period that came to be called the "post-hostilities period," *i.e.,* the time between the end of hostilities and the conclusion of peace treaties. The Declaration of the United Nations of January 1, 1942[10] reaffirmed the ideals which Roosevelt and Churchill, four months earlier, had eloquently expressed in the Atlantic Charter. Beyond this the signatories pledged themselves to employ their full resources, military and economic, for the early defeat of their enemies and to cooperate with each other, and "not to make a separate armistice or peace with the enemies." The public statements made by President Roosevelt after the meeting with Prime Minister Churchill at Casablanca in January 1943[11] announced unconditional surrender as the only terms on which the United States would deal with the Axis Powers. The Soviet Union, apparently still more concerned with the immediate commitment of "all resources, economic and military" by the Western Powers, echoed this demand less vigorously.[12]

The victorious conclusion of the Tunisian and Sicilian campaigns was followed by the invasion of the Italian mainland and the announcement of the Italian surrender.[13] In accordance with the United Nations Declaration of 1942, the Russian government was kept informed about the negotiations, and General Eisenhower signed the surrender of September 3 and the additional document of September 29, 1943* "by the authority of the governments of Great Britain and of the United States and in the interests of the United Nations." But the documents of Italian surrender did not contain a viable policy of the Allies with regard to Italy. The delivery of the Italian Navy and other Allied advantages derived from the Italian surrender were important gains. But Rome and central Italy were not delivered to the Allies, and the new regime of Badoglio was so feeble that it was for some time of little value to the Allies in the administration of Sicily and the invaded parts of southern Italy. Allied military government had to concentrate upon assisting the fighting troops and attending to the most urgent needs of the Italian population. General political considerations for a while took second place.

---

*Appendix II.

The Italian surrender of September 3 contained a general clause binding Italy to comply with the political, economic and financial conditions which the Allied powers might impose in the future. In this respect the surrender was unconditional. It was implemented on September 29 by an instrument which outlined in some detail specific conditions of which a good many soon proved inapplicable owing to the events which followed the escape of the King and Badoglio from Rome. On October 13 the Italian government declared war on Germany.

In these circumstances the conditions of September 29 proved partly impractical, as General Eisenhower had already admitted in a letter to Badoglio of September 29.[14] Whereas it had been originally found that some of the conditions were beyond fulfillment on account of the weakness of the Badoglio government, there were other conditions which would have made it impossible for Italy to cooperate with the Allies against the Nazis. The enforcement of the Italian surrender in itself no longer constituted a feasible course of action. Allied military government, using the general powers it derived from the Italian surrender, had to develop its practical policies by trial and error methods. In this process the divergent attitudes of the American and British peoples, truly reflected in the sentiments of their soldiers in Italy, were not always readily harmonized. The British found it hard to forget the wounds that Italian fascism had inflicted on the Empire and displayed considerable skepticism over the revival of democratic forces in Italy. The Americans were more eager to change from the role of conquerors to that of liberators and felt more optimistic about Italian democracy, though its strength was in Rome and in the north rather than in the south. The evolution of a confident American policy and practice of administration was inevitably delayed by these perplexities of the Italian and international scenes.

The invasion of Italy was carried out by American and British armies, and plans for the military government operations in the combat period had been drafted by combined agencies. However, the first invasion of enemy territory raised the question how other members of the United Nations should cooperate in the formulation of policies preparing for the transformation from war to peace conditions. The assertion was often made that the Soviet Union resented the Anglo-American support of Badoglio. There appears no good reason for such suspicion. The Russian government, which was undoubtedly better informed about the actual conditions of Italy than the American public at that time, obviously believed that the only way to end Italian military resistance was by dealing with the King and Badoglio. Otherwise it would not be understandable why Russia participated not only in the Italian surrender but, on October 13, in the recognition of Royal Italy as a co-belligerent.[15] Nor should it be forgotten that Russia, as late as March 13, 1944, when at least the United States was ready to create a government on a broader democratic basis, took the unusual step of accrediting a diplomatic representative to the Badoglio regime.[16]

It may be assumed that Russia was anxious to be represented in Italian affairs in a form appropriate to her military contribution to the War and to the role which she was bound to play in a Europe freed of the Axis. This desire was understood in London and Washington. The broadcast which Prime Minister Churchill made on August 31 after his meeting with President Roosevelt in Quebec announced: "We shall also be very glad to associate Russian representatives with us in the political decisions which arise out of the victories the Anglo-American forces have gained in the Mediterranean."[17] There was enough common ground to achieve an understanding on Italian affairs at the first conference of the three foreign ministers, which was held in Moscow from the 19th to the 30th of October 1943.

The Moscow Declaration* did not alter the principle underlying Anglo-American policy that it would be the right of the Italian people ultimately to choose their own form of government.[18] But it did define more clearly certain negative and positive measures to stimulate the growth of Italian democracy. On the negative side this meant a strict policy of "defascization," the extirpation of all institutions and organizations created by fascism as well as the removal of all fascist elements from public life. On the other hand this policy envisaged democratic organs of local government and a strengthening of the democratic character of the Italian government by the admission of opponents of fascism. In addition freedom of speech, of religious worship, of political belief, of the press and of public meeting was to be restored and the formation of antifascist groups to be permitted.

These aims were gladly accepted by the United States Government. They had never been seriously questioned by the Americans themselves, but there had been momentary hesitation over deciding how quickly they could be put into practice in the face of the military and political situation existing in Italy. The Russians obviously understood these difficulties, for they agreed to have the Supreme Commander determine, on the basis of instructions received through the Combined Chiefs of Staff, "the time at which it is possible to give full effect to the principles set out." The right of each government to request further consultation on this matter was reserved.

*Appendix IV.

The Moscow Conference also made the first attempt to create tripartite machinery in the field of military government by establishing the Advisory Council for Italy to deal with "day to day questions, other than military operations" and to make "recommendations designed to coordinate Allied policy with regard to Italy." Thus an important pattern was created which in future was largely followed in all other countries occupied by an army under a single command. The responsibility for military government during the combat period rested with the high commander and his government or governments. The terms of surrender and subsequent non-military policies were to be discussed among the Allied governments. Allied representatives were to be attached to the Supreme Commander to advise him on political matters. However, the Supreme Commander was to retain full authority, at least in the early post-surrender period, and military considerations were to have higher priority than the speedy execution of agreed non-military policies. It was along such general lines that inter-Allied cooperation was later modeled in Rumania, Bulgaria, Hungary, and Japan. As will be seen, these principles, though considerably modified, were applied even to the military government of the Western Allies and Russia, in Germany and Austria prior to the establishment of the Allied Control Councils in Vienna and Berlin.

Some aspects of the Moscow Declaration on Italy have a significance far beyond military government. The documents of Italian surrender, as we have seen, spoke of the United States, Great Britian and the United Nations. From the Moscow Conference the United States, Great Britain and the USSR emerged as the big leaders of the United Nations. It was obvious that a place was kept open for China which signed the Moscow Declaration on General Security together with the other three powers. A representative of the French Committee of National Liberation was to be one of the four original members of the Advisory Council for Italy, and this step seemed to indicate that France was finally to join the group of big powers. But representatives of Greece and Yugoslavia were to be added only "in view of their special interests arising out of the aggressions of Fascist Italy upon their territory during the present war." Provisions for the representation of other smaller members of the United Nations were not envisaged. Clearly the scheme already foreshadowed the division of rights and responsibilities worked out on a broader scale at Dumbarton Oaks and San Francisco.

The Moscow Declaration on Italy produced a practical international frame for Allied cooperation there. On November 10, 1943 General Eisenhower announced the establishment of the Allied Control Commission for Italy to enforce the terms of surrender, to organize Italy for active participation in the war against the Nazis, and to assist the growth of democratic life. The Supreme Commander of the Mediterranean Theater, General Eisenhower (and a little later Field Marshal Sir Harold Alexander) was the President of the Allied Control Commission. Field Marshal Alexander delegated his functions to the acting president, Harold Macmillan. A chief commissioner, a position in which General MacFarlane was early succeeded by Rear Admiral Ellery Stone of the U.S. Navy, directed the work of the Allied Control Commission. In contrast to the time of the Allied Military Government of Sicily before the Italian surrender, there existed now at least the nucleus of an Italian government which, as it grew stronger, could assume the actual administration and make it possible for the civil affairs officers to confine themselves to supervisory tasks. Progress was slow in the beginning, largely owing to the long-protracted fighting in southern Italy. The conquest of Rome on June 4, 1944 and of Florence on August 22 quickened the revival of indigenous political authorities, which simultaneously became more representative of the people, though it was impossible yet to think of national elections. The Allied Control Commission could return an increasing number of functions partly or fully to the Italian government. The Allied Control Commission had no jurisdiction in the forward areas of the Army. Here full military government remained a necessity and the military government officers had to be under the command of the tactical commanders. But in January 1944 the chief commissioner of the Allied Control Commission was made at the same time the chief civil affairs officer for military government, thus making coordination of Allied policies in all occupied parts of Italy possible and further accelerating the process of reverting control from the Allies to the Italians themselves. This process was speeded up considerably after the second Quebec Conference of President Roosevelt and Prime Minister Churchill in September 1944. As an outward expression of the new policy the Allied Control Commission was renamed Allied Commission.[19]

The Advisory Council for Italy enabled Russia to get a clear impression of the actual policies of Anglo-American military government and gave the Allied Supreme Commander the benefit of a Soviet view of Italian affairs. At a time when the Polish and Yugoslav issues caused much recrimination and threatened to separate Russia and the Western powers, Italian problems never became a matter of serious argument. The Advisory Council for Italy gradually lost its significance with the appointment of diplomatic envoys to Italy and with the return of government functions to the Italian Cabinet. Its last meeting was held in Rome on September 14, 1945.

Meanwhile, the Allied Commission had begun to liquidate its functions. Its political section was dissolved as of March 1, 1945. The UNRRA Council approved at its London meeting in August 1945 an expanded program of relief for Italy in 1946, which made it possible for the Army to withdraw from the administration of civilian supplies as well.[20] The inability of the big four powers to agree among themselves on the terms of the Italian peace treaty has made it impossible to abolish the Allied Commission altogether. But the revision of the Italian armistice by the conference of the four foreign ministers in London in May 1946 has left but few functions to that Anglo-American agency.

FOOTNOTES, CHAPTER 4

[10]Department of State, *Bulletin*, Vol. VI, p. 3. Also *Documents on American Foreign Relations*, Vol. IV. p. 203, or *War and Peace Aims of the United Nations*, ed. by L. W. Holborn, p. 1, Boston, 1943.

[11]*Documents on American Foreign Relations*, Vol. V. pp. 254-55, 42-44.

[12]Most important Marshal Stalin's Order of the Day of May 1, 1943, *Documents on American Foreign Relations*, Vol. V, pp. 209-10.

[13]The surrender document was signed on September 3 and the event announced on September 8. Allied forces landed in Calabria on September 3, at Salerno on September 10. The documents of surrender were not published before November 1945. See Department of State, *Bulletin*, Vol. XIII (1945), pp. 748-765. Appendix No. II. Cf. M. H. Graham, "Two Armistices and a Surrender," *American Journal of International Law*, Vol. XL (1946), pp. 148-158.

[14]See Department of State, *Bulletin*, Vol. XIII (1945), p. 754. See Appendix No. II C.

[15]Department of State, *Bulletin*, Vol. IX, p. 253; *Documents on American Foreign Relations*, Vol. VI, p. 178.

[16]*Ibid.*, p. 173.

[17]*Ibid.*, p. 225.

[18]It would be more correct to speak of the Moscow Declarations: the three-power communiqué, the declarations on Austria, regarding Italy, on German atrocities, and the four-power declaration on general security. Department of State, *Bulletin*, Vol. IX, (1943), pp. 307ff. *Documents on American Foreign Relations*, Vol. VI, pp. 227ff.

[19]The Allied Commission has issued a report on its activities from 1943 to 1945: Allied Commission for Italy. Public Relations Branch. *A Review of Allied Military Government and of the Allied Commission in Italy. July 10, 1943, D-day Husky to May 2, 1945, German Surrender in Italy.* U. S. Army, APO 394, [Rome, 1945].

[20]See Department of State, *Bulletin*, Vol. XIII (1945), pp. 578-79; 632.

Chapter 5
Tripartite Planning
For Germany and Austria

THE THREE foreign Ministers in their meeting at Moscow provided political arrangements that enabled the civil affairs officers in Italy to work constructively and withdraw early after VE-day, but they did not settle the urgent problems of Allied military government in Germany. It may be surmised that these problems were discussed, but that it was decided further study was needed. Secretary of State Cordell Hull before Congress stated: "The Conference faced many political problems growing out of the military activities in Europe. It was foreseen that problems of common interest to our three governments will continue to arise as our joint efforts hasten the defeat of the enemy. It is impracticable for several governments to come to complete and rapid understanding on such matters through the ordinary channels of diplomatic communication. The Conference accordingly decided to set up a European Advisory Commission with its seat in London. This commission will not of itself have executive powers. Its sole function will be to advise the governments of the United States, Great Britain and the Soviet Union. It is to deal with non-military problems relating to enemy territories and with such other problems as may be referred to it by the participating governments. It will provide a useful instrument for continuing study and formulation of recommendations concerning questions connected with the termination of hostilities."[21]

The European Advisory Commission was composed of the American and Russian Ambassadors in London, Mr. Winant and Mr. Gusev, and Sir William Strang of the British Foreign Office, each of whom was accompanied by a military and naval adviser. The problems referred to the Commission were those of the German surrender and of the organization of Allied military government in Germany and Austria.[22] The Commission had for its guidance on Austria the Moscow Declaration on that country which proclaimed the intention of the three powers to restore a free and independent Austria. As for Germany, the Big Three at their Tehran Conference late in November 1943 agreed in principle that Germany was to be divided into three zones of occupation, but that there was to be in addition an inter-Allied zone to serve as the seat for an inter-Allied Commission to deal with common policies of the three Allies. This decision made it clear that Germany was not to be partitioned along the zonal lines but was still to be considered as a national unit. But to what extent Allied policies in all zones would be unified or how far Germany would be decentralized remained an open question.

The European Advisory Commission, after a preliminary meeting on December 15, 1943, held its first formal meeting on January 14, 1944. The tasks assigned to it proved more complex than had been expected. The demarcation of the German zone to be occupied by the Russian army proved relatively simple. But no agreement was reached between the British and Americans on their zones and the impasse was not solved until President Roosevelt and Prime Minister Churchill met again eight months later in Quebec in August 1944. The zonal system of occupation itself was never contested. A Combined military government staff of the type formed by the American and British in Italy could not be created on a tripartite basis. The language barrier, the contrasts in legal and administrative practices were insuperable. A fully unified Allied administration on a tripartite basis would also have required the establishment of a Combined Chiefs of Staff organization which was unattainable.

The question was raised whether it would not be preferable to have two zones, namely a Western Anglo-American and a Soviet zone, instead of three areas laid out along national lines. In this case the Combined Chiefs of Staff and the Combined command of General Eisenhower would have been continued during the post-hostilities period. The technical operational advantages of a two-zone system made General Eisenhower at times favor such a plan.[23] But inevitable as combined Anglo-American operations were in the combat phase, the continuation of this arrangement would have severely limited the freedom of American policy in Germany and Europe. From the American point of view cooperation with Soviet Russia was as important as association with Britain. In certain respects the United States had to pay even greater attention to Russia. Allied military government of Germany was to become the first practical test of the ability of the United States and Soviet Russia to work together intimately in the practical solution of a political task of the first magnitude. To the Russians the future of Germany appeared as the foremost problem of their national security. Russia's attitude to American policies in the Far East and to American-Soviet cooperation in the development of a world-wide security organization was bound to be profoundly affected by the relations which Russian and American administrators would be able to establish in discharging a common mission. It was also to be expected that British and Russian policies in Germany would not be easily harmonized and that American policy would be unable to mediate between the two powers if American military government was not separated from that of the British.

The creation of national zones in Germany was inevitable, but the coordination of the zonal administrations by the formulation of common policies remained the true political objective. For these reasons authority over Germany was to be vested in an Allied Control Council to be composed of the high commanders of the three armies of occupation. They were to meet at regular intervals and legislate on matters of common concern for all of Germany. Laws and orders for the approval by the Allied Control Council were to be prepared by the deputy military governors of the three nations, who, supported by technical staffs, were to form the Allied Coordinating Committee. The Committee was to supervise the execution of policies adopted by the Council and direct any central German agency the Council might care to revive and charge with administrative functions.

The charter for the inter-Allied control machinery which the European Advisory Commission drafted and finally accepted in May 1944 thus provided for inter-Allied agencies capable of formulating parallel and even identical administrative policies. However, the contemplated inter-Allied control machinery was likely to remain a liaison agency rather than to become an organ of cooperation if the three governments failed to reach an understanding on the fundamental aims of their German policies. Otherwise the three governors could not work together effectively. The unanimity rule which the Allied Control Council was to follow was only the logical expression of this situation. Military government is never an end in itself but merely an instrument temporarily used to realize aims of national policy. The three military chiefs, in General Eisenhower's words, were to act as the "pro-consuls" of their governments. If their consuls could not show them a common goal the pro-consuls could not hope to discover a path that would lead there.

The charter on the organization of inter-Allied control machinery could prove useful only insofar as concrete military government policies could be devised by the three powers. In a way that had been recognized by the Big Three when they assigned to the European Advisory Commission not only the preparation of inter-Allied machinery for Germany but of the terms of a German surrender as well. But it proved extremely difficult to define the scope of such a surrender document. The British were originally inclined to model the German document along the lines of the Italian surrender and to include many political and economic conditions. The Americans were no longer convinced that such specific documents were politically useful. The Italian experiences had shown that developments after the defeat of an enemy were largely unforeseeable. In Italy the continued existence of an Italian government with which the Allied commanders were to deal beyond the time of surrender led understandably to an attempt at putting political demands on paper. The German case was very different. It was very doubtful whether or not there would still be a government in being at the time of the collapse of German military resistance. In either circumstance no German government would be in a position to exercise effective control over Germany after the surrender. Military government, therefore, could not expect any advantage from maintaining a German central authority, quite apart from the fact that even temporary acceptance of a "Badoglio regime" would have compromised United States policy. But if no German government survived the surrender, no reason existed for writing the future Allied policy into the German terms of surrender. The Allied policy with regard to Germany was a subject exclusively for Allied discussion, to be made public by a proclamation of the Allied commanders at the moment when they assumed the direction of German affairs as military governors. The American approach to the negotiations favored a brief German surrender document, but hoped that the European Advisory Commission would thereafter proceed to formulate common military government policies in much the same way as the Combined Civil Affairs Committee had done for Italy.

The Russians insisted from the beginning on a document which would cover exclusively military problems. But even their draft seemed to demonstrate the difficulty of achieving agreement on the first step without at least thinking about subsequent policies. The Western Allies felt themselves bound by the Geneva Convention with regard to prisoners of war, whereas Soviet Russia was never a partner to that Convention and many hundred thousands of starved and maltreated Russian prisoners of war in Nazi hands bore witness to the complete disregard of the Geneva Convention and the most primitive rules of humanity by the Nazis. Was it under these conditions possible or even desirable to reach a common policy on the fate of all German prisoners of war for insertion in the German surrender?

The Russians indicated that they planned to use German prisoners of war as labor in the reconstruction of their devastated provinces, and this plan raised not merely a problem of international law but indirectly the whole issue of future German reparations and of their impact on the growth of a democratic Germany. Soon the members of the European Advisory Commission found themselves in deep political waters from which only the acceptance of a more modest program could eventually save them. The Commission was not organized or properly staffed to serve as a sort of preliminary peace conference. It was an advisory body charged with framing recommendations but not with making decisions for the governments. The big issues of future policy called for direct discussions among the Big Three.

It can also be doubted whether in the spring of 1944 the time was quite ripe for an agreement on an Allied long-range policy with regard to Germany. Probably none of the governments had fully thought out its future German policies. At least in England and America it was apparent in 1944 that public opinion in these countries was very uncertain and confused in its ideas about Germany, and in each country schools of thought developed which left the future trend of their national policies shrouded in doubt. It was inadvisable for either government to place the issue more clearly before the people at a time when the fighting on the greatest scale was about to begin. Public controversy might have seriously impaired popular unity, then more urgently needed than ever before.

The European Advisory Commission finally agreed on a document of German surrender which dealt almost exclusively with the disarmament of Germany. The question of the treatment of prisoners of war was side-stepped by the statement in Article 2B that they would be subject "to such conditions and directions as may be prescribed by the respective Allied representatives."* But in the political field the Germans were told in Article 13 that the three governments would assume "supreme authority with regard to Germany" and would not only take additional steps to complete the disarmament and the demilitarization of Germany in the interest of future peace and security but would "impose on Germany additional political, administrative, economic, financial, military and other requirements arising from the complete defeat of Germany." Seen in the perspective of the discussions of the European Advisory Commission these statements proclaimed the intention of the three powers to act together once the military capitulation was effected. But to define the concrete nature of such common inter-Allied policy went beyond the strength of the European Advisory Commission. The debates and conversations contributed greatly to clarification of the issues which the governments would have to solve and of the attitude in which the individual governments would approach them. In this respect the work of the European Advisory Commission helped to prepare the next conference of the Big Three which, on account of the American elections, unfortunately could not be held before February 1945.

*Appendix X.

Meanwhile the European Advisory Commission rounded out its results by drawing zonal divisions and providing inter-Allied control machinery for Austria. But here, too, no specific agreement on subsequent policies was achieved.

FOOTNOTES, CHAPTER 5

[21]Department of State, *Bulletin*, Vol. IX, pp. 341ff. *Documents on American Foreign Relations*, Vol. VI, p. 14.

[22]See the statement on the work of the European Advisory Commission in the Potsdam Declaration of August 2, 1945. Department of State, *Bulletin*, Vol. XIII (1945), pp. 753ff. Appendix No. XII, p. 196.

[23]H. C. Butcher, *My Three Years with Eisenhower*, New York, 1946, p. 699.

Chapter 6
Combined Planning for the
Northwestern European Theater

I: CIVIL AFFAIRS IN WESTERN EUROPE

AT THE time of the Tehran Conference the Allied Forces assembling on the British Isles began to reach a strength that made it possible to set a date for the Western invasion of Europe. The operation Overlord was planned for the early summer of 1944. General Eisenhower was appointed Supreme Commander of the Allied Expeditionary Force in the European Theater of Operations and arrived at his headquarters (SHAEF) in the second week of January. In the five months just prior to D-day innumerable feats had to be performed in planning actual operations as well as in creating and training the organizations which would execute the original plans. In the civil affairs and military government field these responsibilities were heavier than ever before. Many military and political considerations had to be taken into account.

The operation Overlord envisaged the invasion of France, Belgium, Luxembourg, and the Netherlands to be followed by a decisive thrust into the heart of Germany. The annihilation of the bulk of Germany's western armies and the conquest of her major industrial regions would, it was rightly thought, make further German resistance impossible. But it was at least possible that German forces might try to hold out in Norway and Denmark even after the surrender of the Nazi forces in Germany. Then special landings would have to be made and protracted fighting and serious devastation might have ensued in these countries. In other words, although it was clear from the outset that plans had to be made for all of Western Europe, it was hardly possible to predict of some of the planned operations whether they would take place in the combat or in the post-hostilities period and what devastation and deprivation the peoples of Western Europe might suffer before the Allies would be able to assist them.

Nobody can question the soundness of the general strategic conception of the operation Overlord. Events have clearly shown that there was no better and shorter route to the defeat of Germany. Events proved, too, that the military strength of the Western armies and their flow of supplies were barely adequate to achieve the strategic aims before German production of new weapons might have tipped the balance again, thus prolonging the sufferings of the nations of

Western Europe. Civil affairs operations had to be strictly subordinated to the paramount needs of the fighting armies. Highest priority had to be given to the restoration of lines of communication and to the use of the resources of Western Europe for the maintenance of the offensive power of the Allied armies. Assistance to the civilian population could be given only to the extent required for the maintenance of public order and health.

Apart from the unpredictable course of the actual fighting, the whole military program for the civilian population depended greatly on certain political factors not clearly foreseeable. The exiled governments of Norway, the Netherlands, Belgium, and Luxembourg and also the French Committee of National Liberation had made careful studies about the restoration of their national administrations and had prepared estimates of the civilian supplies that would be needed after the Allied invasion of the Continent. The information about economic and political conditions of the occupied countries which the exiled governments possessed was most valuable and on the whole correct. But none of their Cabinets could feel sure whether or not it would be easily accepted by the people at home, even as a temporary national government acting in the period between liberation and new elections. It was imperative to add to each Cabinet at the earliest moment men who had gained a national reputation while leading the resistance against the Nazi oppression in these countries.

Such a reorganization of governments-in-exile was greatly facilitated by the unwavering loyalty which the Norwegian and Dutch monarchs inspired among their peoples. King Leopold of Belgium, however, was a prisoner of the Germans and considered unfit by many Belgians to represent the national interest. The reform of the Belgian Cabinet was likely to face difficulties. The American and British governments were allied through the United Nations Declaration with the governments of Norway, the Netherlands, Belgium, and Luxembourg. Their only political aim was the restoration of the independence of these victims of Nazi aggression. But they had no wish to compromise that policy by an act of intervention in the internal affairs of these countries. If after the liberation the American and British governments had imposed the London cabinets upon the people, they would have laid themselves open to such accusations. On the other hand, the purpose of Allied policy would have been defeated if the exiled governments after their return had been greatly weakened by party strife, or had been otherwise incapable of exercising effective leadership. In such circumstances the chiefs of the Allied armies would have been compelled to assume control, since administrative chaos in the communication zone of the armies would have jeopardized the defeat of the Nazis and the liberation of Western Europe.

These political and military considerations caused particular concern with regard to France. Militarily the liberation of France was the immediate strategic objective of the invasion of Europe and France was to furnish the major bases for the offensive into Germany. Moreover, French divisions were to participate in the fight and it was to be expected that the contributions of France in the use of her manpower and her other resources would carry great weight in the final phase of the war. From a political point of view the abstention from any interference with the democratic wishes of the French people was even more necessary than it was in other Western European countries, since what happened in France was bound to affect the rest of Europe. It could be argued that the French Committee of National Liberation was less representative of the national sentiment than some of the exiled governments were of theirs. It was feared that the authority of the Committee might be challenged by large groups of Frenchmen and, even if strengthened by the appointment of resistance leaders, might not acquire a truly democratic position. General de Gaulle's highly personal philosophy often seemed at variance with prevalent ideas of the resistance movement about the future French policy, and it was not clear where those silent citizens of France would fit in who had been neither Vichy men nor members of the *maquis*.

The Third Republic, on the other side, was totally discredited. Not even single institutions, like the presidency, senate, or chamber of the Republic, could be used for a restoration of the French state. De Gaulle and the Committee of National Liberation had become the strongest symbol of the will to fight for the rebirth of France. Even those who were inclined to believe that France would choose to make an entirely new start in her political life were finally persuaded that the French Committee would rally the full support of the French people during the military period of the liberation. Cooperation with the Committee would not be judged to constitute an act of Anglo-American intervention in the domestic affairs of France if the way to its reorganization on a broader political basis were kept open. For this reason the two powers did not recognize the French Committee as the Provisional French Government but only decided to have their military chiefs freely cooperate with members of the French Committee for the management of civil affairs in France.

General Eisenhower consequently was authorized to sign agreements for the administration of civil affairs not only with the Norwegian, Netherlands, and Belgian governments but with the French

Committee of National Liberation as well.* The agreements followed the same general pattern.[24] Under their terms the Supreme Allied Commander held paramount power over civil administration during the period of hostilities. He was to exercise his powers in accordance with indigenous law through a national of the country appointed as civil affairs commissioner by General Eisenhower. The Supreme Commander could determine how far the successful prosecution of the war required the use of his full powers and at what time military conditions would permit the return of these powers to the governments.

The agreements on the administration of civil affairs in the liberated countries of Western Europe proved highly successful. It never became necessary for the Supreme Allied Commander to invoke his full powers. The indigenous civilian administrations of the different countries were cooperating cheerfully and effectively. As early as October 24, 1944 most of France was declared a "zone of the interior," which restored practically complete control to the French Provisional Government as the duly recognized successor to the French Committee of National Liberation. Nowhere did the agreements impede the revival of independent political life.

The only crisis arose in Belgium, where certain groups for a while seemed willing to withhold support from their own government and indicated preference for having an Allied Mission assume the responsibilities of government. However, this was a brief episode and the conduct of Allied policy was such as not to discredit the general line followed of claiming no other authority in United Nations countries than was absolutely necessary for the military defeat of the common enemy.

The main emphasis in Allied civil affairs operations could be laid upon economic matters. Exchange rates had been fixed in free negotiations with the Western European countries before D-day. If these rates were criticized later on it should not be forgotten that they did not represent decisions made by the United States but rather constituted a further demonstration of respect for the political independence of the countries concerned.

The import of civilian supplies formed another subject of long negotiations before the invasion and the chief administrative task of Allied civil affairs officers for the year thereafter. Shipping was the main factor limiting the amount of relief goods to be brought to the liberated areas. Military and civilian supplies keenly competed for available shipping space and, as later events showed, the volume of military supplies needed in the battles of Northwestern Europe

*Appendix VI.

was rather underestimated than exaggerated by the Allied chiefs of supply. Fortunately certain high priority needs of the Army would in due time serve the civilian population as well. Particularly did the rehabilitation of transportation, railroads, roads, bridges, and ports, for which Allied military personnel and imported supplies were freely employed, benefit the civilian population. Projects for the restoration of selected industries in order to get production of greatly needed commodities started and thus relieve the strain on shipping were another contribution to the first recovery of economic life in Western Europe.

As far as military programs of highest priority permitted, plans for the import of civilian supplies were made and the promises contained in these plans were kept, though there were delays in delivery as a consequence of the continuing German occupation of a number of French ports and the serious destruction of others like Le Havre and Rouen. These delays were aggravated by the devastation of railroad and highway bridges in the interior of France which made distribution of the goods by the French government extremely difficult. The winter of 1944-45 was a bleak winter all over Western Europe, but the Allied armies not only did battle with the Germans but fought successfully starvation, hunger, and epidemics among the peoples of the liberated countries, and laid the foundations for a revival of economic and political life in Western Europe.

The direction of this task was in the hands of Allied Military Missions which had been set up well before D-day so that they were able to prepare their plans in conversations with the military missions which the Western European governments and the French Committee maintained at SHAEF. After the invasion of the Continent the Allied Military Missions accompanied the governments to their capitals. With the early establishment of embassies political relations were returned to civilians, but the administration of supply programs* remained an Army responsibility up to the early fall of 1945.[25]

II: MILITARY GOVERNMENT OF GERMANY

The planning for the administration of civil affairs in Western Europe was the first great problem that had to be solved between London and Washington before D-day. But it was equally important that plans and personnel would be ready for setting up military government in Germany. Nobody could, or even cared to, predict on what date Allied armies would enter Germany. Actually the First U. S. Army crossed the German frontier on September 11, 1944 (D plus

*Appendix XX.

96). But the forward march of the Allied armies came to a standstill soon afterward in front of the Siegfried Line and only small areas of Germany were occupied prior to March 1945. Of course, events might have turned out differently if the Allied forces could have maintained their thrust towards the Rhine and Ruhr beyond September or if German resistance, possibly as a result of the Goerdeler conspiracy of July, had collapsed earlier.

In any event, the plans and organization for the military government of Germany had to be generally completed well before D-day, thus allowing time to acquaint officers and men with their mission. Ideally, directives for the military government of Germany should have been issued to the Supreme Allied Commander early in 1944 to enable SHAEF to prepare its more detailed plans and procure and train the personnel required. However, in the first months of 1944 it was still hoped that the European Advisory Commission would at an early moment finish the subjects which the Big Three had assigned to it and would be able to enter upon a discussion of common occupation policies. But it soon became clear that the European Advisory Commission would not produce more than the organization charter of the Allied Control Council, an agreement on zonal divisions, and a document of German surrender. Hope for coordination of the principles of Anglo-American and Russian military government policies prior to the surrender of Germany had to be abandoned. Thus plans for the military government of Germany during the period of hostilities had to be made on a combined Anglo-American level. On April 28, 1944 the Combined Chiefs of Staff sent to General Eisenhower directives for the military government of Germany "prior to defeat or surrender." *

This delay had some unfortunate consequences. It was understandable that the policy-makers hesitated to act before international developments could be more clearly judged. But SHAEF could not afford to postpone the start of its complex job of planning and organizing all its operations of which military government was an integral part. In the absence of directives from Washington, G-5 of SHAEF was compelled to formulate its own plans and use them as the basis for its operational instructions on the military government of Germany. But expecting final orders from Washington with regard to general policies, and not knowing whether these official directives from the Combined Chiefs of Staff would be fully identical with their own tentative policy assumptions, the members of SHAEF were rather cautious in the political indoctrination of the military government officers then

*Appendix V.

assembling in England. The last opportunity for giving the officers a clear political orientation was largely lost.

As a matter of fact, the early draft plans for the military government of Germany prepared by G-5, SHAEF, and embodied in the so-called SHAEF Handbook for Military Government in Germany, differed in certain respects from the Combined Chiefs of Staff directives of April 28, 1944. This was not surprising. The April directives could take advantage of the work done by various government agencies which had helped to crystallize political thinking with regard to the treatment of Germany. Some problems could be more clearly judged in Washington than in London. For example the question of civilian supplies for Germany depended largely on the programs for Western Europe which were under discussion at the same time, and they in turn had to be decided in the light of available world supplies and worldwide Allied shipping needs. In all these discussions which preceded the official directives of the Combined Chiefs, the opinions presented by individuals and agencies were colored, consciously or unconsciously, by conceptions about the ultimate policy of the United States and her Allies with regard to the final treatment of Germany. But the material conditions under which Allied military government was to operate in the pre-surrender period introduced a useful brake on an exaggeration of the political approach.

The Allied armies were to enter a country in a state of utter devastation. The first and major aim of the military government officers was to support the Allied troops by restoring lines of communication, by discovering German resources useful to the Allied war effort, maintaining public safety, taking measures against epidemics, etc. High priority had also to be given to lending immediate assistance to United Nations nationals, of whom more than six millions were expected to be encountered in the Western zone of Germany. In addition, property of the Allies or of the United Nations held or robbed by the Nazis was to be taken in custody.

These by themselves were staggering tasks for the relatively small group of 7,500 officers and enlisted men available for the U. S. military government of Germany. It was entirely unrealistic to expect that military government in the pre-surrender period would be capable of creating a Germany in accordance with any ambitious plan. However, it was important that mere exigency did not become a naïve excuse for a thoughtlessness which could have frustrated what Allied fighting men were to gain by their exertions. On the one side there was a constant danger that military government might aim at creating order and normalcy to a degree that could be purchased only by neglect of a political purge of German officialdom in disregard of other vital interests of the United Nations. On the other side, it was beyond the physical power of Allied military government to sweep out every Nazi and impose a democratic pattern upon Germany in the pre-defeat period. This policy would also have been incompatible with one of full assistance to the fighting troops.

A practical program of military government prior to the surrender of Germany had to concentrate on those measures which could directly benefit the Allied troops and alleviate the plight of the Allied prisoners of war and the slave laborers from the United Nations. The actions of Allied military government in the first period had also to demonstrate as clearly as possible to the German people and to the world the general political intentions of the Allied powers, but it was sufficient to take only key measures, leaving a full implementation and elaboration to the post-surrender period.

From this it followed that it could not be the function of Allied military government prior to the defeat of the enemy to assume the responsibility for the direction of German economic life. As a rule its actual management was to be left in German hands. Allied supervision, however, was to achieve certain immediate results by making available German resources for the support of military operations and the assistance of the displaced persons of the United Nations. For this special purpose even the rehabiliation of suitable industrial installations was permissible. In addition military government was to see to it that the Germans would husband their food stocks and supplies and would make every effort at maintaining a subsistence economy. Such a limited program included all agrarian production and related industries, the production of fertilizers, of all kinds of fuel, soap, and medical goods. Even this required in practice the maintenance and at times the restoration of the administrative controls which the Nazis had built up in their war economy. These controls, like price control and rationing, had already grown shaky under the impact of the Allied bombing offensive from the air; land warfare and the disappearance of central German agencies was bound to shatter them badly. It was highly doubtful to what extent they could be made effective again on a mere local and regional basis, but it seemed worthwhile to have the Germans try to maintain their bare necessities of life.

It was hoped that this policy would not only be useful to the Allies during the hostilities period by relieving military government officers of additional work, but would also avoid the necessity of importing relief goods at a later date. For the first period it was decided to import no food or other civilian supplies at all. It was estimated that

German food supplies were ample to carry the German people through to the fall of 1945, even if they were made responsible for the feeding of the displaced persons. There were certain unknown factors in this appraisal, since the amount of destruction and wastage during the fighting was unforeseeable. Moreover, since the Allied invasion of Germany would proceed on a regional basis, a considerable variation of local conditions could be anticipated. But German food supplies were richer than those of all the countries which had become victims of Nazi occupation, and it could be assumed that if any dangerous shortages occurred in Germany they would be only local in character and could be met by the release of army supplies. In these circumstances it would have been irresponsible to consider a civilian supply program for Germany instead of concentrating on the relief of the Nazi dominated countries which were in such dire straits.

The economic and relief policy for Germany contained in the pre-surrender directives of the Combined Chiefs of Staff was a short-term program reducing military government activities in this field to a few essential responsibilities. No power on earth could have prevented or undone the collapse of the industrial productivity of Germany. Any unnecessary intervention by the Allies would only have given the Germans a chance to switch the blame from the Nazis to the Allies. But it was desirable that the Allies should enter upon the period following the surrender with more specific ideas on a peaceful German economy.

The economic program of the Allies for the pre-defeat period was thus one of relative aloofness, with no attempt made to sketch out even briefly the future policies. But the political sections of the Combined Chiefs directives were more explicit, based on a clearer conception of the measures to be adopted at the subsequent stage. The general aim of the Allied military government, broadly stated, was the imposition of the will of the Allies upon Germany through disarmament, demilitarization, and denazification, and through positive steps looking towards the restoration and maintenance of law and order and the preservation and establishment of a civil administration.

Disarmament was, of course, chiefly a responsibility of the tactical forces and military government held only a subordinate role in its accomplishment. The term demilitarization was still used somewhat vaguely in early 1944. Its economic implications had hardly been recognized as yet. The word still implied in the first place the suppression of manifestations of nationalism in press, radio, and education, but it was applied to the capture of war criminals as well. Denazification meant the destruction of the National Socialist Party and the removal of all active Nazis and ardent Nazi sympathizers from positions of authority. The Combined Chiefs' directives ordered the complete dissolution of the Party and all its affiliated organizations by the seizure of all their offices and property and the arrest of high Party officials. Simultaneously the fundamental laws by which the Nazis had imposed their arbitrary power and introduced their discriminatory practices were to be declared void.

The main problem was how far the denazification of German public life should be carried and how speedily the program should be executed. It was obvious that the program could not be accomplished all at once, even if one excluded certain public agencies altogether in the first period. The directives ordered the closing of all German courts, schools, and universities until suitable substitutes for the Nazi judges and instructors could be found. But it was obviously impossible to do the same with general administrative offices or with technical services, like railroads and public utilities. Military considerations had to be taken into account in order to permit them to function for necessary military operations. The military commanders therefore had to be left with sufficient discretionary power to make such practical decisions. However, the directives and subsequent instructions established not merely the principle that all Nazis and ardent Nazi sympathizers should be replaced by non-Nazis but laid down very extensive categories of Nazis and other office holders whose removal, and in many cases whose detainment, was made mandatory.

The denazification policy was thus given from the outset the strongest impetus, and it was always understood that it was to gain even greater momentum once the Allies achieved full control of German affairs. The policy of denazification was the logical expression of American sentiment and interest. In order to make a third war between the United States and Germany impossible, it was necessary to exclude the chief agents of a reckless German militarism from the political scene and to promote the growth of democratic forces.

Nobody could seriously believe that these forces would be strong. They had been weak even before 1933. Twelve years of ruthless extirpation of all liberal and dissenting organizations had probably left few potential democratic leaders and administrators. It was imperative, therefore, to encourage men of good faith and conscience to step forward and acquire the experience of political office. If Allied military government had given the impression that it was not earnestly striving to destroy the Nazi forces in German life, it was improbable that the Germans could ever be induced to develop free institutions. Nor was it desirable that other nations should suspect the United States of protecting those German elements which had been the deadliest threat to all the neighbors of Germany. Such suspicion would have poisoned in particular the cooperation with Soviet Russia.

In contrast to the economic policy of the Combined Chiefs' directives, which was strictly temporary, the political policies, though calling for elaboration and intensification, looked beyond the pre-defeat period. Practical limitations imposed by hostilities and other contingencies had led its authors to be selective in stating the aims for the first period, but the political program of the directives was already conceived with a knowledge of the political objectives of the subsequent period. It rested on the assumption that the rebuilding of a German administrative structure would have to start with local offices, progressing to the regional and finally to the state or provincial level. The adoption of this slow and difficult method which the circumstances of the German collapse made inevitable had at least one possible advantage in that it would strengthen the local and regional autonomy, the absence of which had proved to work in favor of a centrally directed German expansionism. This was also one of the reasons why it was not deemed wise to think of the early appointment of a German government, though it was considered necessary to aim at the establishment of central German administrative agencies of a purely technical character, working under instructions from the Allied Control Council.

After a German administrative system had been reconstructed, the revival of German political life could be begun by inaugurating a free press and radio and by permitting democratic parties and labor unions. Ultimately elections could be held, first in the municipalities, then in the states and provinces. Together with these actions, which were estimated to require about a year, a contraction of Allied military government operations and personnel was envisaged by confining these increasingly to supervisory functions.

This was the general conception of American military government policies which underlay the directives for the prior-to-defeat period. It was not fully written into the directives, because only a start in this direction could be made during hostilities. Moreover, the policies of the post-surrender period were to be tripartite policies which consequently did not belong in *combined* directives but had to be presented as United States recommendations to tripartite agencies, such as the European Advisory Commission or the Allied Control Council. But before this could be done an economic policy had to be developed.

The second half of 1944 was largely dedicated to these problems. Russian statements and articles as well as the Russian armistice with Finland indicated that the Soviet Union would demand reparations from Germany. Other Allied nations which had been despoiled by the Nazis were considering similar claims. The moral right and the practical urgency of these demands was undeniable. The mere restoration of stolen property and machinery from Germany would make up for only an infinitely small part of the losses suffered by the countries which the Nazis had invaded, but in no conceivable conditions would Germany be capable of repairing the full damage she had caused. It was supremely important, however, that the despoiled countries should be enabled to begin the rehabilitation of their economic life without delay. Foreign loans, assuming for a moment that they had been available at all, would not have solved the problem, since in the period of worldwide reconstruction it would not be possible for any amount of money to buy the equipment needed for the full restoration of the productive capacity of any of these countries. The transfer of German machinery to the liberated areas appeared to be the only means to speed up the recovery of the devastated areas, which even then would be a problem of years.

Here new and most far-reaching political problems confronted Allied military government. It had always been a guiding principle of American planning that it would be one of the major functions of military government to assist in creating conditions which would facilitate the work of the peacemakers. But at the same time, military government planners shied away from many fundamental decisions in order not to prejudge what actions would be taken by the statesmen. However, in politics lack of action and even delay of decision often produce results comparable to those of actual moves. If a decision on reparations had been postponed not only would the recovery of the liberated Eastern and Western European countries have been gravely handicapped but also Germany might again have retained, as after 1919, her economic preponderance over the rest of Europe, which she employed to strangle the defense of the smaller nations before conquering them. With internal law and order maintained by military government, Germany, still richly endowed with industrial facilities, might have found the road towards rehabilitation easier than her former victims. A policy of mere disarmament would not meet the situation in the period prior to the peace conference. It had to be combined with a reparations policy. And only after an inter-Allied agreement on these questions had been reached was it possible to outline a policy with regard to the future peacetime economy of Germany.

The consideration of this question showed that the process of peacemaking could not be broken up into neatly defined stages according to historical precedent. The old sequence of an armistice, followed in due course by a peace conference, or possibly first by a preliminary and then a final peace, had become meaningless. Nor was it possible to draw a clear division between a military government and a diplomatic period. Military government can only function as an arm of national policy, which in the case of Germany has to be harmonized with the policies of America's Allies. Without an active national policy as basis military policy would be blocked. It has never been well enough understood by the public, or even by people professionally concerned with the conduct of foreign affairs, that American overseas administration cannot function in a political vacuum, that on the contrary it is an essential part in the very process of peacemaking.

The formulation of an economic policy for the post-surrender period brought these problems into full relief. Undoubtedly this policy could not be an interim solution. It had to be the first part of a long-term course of action. The questions involved were most complex and schools of thought existing in the government held widely differing views upon them. And the American public had not shown great interest in a concrete discussion of the German problem.[26] In the summer of 1944, while the battle of France was being fought and representatives of the big four powers met at Dumbarton Oaks, the chief interest in international affairs centered around the winning of the war and the creation of a world organization. These events, together with the presidential campaign, overshadowed any debates on the German peace. President Roosevelt, turning his attention to the planning for German military government which was on the agenda of his meeting with the British Prime Minister at Quebec, September 11-16, 1944, did not find clear and practical proposals for a United States policy with regard to Germany.

Among the suggestions then offered to the President those of the Secretary of the Treasury became known to the public by unauthorized publication in the press. The so-called "Morgenthau Plan" evoked little approving press comment, some half-hearted support, and a great deal of negative criticism. It proposed the cession of large borderlands to Russia, Poland, France and Denmark as well as the partition of Germany into three zones, one of which, a greatly and curiously expanded Ruhr region, was to be internationalized, while the two others were to form separate states. The memorandum recommended in addition the complete destruction of all heavy industries and a reagrarianization or "pastoralization" of Germany.

The Morgenthau Plan did not become, as many people including its author seemed to believe, the official United States policy after

Quebec, but the plan did make a few important contributions towards the evolution of American policy.[27] It had always been the keynote of all American planning for military government that Germany's capacity to make war should be broken. It was also recognized that the mere destruction of all military organization and armament, and the dismantling of arms factories would not achieve this result, but that the whole structure of the German heavy industries had to be attacked. But how far such intervention should go and exactly at what moment it should be undertaken was never settled. Some argued that it would be desirable to use existing German industries to produce for reparations and for the rehabilitation of Europe, a statement to which others took exception by pointing out that, irrespective of the political consequences, the restoration of German industries would be much too costly to be undertaken for a limited time only.

The "Morgenthau Plan" forced a clear decision with regard to these and other ideas which had not been clearly worked out. President Roosevelt accepted the theory that the mere disarmament of Germany would contribute little to world security if it were not accompanied by the extinction of certain German industries and, in general, by a considerable diminution of German heavy industries. This was to be achieved by a reparations policy which would emphasize the delivery of capital equipment as far as it was in excess of normal peacetime needs of German economy.

On September 28 the President directed the Foreign Economic Administrator, Mr. Crowley, to "accelerate studies from the economic standpoint of what should be done after the surrender of Germany to control its power and capacity to make war in the future."[28] While these technical studies were pursued, the Yalta Conference afforded an opportunity for gaining an impression of Russian thinking about these matters and it became then possible to outline a United States policy with regard to the military government of Germany in the initial period after the surrender, a document to be used either as a directive for the commanding general in the American zone or as an American proposal for a common inter-Allied policy to be issued by the Allied Control Council in Berlin.

The statement, known under its file number as JCS-1067*, was completed in April 1945 as the result of the deliberations of the Informal Policy Committee on Germany, a committee which was established shortly after the President's return from the Crimea and which was composed of four Assistant Secretaries of the State, Treasury, War and Navy Departments, and the Foreign Economic Admin-

*Appendix VIII.

istrator.[29] These new directives contained nothing basically new in the political field, though certain rules were tightened. The chief difference between the political sections of the pre-defeat and the post-surrender directives was not in their underlying theories but in their application. While the scope of denazification for the pre-defeat period had been limited so as to avoid adding to the immediate responsibilities of military government officers during fighting, the program was now considerably broadened. Simultaneously the mandatory character of the orders was strengthened.

The economic program was new, and it had not even been foreshadowed in the pre-surrender directives, with the possible exception of the principle that the responsibility for German economy rested with the Germans and that military government would assist them only to fight starvation and disease. But a policy of industrial disarmament and demilitarization was now inserted, and it was definitely stated that in the initial period reparations and relief from German sources for the liberated countries would take precedence over the German standard of living. However, it also became American policy to see in "the preparation for an eventual reconstruction of German political life on a democratic basis" an essential step towards the demilitarization of Germany comparable to denazification, the apprehension of war criminals, industrial demilitarization and future international control of German industries.

FOOTNOTES, CHAPTER 6

[24]These agreements have not been published before. A State Department release of May 16, 1944, described briefly the Norwegian, Dutch, and Belgian agreements. See Department of State, *Bulletin*, Vol. X, p. 479, on the civil affairs agreement with Luxembourg, *ibid*. Vol. XI (1944), p. 125. Cf. also *Documents of American Foreign Relations*, Vol. VI, p. 698, and General Marshall's Report, *The Winning of the War in Europe and the Pacific*, p. 91. The text of the French agreement appears in Appendix No. VI.

[25]See the statistical figures given in the Appendix, No. XX. Cf. also Assistant Secretary Hilldring, "U. S. Aid in Economic Reconstruction of France," Department of State, *Bulletin*, Vol. XIV (1946), pp. 674-676. A brief description of civil affairs operations in Western Europe during the combat period is contained in the article by D. M. Gunn, "The Civil Affairs Detachment," *Military Review*, Vol. XXV (September 1945), pp. 75-78.

[26]Among the books on the German problem then available Sumner Welles' *Time for Decision*, and L. Nizer, *What To Do With Germany*, probably had reached the widest audience.

[27]Cf. Henry Morgenthau, Jr., *Germany is Our Problem*, New York, 1945.

[28]The first interim report was presented on January 10, 1945, another on April 15. During the spring and summer of 1945 thirty-two committees were formed to examine the various aspects of the German disarmament problem. These "Technical Industrial Disarmament Study" committees were staffed not only by FEA but by State, War, Navy, the Office of Strategic Services, War Production Board and other agencies. The final report of the Foreign Economic Administration was made on December 19, 1945, and presented in addition to government agencies to the Kilgore Committee of the U. S. Senate: *A Program for German Economic and Industrial Disarmament*, Final Report. Enemy Branch, Foreign Economic Administration.

[29]See V. H. Cassidy, "American Policy in Occupied Areas," Department of State *Bulletin*, Vol. XV (1946), pp. 291-296.

Chapter 7

Allied Military Government of Germany
in the Pre-Defeat Period

WHEN THE United States directives on American policies in the post-surrender period, which came to be known as JCS-1067, were first drafted during the summer of 1944, the American goverment still hoped that the European Advisory Commission would soon complete the document of German surrender, the organization charter of the Allied Control Council, and an agreement with regard to the zonal division of Germany. It was further hoped that the Commission would then enter upon a discussion of substantive policies to be executed jointly by the Allied Control Council in Germany. The United States was even prepared to have the *pre-defeat* directives reviewed in the light of any decision which the European Advisory Commission might make with regard to common policies of the three powers after Germany's surrender. The preamble of the pre-defeat directives warned the Supreme Commander that modification of policies might be found necessary by the European Advisory Commission.

It was with a view to an unprejudiced tripartite agreement that JCS-1067 was not presented to the British for their concurrence. The post-surrender directives were a statement of United States policy to be presented simultaneously to the British and Russians. However, the European Advisory Commission never took up the discussion of substantive policies. After the Quebec meeting of President Roosevelt and Prime Minister Churchill in September 1944, the Commission finally agreed on the delineation of occupation zones in Germany. Subsequently the Commission turned its attention mainly to the Austrian problem, though it was called back to the consideration of German zones once more after the Crimea Conference of February 1945, when the addition of France to the Allied Control Council made it necessary to devise French zones in Germany and Austria.

A solution of this question was achieved, but with some difficulties that foreshadowed a good many future problems of Allied military government. The French displayed their desire for control of the Rhinelands which under the earlier agreement had been assigned to Britain, and in general they showed their displeasure with the results of the Crimean Conference to which they had not been invited. The tension was temporarily resolved by the willingness of the United States and Britain to cede parts of their zones to the French. France received what actually amounted to two zones, the one between and around the Moselle and central Rhine, chiefly composed of the Saar district and the Palatinate, the other around the Upper Rhine, Black Forest, and Lake Constance, consisting of the southern parts of Baden and Württemberg. With this region France gained a bridge to Tyrol and Vorarlberg, the zone of Austria which was to be occupied by French troops.

This arrangement was a weak compromise, and an American note to the French government recognized that it should be kept open for reconsideration at a later date.[30] The agreement did not really satisfy the French, since it left the British in control of the major industries of the lower Rhine and Ruhr. At the same time it weakened the chances of an effective decentralization of Germany. If such a policy was to be launched its natural aim was the strengthening of regional sentiment, which next to that in Bavaria was strongest in the Rhinelands, Württemberg, and Baden. The original tripartite zonal system had wisely adhered to the principle that zonal boundaries should follow the old provincial and state lines in Germany. By departing from this rule the Allied administrators would become gravely handicapped in their attempts to make the regions of Germany more self-contained in their political aspirations.

The European Advisory Commission did not go beyond the discussion of the mere organizational structure of the future Allied military government of Germany. Any hope that a formal agreement on concrete policies to be executed by the Allied Control Council could be achieved through the London Commission proved to be disappointing. Nor was there much of an exchange of ideas among the Allied officers who were to form the staff of the future Allied Control Council in Berlin. In June 1944 the nucleus of what was to become the American component of the Allied Control Council, the so-called United States Group, Control Council (US,CC), began to assemble in England and started planning its operations in September. But not even on an informal basis did cooperation between the functionaries of Allied military government extend beyond Anglo-American relations.

The absence of a formal agreement on joint Allied policies for the post-surrender period, and the lack of official contacts among the Allied officers planning the technical aspects of the occupation of Germany, made it improbable that the quadripartite government of Germany could be established immediately after the day of German surrender. However, as mentioned before, the formulation of these policies called for some major decisions that could be made only on the highest level. The nature of future economic policies depended entirely on the question of German reparations. It was also obvious that the Polish question had to be settled not only because it undermined the mutual confidence of the Allies but also because it augured ill for the future Allied administration of Germany. It was unfortunate that a meeting of the Big Three could not take place before February 1945.

The Crimea Conference of February 3-11, 1945 first of all agreed on the coördination of Allied strategies for the final defeat of Nazi Germany which were revealed to the world a few weeks later, when on March 7 the Western Allies crossed the Rhine and the Russians crossed the Oder in strength. Much attention was also given to the Allied occupation of Germany. The German surrender document, the organization charter of the Allied Control Council, and the zonal division of Germany were finally approved, though with the provisos that France was to be invited to join the Council and that a French zone was to be created by the European Advisory Commission.

Still no detailed policies for the post-surrender period were agreed upon by the three statesmen, though common general aims were stated for the first time. "It is our inflexible purpose," the Report of the Crimea Conference said,* "to destroy German militarism and Nazism to ensure that Germany will never again be able to disturb the peace of the world. We are determined to disarm and disband all German armed forces; break up for all time the German General Staff that has repeatedly contrived the resurgence of German militarism; remove or destroy all German military equipment; eliminate or control all German industry that could be used for military production; bring all war criminals to just and swift punishment and exact reparations in kind for the destruction wrought by the Germans; wipe out the Nazi Party, Nazi laws, organizations and institutions, remove all Nazi and militarist influences from public office and from the cultural and economic life of the German people; and take in harmony such other measures in Germany as may be necessary to the future peace and safety of the world. It is not our purpose to destroy the people of Germany, but only when Naziism and militarism have been extirpated will there be hope for a decent life for Germans, and a place for them in the community of nations."

The Yalta Report read in its political parts like a summary of what had been written into the pre-defeat directives by the Combined Chiefs, and in its economic demands it reflected rather closely the official American thinking as it had crystallized during the last preceding months. Undoubtedly, President Roosevelt found his political philo-

---

*Appendix VII.

sophy fully expressed in the Crimean Report. However, most of the aims were only stated broadly and a great deal would depend on their practical application. What did the sentence mean—"eliminate or control all German industry that could be used for military production?" And how was the general policy of ensuring that Germany would never again be able to disturb the peace of the world to be harmonized with the promise of a decent life for the Germans in a later period? The Crimea Conference left these questions to future negotiations, but not without creating machinery for the study of the question "of the extent and methods for compensating damage caused by Germany to the Allied countries." It would have been better if the Crimea Conference could have agreed on the methods and left only the extent of the compensation to the new Allied Commission on Reparations in Moscow. But the other two powers did not accept the Russian proposal of fixing a total sum of twenty billion dollars of which one half was to go to Russia. This proposal was only passed on "for initial discussion and study" to the Reparations Commission. The Commission was thus charged not merely with an implementation of the results of the Yalta Conference but rather with a continuation of the debate, and this made it likely that the reparations question would not get out of the discussion stage till the Big Three could meet again.

Compared to the events which took place after World War I, when reparations were not discussed until after Germany had requested the conclusion of an armistice, it was a hopeful sign that the Allies of World War II were willing to attack the reparations problem before the collapse of Germany. It also became apparent at Yalta that all the Allies had learned their lesson from the financial history of the last twenty-five years and realized that large reparations in the form of money payments were impracticable. But in spite of this better understanding of international economics, a generally acceptable plan could not be drafted in a few days or even a few weeks. And as long as no agreement could be reached on this fundamental question it was idle to hope for a formal agreement on joint Allied policies in Germany. The work of the European Advisory Commission on the terms of the German surrender and the organizational structure of Allied control over Germany and Austria, together with the broad political aims stated in the Crimea Report remained the basis of Allied cooperation in the occupation of Germany.

In these circumstances it became doubtful whether the Allied Control Council would be able to assume the political direction of Allied military government immediately after the German surrender, except in name only. It became likely that after the hostilities period in which the three Western armies were under the command of General Eisenhower, while the Russians were independent in their theater of operations, there would be at least a brief interim period in which all four commanders-in-chief would have to follow their own national policies. Therefore, JCS-1067 was issued in April 1945 to General Eisenhower, not in his capacity of Supreme Commander of the Allied Expeditionary Force, but as Commanding General of the United States Forces of Occupation in Germany. However, as a member of the Allied Control Council he was supposed to urge the adoption of the policies set forth in JCS-1067 by the other occupying powers. In other words, the United States government felt that it had a definite policy which would not only serve the needs of the United States zone but should be presented to all inter-Allied bodies, such as the Control Council or a future meeting of the Big Three.

Shortly after the Yalta Conference the final phase of the European War opened and within two months the German armies were shattered and the Nazi regime wrecked. Events moved so fast that military government had no need for very detailed instructions, for they could attend only to the most urgent immediate tasks. However, the future was not altogether forgotten. Every effort was made to maintain agricultural production even in the period of fighting, with the result that eighty-five per cent of the arable land in the American zone was under cultivation at VE-day, although the furor of modern machine war had passed over it in the crucial months of spring. Not only the rapidity of movement but the wide spread of the American troops made intensive military government operations difficult. The American troops went as far north as Wismar on the Baltic coast, occupied the Saar, the Palatinate, most of the Rhinelands, Westphalia, Hannover, all of the provinces of Saxony and Thuringia, and the major part of the State of Saxony. In addition to the American zone, the Americans occupied one half of the French and Russian zones and probably up to two-thirds of the British zone.

American military government officers were consequently spread very thin over the map of Germany. However, the early termination of fighting made it possible to assign men from the combat forces to military government duty, and the number of officers and enlisted men serving in the United States military government was almost doubled by two months after VE-day. Even more important, the surrender made it possible to use army transport to help in the execution of certain major functions. The greatest achievement in this respect was the location and speedy repatriation of United Nations and neutral displaced persons. Six and a half million of them were found in the SHAEF zone and four million were repatriated within a three-month period, a unique achievement in the movement of populations. The original plan had assigned to military government personnel chiefly the location and care of DPs during the battle period, while the administration of assembly centers in the rear zone of the Army was to be taken over more and more by UNRRA personnel, which also was to provide certain specialized services. But with events moving so fast the UNRRA teams came into it rather late.[31] The Army deserves credit for solving two-thirds of this extremely difficult problem. On the other hand, even with the numbers of DPs substantially reduced, the members of UNRRA found a big task. They were confronted with the hard core of the problem—chiefly with those displaced persons who for one reason or another did not choose to be repatriated. UNRRA, working under the authority of military government, had to concentrate on the DP camps in the United States, United Kingdom, and French zones rather than on repatriation.

The months of May and June 1945 were months of feverish redeployment. It would have been unfeasible to withdraw all those American troops in the areas assigned to the zones of the other three powers and assemble them in the American zone before their departure to the United States and to the Far East. This would have delayed redeployment. Moreover, the small American zone would not have been capable of holding the mass of American soldiers. In addition to the transfer of low-point men from divisions earmarked for demobilization to divisions remaining in Europe or going to the Far East, the reverse process involving high-point men was going on. The administration of army affairs was never more perplexing than in these months and transportation in Germany was heavily taxed. Furthermore, the sudden dissolution of SHAEF would have been most embarrassing to the British who relied so greatly on the supply services of SHAEF which the British could not replace by their own at short notice. The British zone, including the Ruhr and other highly urbanized regions, was always dependent on imports from other regions for its sustenance. The British, who had to cut the rations of their own people after VE-day, were understandably concerned about a sudden shift.

At the same time United States military government operations assumed a new place in the Army. During the battle period the military government officers were attached and under the command of the tactical commanders.[32] In the case of SHAEF General Eisenhower had delegated his authority as military governor to the commanding generals of the Army groups, retaining only the making of certain major decisions and, of course, general supervision. However, the actual direction of military government operations did not rest with SHAEF nor with the Army groups but with the individual armies, and it could be doubted whether even they exercised any great control over the operations from March to May 1945.

The breakdown of all means of civilian transportation and communication in Germany was complete and left the military government officer isolated in the precincts of the town and city which happened to come under his charge.[33] The rapid movement of the armies and the extension of American operations beyond the American zone played havoc with the original plan of training and "pin-pointing" the individual military government teams for certain districts. The individual officer found himself often enough in a region unknown to him by preparatory study and struggling with local conditions which had to be settled by expediency rather than by principle. These were the days in which any central direction of military government operations could hardly be attempted and the officer in the field had to find his own solutions. The natural result was considerable divergence of policies which was only slowly overcome after VE-day.

Little was gained in the beginning by making the American military districts conform to the German regional system. For the German administrative agencies had ceased functioning and the appointment of district and provincial German officers did not mean much as long as they were physically unable to move within their districts. Nor did the stronger interest of the army commanders in military government, shown after the end of hostilities, always contribute to making American military government practices uniform throughout the American zone. The subordination of military government under the tactical commanders was necessary in the combat period, but undesirable thereafter. Once the German armed forces had been completely disbanded and the army of occupation had been securely established, the command and staff channels of military government had to be separated step by step from the general chain of command in the Army.

The appointment of Lieutenant General Lucius D. Clay as Deputy Commander of the United States Forces in the European Theater indicated the significance which military government assumed in the post-surrender period. General Clay was to act as the chief of the United States Group of the Control Council, while at the American headquarters in Frankfurt the Office of Military Government in the American Zone (OMGUS) was created which in due course was to assume direct control of all operations in the American zone.

In thus inaugurating a separation of military government from military occupation duties the eventual transfer of the German administration to civilian officers was prepared. The Army, both in the Theater and in Washington, never lost sight of this ultimate aim. On the contrary, it did everything in its power to press for an early transfer of its governmental duties to civil authority. General Eisenhower hoped that the Army could be relieved of its governmental responsibility in Germany by June 1, 1946.[34] In order to facilitate the change the Army strove to give qualified civilians an opportunity for gaining experience in overseas administration. The United States Group, Control Council, contained from its early beginning a large number of civilian experts who received temporary army commissions, and the same practice was adopted in staffing the Office of Military Government in the American zone.

The two months after VE-day saw the Army staffs busy with a great host of the most complex and delicate administrative problems. Overseas redeployment, relocation, and reorganization of the troops earmarked for further duty in Europe, demobilization, together with the care for millions of displaced persons and the handling of millions of prisoners of war constituted the major tasks which had to be performed. In the last days of June 1945 the huge organization of SHAEF was officially dissolved and though naturally a few combined committees remained for a while in existence to liquidate all combined commitments, the three Western Powers established separate headquarters in Frankfurt, Herford, and Baden-Baden.

At about the same time that part of the Soviet zone which was occupied by troops under General Eisenhower's command was turned over to the Russians. A little later American, British, and French troops proceeded to Berlin to take possession of their zones and establish, together with the Russians, the local allied military government under the so-called *Kommandatura*. On July 4, 1945, the American flag was hoisted in the presence of General Bradley in the southwestern section of Berlin. With this act the zonal occupation of Germany became complete and the zonal administrations could begin their work.[35] The question remained whether the inter-Allied agencies would prove capable of developing common policies and of assuming more than a nominal direction of the military government of Germany.

FOOTNOTES, CHAPTER 7

[30]See Department of State, *Bulletin,* Vol. XIII, 1945, p. 276.

[31]For Army operations in the early period see the report on "Displaced Persons in Germany, Present Operations," Department of State, *Bulletin,* Vol. XII, 1945, pp. 1014-1016. On UNRRA, F. K. Hoehler, *Europe's Homeless Millions,* Foreign Policy Headline Series, No. 54, New York, 1946.

[32]A brief description of the organization of civil affairs operations in the Northwestern European Theater can be found in the instructive article by H. M. Pendleton "The European Civil Affairs Division," *Military Review,* Vol. XXVI, No. 1, (April 1946), pp. 49-51.

[33]The best article on the problems confronting Allied military government in the initial period comes from a well informed English author in *The World Today,* February 1946 (Royal Institute of International Affairs).

[34]See the letter from General Eisenhower to President Truman of October 26, 1945. Department of State, *Bulletin,* Vol. XIII, 1945, p. 711.

[35]See the statistical analysis of the German zones by L. A. Hoffmann, "Germany: Zones of Occupation," Department of State, *Bulletin,* Vol. XIV, 1946, pp. 599-607.

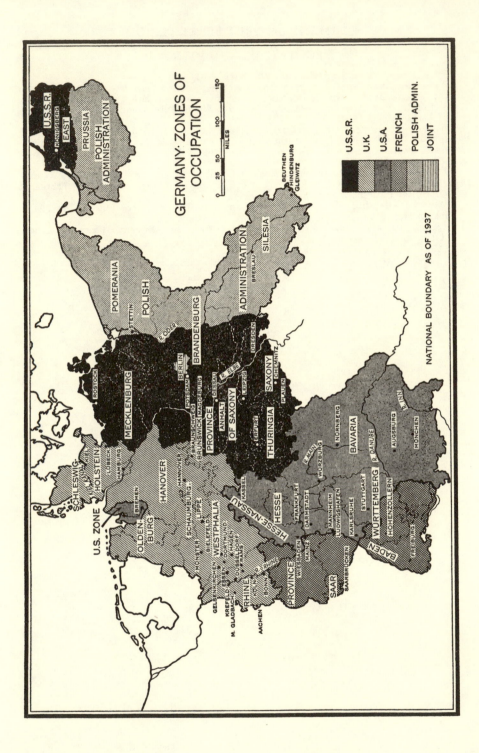

GERMANY: ZONES OF OCCUPATION

U.S.S.R.
U.K.
U.S.A.
FRENCH
POLISH ADMIN.
JOINT

0 25 50 100 150
MILES

NATIONAL BOUNDARY AS OF 1937

Chapter 8
Allied Military Government of Germany
After the Surrender

THE GERMAN SURRENDER of May 8 was a mere act of military surrender.* It was signed by representatives of the German High Command, not of the German Government. From a political point of view the most important article was the fourth which stated: "This act of military surrender is without prejudice to, and will be superseded by any general instrument of surrender imposed by, or on behalf of the United Nations and applicable to GERMANY and the German armed forces as a whole.[36] The Allies thus indicated at once that from this day on they would write the law without recognizing German political authorities. It was equally significant that the Allies stressed that theirs was a common responsibility and that future policy would have to be issued by them in concert. General Eisenhower, Marshal Zhukov, Field Marshal Montgomery, and General De Lattre de Tassigny met in Berlin on June 5 and proclaimed the assumption of "supreme authority with respect to Germany, including all the powers possessed by the German Government, the High Command and any state, municipal, or local government or authority."** They declared, however, that this assumption of power did not effect the annexation of Germany, although the governments of the United States, the Soviet Union, Britain, and France would later determine German boundaries and "the status of Germany or of any area at present being part of German territory." Under the terms of the Declaration of Berlin Germany remained a political entity whose sovereignty was temporarily exercised by a group of occupying powers. Whatever the individual powers might have in mind with regard to the eventual solution of the German problem, they occupied Germany as a group "in the interests of the United Nations" and with the intention of acting together in German affairs. The zones were not even mentioned in the Declaration and a simultaneous statement of the four governments only said that they were created "for the purposes of occupation."[37] Legally speaking, the zones were established for the convenience of Allied administration but constituted neither an annexation by individual powers nor a political partition of Germany.

The Declaration of Berlin of June 5, 1945 proved a disappointment to those who had hoped that a meeting of the military chiefs would

---

*Appendix IX.
**Appendix X.

result in the approval of substantive occupation policies. The Declaration announced only "the immediate requirements with which Germany must comply," while reserving to the Allied governments absolute power to "impose on Germany additional political, administrative, economic, financial, military, and other requirements arising from the complete defeat of Germany." The Declaration was confined almost completely to the military disarmament of Germany. The reasons for its meager political contents can be found in the history of inter-Allied negotiations which at the Yalta Conference had not led to an agreement on essential points. Only the Big Three could set the machinery of the Allied administration of Germany in motion by settling those major political issues which would determine the basic occupation policies. Their decisions* have to be judged not only in the light of European developments but of the general world situation as well which the three statesmen tried to shape.

The problems which President Truman, Prime Ministers Churchill and Attlee, and Generalissimo Stalin had to solve could be arranged in three groups. First, they had to reach agreement on the military and political strategy for the final defeat of Japan and on the general outlines of a peaceful organization of the Far East after the surrender of Japan. Second, they had to define the methods and procedures which the Allies would employ to draft peace treaties with the Axis Powers and their satellites. Third, provisions had to be made for the interim period in Europe.

It is almost exclusively with the third group of questions we have to deal in this chapter. This group included in the first place the reconstruction of democratic governments of the defeated nations. The United States and Britain pressed for access of their representatives to the Russian-occupied Hungary, Rumania, and Bulgaria, and for a broader foundation of the governments which had emerged in connection with the armistices concluded by Russia in southeastern Europe. The Italian government had long been recognized and the Italian treaty could therefore be given high priority in the process of future peacemaking.

But it was not always possible to draw a clear distinction between problems of peacemaking and those of the interim period. Particularly where a postponement would seriously hinder the rehabilitation of invaded countries any delay seemed undesirable. The problem of reparations is a case in point. An early settlement became very urgent because the recovery of the liberated areas depended on it. The Russians claimed that the drawing of a western frontier of the new Polish state

---

*Appendix XII.

was equally imperative. Since the fall of 1943 Stalin had hinted that Poland was to receive compensation for her eastern territories which Russia intended to keep by a westward expansion to the Oder. Neither the American nor the British government had ever given an indication of approving such a program. But at the Crimea Conference the matter was discussed officially and, if the amount of evasiveness displayed in the official report can be used as a yardstick, must have caused considerable uneasiness. After accepting a slightly modified "Curzon Line" as Poland's eastern boundary, the report continued: "[the three heads of government] recognize that Poland must receive substantial accessions of territory in the north and west. They feel that the opinion of the new Polish Provisional Government of National Unity should be sought in due course on the extent of these accessions and that the final delimitation of the western frontier of Poland should thereafter await the peace conference."

A close scrutiny of the Crimea Report leaves uncertainty about the exact meaning of its Polish section.[38] It cannot be denied, however, that most of the Potsdam award to Poland can be read into the Crimea Report. The American thesis that all territorial questions were to be left to the peace conference was already impaired by the Yalta Report. For there was no clear reason why the Polish government should be consulted "in due course" instead of being called to the peace conference. The American thesis that territorial questions should await the peace conference was not always practicable. Once it was admitted that Poland was to get substantial territorial accessions, it was hardly possible to postpone such a change for another two years or more till a peace with Germany could be concluded. Poland was the most cruelly devastated country, with most of her cities and many hundreds of her villages shattered. It could not be expected that she could resettle her homeless people, both her war victims and those who preferred to migrate from the parts ceded to Russia, without knowledge of her future frontiers. It would have been unrealistic to assume that with millions of Poles crying for a roof and land of their own the settlement of the German-Polish frontier could be put on ice for a considerable period of time. It would have meant the continuation of chaos in a country which had already suffered too much.

It was not surprising, therefore, that such a line was drawn at Potsdam, but it was astounding to see the maximum demand of Poland and Russia accepted. The principle that the final settlement of the border question would be left to the peace conference was expressly reaffirmed, but the whole of eastern Germany to the Oder and western Neisse, even going farther west at the Baltic coast to include the whole

Oder estuary, was turned over to Polish administration and exempted from the rule of the Allied Control Council in Berlin. The future peace conference was thereby gravely impaired in its freedom of decision, and in the interim period the Allied Control Council was made a mere servant in the execution of the Polish policy of de-Germanization. The Allied military government of rump-Germany had to find shelter, food, and homes for the many millions of Germans driven out of the areas under Polish administration. Together with other millions of Germans from Czechoslovakia and Hungary, the eventual transfer of Germans was the biggest migration in a thousand years of European history and the greatest potential threat to an orderly operation of military government in Germany. The tragic decision of Potsdam cast a deep shadow over the Allied occupation.

Another question which had already figured on the agenda of the Crimea Conference was debated again at Potsdam. At Yalta the Russians proposed to extract twenty billion dollars from Germany, half of which the Soviet Union was to receive. Britain and the United States took the view that Germany would be incapable of paying such a sum without rebuilding and even expanding her industries and that she would thus regain a great war potential. It also seemed impractical to express the removal of plant equipment and other deliveries in terms of money values. Goods would have a very different value depending upon whether, for example, they were received in Rostow or in Lille. Individual countries then might claim that deliveries did not come up to the figure set as their share in the German reparations.

The Reparations Commission in Moscow, which had been created by the Crimea Conference and charged with the formulation of a common reparations policy, did not succeed in its tasks. The Potsdam Conference tried to break the deadlock by a fundamentally different method which was in the end adopted. Under the Potsdam agreement only the division of reparations as it had been discussed in Yalta was retained. That is to say, Russia was to get fifty per cent out of which Poland was to receive a share. But reparations were now confined to the seizure of capital equipment and German external assets. In addition, a new system of administration was agreed upon. Russia, which by July 1945 had already started to remove a great amount of industrial equipment from her zone, was supposed to collect her share of reparations in that zone and was also to receive shares of German enterprises in Bulgaria, Finland, Hungary, Rumania, and Eastern Austria. Since the Soviet occupied the area of Germany which contained a proportionately smaller part of the German industries, she was to be given in addition "ten per cent of such industrial equipment as is unnecessary for the German peace economy and should be removed from the western zones—without payment or exchange of any kind." Furthermore, she was to receive another fifteen per cent in exchange for an equivalent value of commodities of which the Russian zone had richer resources.

This settlement was designed to simplify the administration of reparations. It made a review of the removals which had been effected in the Russian zone unnecessary, and equally, a decision whether or not removals from the areas which the Potsdam Declaration assigned to Polish administration should be considered Russian or Polish receipts. The latter question was to be worked out between Russia and Poland. With reparations restricted to existing assets, they were likely to cease after two years, for by that time Germany would probably be incapable of making further deliveries. But whereas the Potsdam decisions would ultimately ease the administration of reparations, they laid a very heavy burden upon the Allied Control Council during the initial months.[39]

The Potsdam program of reparations was based on the assumption that German industries had expanded far beyond the peaceful needs of the German people, and that consequently a large part of the German industrial capacity could be removed without in the long run impairing the peacetime German economy. Naturally the additional assumption was made that the restoration of German economy was subordinate to the rehabilitation of her neighbors. However, this approach, which attempted to kill two birds with one stone by linking reparations with demilitarization, raised the question of defining the peaceful needs of the German people. The Potsdam agreement permitted a standard of living not higher than the average of the standard of living of European countries excluding Great Britain and the Soviet Union. But it provided that the payment of reparations, or as we may as well call it, the degree of German de-industrialization, "should leave enough resources to enable the German people to subsist without external assistance."

The Potsdam program made the Allied Control Council responsible for the execution of this program. The Council had the duty of determining what industries should be altogether abolished because they served exclusively military purposes or were easily convertible into war industries. Beyond this, each single industrial plant had to be surveyed and finally a decision had to be reached with regard to the industrial equipment which Germany would have to retain if she was to achieve the standard of living agreed upon by the three powers at Potsdam. Any plant or equipment beyond this level was to be earmarked for reparations or destruction. Obviously the Potsdam decisions rested on the belief that it would be impossible to turn Germany into an agrarian state, an idea which was made even more unrealistic by the award of the major agrarian regions of Germany to Polish administration and by the dumping of more than ten million Germans upon the rest of Germany. The Potsdam Declaration stated clearly that Germany would have to export in order to pay for the import of food and such essential commodities as she was forbidden to produce herself as a result of the abolition of certain potential war industries. The Declaration proclaimed that "in organizing the German economy, primary emphasis shall be given to the development of agriculture and peaceful domestic industries." But those who drafted the Potsdam Declaration were under no illusion with regard to the inevitable need for imports to Germany and the resulting necessity of German exports. "In working out the economic balance of Germany the necessary means must be provided to pay for imports approved by the Control Council. The proceeds of exports from current production and stocks shall be available in the first place for payment of such imports." The Potsdam Declaration obviously wished to exclude a degree of de-industrialization that would make Germany dependent on foreign charity, though it implied a change in the character of German exports away from heavy to light industries and to raw materials.

These were the outlines of the Potsdam agreement on reparations, which correspond closely to the economic principles of JCS-1067.[40] With this agreement the Allied Control Council was given a common program but at the same time one of the most difficult practical tasks. In its hands a great responsibility was placed for the restoration of the economic life of the invaded countries and eventually, through the establishment of a peaceful German economy, for a general pacification of Europe. But there were many pitfalls ahead on the way towards the practical realization of the economic objectives agreed upon by the three Allies, and the most important and urgent assignment given to the Allied Control Council was bound to become one of its severest tests. Undoubtedly the practical solution of the question of German reparations will fundamentally decide whether or not the barriers between the zones can be torn down and a strong inter-Allied policy appear.

In the economic field the Potsdam Declaration made the greatest effort to overcome the zonal division. A very important step in this direction had already been taken in the reparations chapter of the Declaration. The provision for meeting part of the Russian claims by handing over from the western zones fifteen percent of the removable industrial equipment against deliveries of food, coal, potash, zinc, clay products, petroleum products, etc., was an attempt to use to some extent the larger agrarian resources, together with the more variegated raw materials of the eastern zone, for the general German economy. The scheme would seem mutually beneficial. If the Russians agreed to make up some deficiencies in the western zones they would need smaller imports from overseas and, consequently, industrial plants became more readily available for purposes of reparations. The same general objective is specifically stated in the chapter of the Potsdam Declaration dealing with economic policy, in which the Allied Control Council is encouraged to aim at "the equitable distribution of essential commodities between the several zones so as to produce a balanced economy throughout Germany and reduce the need for imports."

These Allied policies clearly envisaged an Allied Control Council that would wield great authority and become most active in assuming the direction of German affairs. The Declaration stated unequivocally "that during the period of occupation Germany shall be treated as a single economic unit" and charged the Allied Control Council specifically to establish common policies with regard to (a) mining, industrial production, and allocations; (b) agriculture, forestry, and fishing; (c) wages, prices, and rationing; (d) import and export programs for Germany as a whole; (e) currency and banking, central taxation, and customs; (f) reparations and removal of industrial war potential; (g) transportation and communications. The Declaration of Potsdam could hardly have gone much farther in its demand for an integrated inter-Allied economic policy in Germany. It inserted an important reservation by ruling that the German economy should be decentralized at the earliest practicable date. But it was made clear that this applied only to a dissolution of economic power as exercised by German cartels and monopolies, and not to a replacement of the general German economic system by various regional, not to speak of zonal, systems.

The Declaration of Potsdam suggested in addition that "in the imposition and maintenance of economic controls established by the Control Council, German administrative machinery shall be created and the German authorities shall be required to the fullest extent practicable to proclaim and assume administration of such controls." The exact meaning of this stipulation soon became controversial. There is no doubt whatsoever that it did not imply the introduction of a German government. It meant in the first place that the Allied Control Council would use "to the fullest extent practicable" the same indirect system of administration which was adopted by the zonal commands. But although the new state governments in the zones were to be composed of ministers, the German central agencies were to be headed by senior civil servants. The Declaration described them as "state secretaries" using the German title instead of the clearer American description "under-secretaries." The central agencies, which were confined to finance, transport, communications, foreign trade and industry, were obviously designed to support the Allied Control Council in a merely technical capacity. At the same time, however, their establishment emphasized the character of the Council as a political body that would not merely deliberate and coordinate, but would eventually take the initiative in the formulation of basic policies and see to it that they were firmly applied in all the zones.

The establishment of German central administrative agencies as contemplated by the Potsdam Conference leads us from the agreement on reparations and economic policies over to that on general political principles. Here the influence of American ideas and plans is even more clearly apparent. All the general objectives contained in the American post-defeat Directives on the Military Government of Germany (JCS-1067) reappear in the Potsdam Declaration, often enough couched in the same language. On the whole the Declaration is less specific in its recommendations than the Joint Chiefs' directives, but only with respect to the methods of administration and not in regard to the principles themselves. There is one major distinction between the Declaration and the directives. Whereas the directives to General Eisenhower flatly said: "No political activities of any kind shall be countenanced unless authorized by you," the Declaration called not only for the early restoration of local government but for the admission and encouragement of democratic political parties throughout Germany. The Declaration postulated the introduction of representative and elective principles into regional, provincial, and state administration "as rapidly as may be justified by the application of these principles in local self-government." But the policies enunciated by the Declaration were exactly what the authors of JCS-1067 had all the time hoped for. They wanted a democratic development of German political life along these lines. But they felt, perhaps overcautiously, that it would be useless to inaugurate democratic institutions on a mere zonal level. They also believed that no time would be lost by waiting for the announcement of an Allied policy, since the first practical problem in the restoration of democratic processes, the rebuilding of a free press and radio, would have to precede the active stimulation of German parties and trade unions. The Russian practice of encouraging German political life as soon as they had entered the country set a new pace. Thus we could not postpone the revival of political life in the western zones.

The Potsdam Conference produced a comprehensive and rather detailed blueprint for the Allied administration of Germany, and it could be confidently said that the American contribution to the conference work in this field was particularly significant. General agreement on disarmament, demilitarization, and denazification was achieved. But the Declaration also showed an understanding that the harsh conditions imposed upon Germany had to be supplemented by policies looking towards the final restoration of free political life in Germany, and even an ultimate readmission of Germany into the society of nations. The Declaration reaffirmed this pledge, which had been proclaimed by the Crimea Conference, and made it one of the major tasks of Allied military government " to prepare for the eventual reconstruction of German political life on a democratic basis and for eventual peaceful cooperation in international life by Germany." It was recognized that the new economic system could be maintained only if the Germans themselves would put their shoulders to the wheel; and even more that the future of political and cultural life depended on the growth of democratic forces in Germany able to stand on their own feet.

Unanimity prevailed in Potsdam that "for the time being" no central German government should be established. It may be surmised that the statesmen wished to wait until democratic German administration on the local, regional, and state level had come into existence and demonstrated its reliability. Moreover, it would have been unwise to have a German government connected with the administration of the reparations program, for this would have hampered the government's later usefulness. The reparations agreement provided definite dates for its fulfillment. By February 2, 1946 the amount of equipment to be removed from the western zones was to be determined and two years later the removals were to be completed. It could be assumed that thereafter the remaining resources of Germany could be used to raise the standard of living to the average European level. Possibly this would constitute the right moment for the establishment of a central German government, provided the powers had solved by that time other political problems connected with such a move. Over what territories was such a German government to rule? Was it to be a government elected by a national parliament, or rather a federal council, consisting of delegates from the state government? What Allied or United Nations controls were to be continued after the introduction of a German government? Obviously these questions were not debated at Potsdam. They required further study of the German reaction to the new conditions and could not be discussed profitably except in connection with the drafting of a German peace treaty, which was unlikely to be undertaken for another one or two years.

Whether or not the Potsdam agreement on Germany would prove a workable plan and would achieve its aim of making the Allied Control Council an effective government of Germany depended chiefly on a successful implementation of the reparations settlement by the Allied Control Council. Its members had to determine what German industries in addition to arms factories had to be eliminated as producing other essential sinews of war. The Allied Control Council achieved an understanding on this question in January 1946. But besides this, a ceiling on the remaining production of German heavy industries had to be found, a ceiling low enough to make removals for reparations possible and high enough to enable Germany to achieve the standard of living allowed by the Potsdam Declaration. This necessitated a detailed survey of existing German plant facilities, a cumbersome process which however was completed by the end of the year 1945. It called at the same time for very difficult economic investigations to clarify the terms of the Potsdam Declaration and to devise suitable methods for its execution. On December 11, 1945 the Department of State made known its interpretation of the economic policy contained in the Potsdam Declaration.* The document was drafted for the guidance of the American authorities in Germany but was presented to the British, French, and Russian governments as well. Through this memorandum the American government demonstrated again its eagerness to fulfill the Potsdam policy.

The position taken by the American representatives in the discussions of the Control Council in Berlin has been one of mediation between the British and Russian viewpoints. The British were very reluctant to accept a policy which would place strict limitations on the productive capacity of German heavy industries while the Russians pressed for their imposition. But it would be a mistake to assume that American policy has been motivated merely by a desire to bring Russia and Britain together. It is true that United States policy desired to maintain the unity of the Allied Powers and to prove that the big Powers were able to work together in times of peace as in war. The achievement of this major political aim will occasionally require the suppression of minor American political concepts and interests. In this respect American policy was kept more flexible than that of Britain, France, and the Soviet Union which, as immediate neighbors of Germany, are naturally less inclined to compromise on their ideas about the future of Germany. However, American policy, conscious

*Appendix XVI.

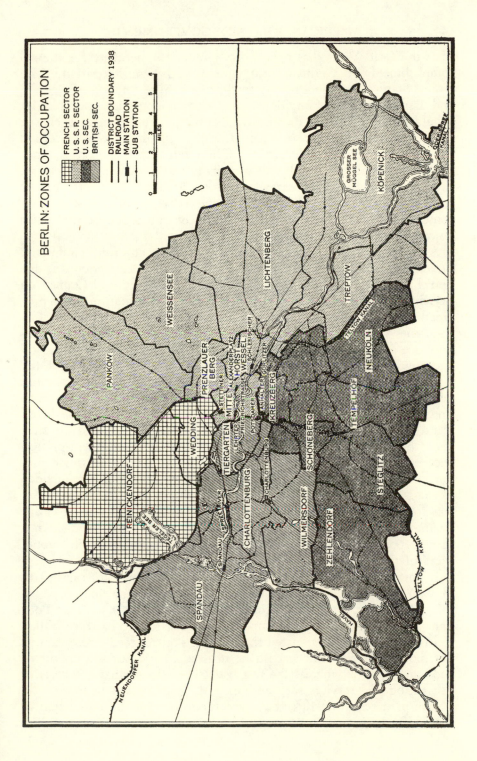

BERLIN: ZONES OF OCCUPATION

FRENCH SECTOR
U. S. S. R. SECTOR
U. S. SEC.
BRITISH SEC.

DISTRICT BOUNDARY 1938
RAILROAD
MAIN STATION
SUB STATION

MILES
0 1 2 3 4 5 6

of two World Wars, has never lost sight of the necessity for the accomplishment of German disarmament and demilitarization. The United States also cannot be indifferent to a final restoration of German and European living conditions. If German industrial opportunities should be curtailed too drastically, Germany would remain a charge of American charity. There is also a limit to the destruction of certain unremovable German industries. While removable industries, once they have been transferred, will contribute to the general economy of Europe again, the disappearance of some immovable plants will be felt not only by Germany but by Europe as well, and the speedy reconstruction of European economy must constitute one of the major objectives of American foreign policy.

An agreement on the German standard of living and future industrial production, which under the terms of the Potsdam Declaration was due by February 2, 1946, was announced by the Allied Control Council on March 26.* The plan for the level of postwar German industry provided for the division of German industries in four major groups: (1) Industries which were to be prohibited on account of their special importance as war potential, but certain of which, like the synthetic oil and rubber industries, were to be retained temporarily to meet the domestic requirements of Germany until the necessary imports could be received and paid for. (2) Industries for which ceilings of production were fixed so that production capacity in excess of these levels could be removed for reparations. These industries included the steel and other metallurgical industries, heavy and light engineering, electrical and chemical industries. (3) Certain industries for which production levels were fixed for 1949, but from which it was not intended to exact reparations. The most important single industry of this class was coal mining which was to achieve maximum production. (4) Industries which were left completely unrestricted, since they did not seem to possess any war potential. This group was supposed to supply some of Germany's need for making exports.

Exports were planned to reach the level of three billion Reichsmarks in 1949 and sufficient capacity was to be retained to produce goods to this value and cover internal requirements in accordance with the Potsdam Declaration. Approved imports were not to exceed three billion Reichsmarks. It was estimated that of the total proceeds from exports not more than 1.5 billion could be utilized to pay for the import of food and fodder, whereas the rest was to be used to pay the costs of occupation and services such as transport, insurances, and so on.

The plan rested on three basic assumptions: that the population of

*Appendix XVIII.

postwar Germany would be 66.5 millions, that Germany would be treated as a single economic unit, and that exports from Germany would prove acceptable in the international markets. It may be said then that the plan would be subject to review by the Control Council if its fundamental assumptions are found to have changed. The German population may very well be larger and closer to 70 millions, if the eastern European countries enforce the expulsion of Germans from their territories in a radical manner. On the other hand, the population of Germany may be even smaller if the powers should decide upon the cession of western regions, such as the Saar or the Rhinelands. In that case the principle that Germany as a whole would be treated as an economic unit would be violated and Germany would not possess the industries like coal mining which were supposed to contribute substantially to her future exports.

The plan for the level of postwar German industry was the most important single achievement of the Allied Control Council in formulating an inter-Allied policy. Each of the four powers made considerable concessions, though the United States probably least of all, since its attitude aimed from the outset at inter-Allied unity rather than at the attainment of specific national advantages. To what extent the plan will have to be modified in order to be approved by all powers as part of the final German peace settlement will have to be seen. At this early moment nobody could make an exact estimate of future world trade or of Germany's recuperative power. Not only the British but the Russians as well may desire changes at some future date, as may the United States. Meanwhile the inter-Allied program does not only make it possible to start the delivery of German reparations and thus make contributions to the rehabilitation of the invaded countries, but at the same time to begin the rebuilding of German economic life. There can be no question that Germany would be unable to reach the levels of production set in the inter-Allied agreement if the zonal barriers could not be lifted. As a matter of fact, it could even be doubted whether Germany's industrial production would reach these levels as fast as the authors of the plan seemed to expect if Germany were treated as an economic unit. The extremely slow rehabilitation of German coal mining, chiefly in the British zone, has proved so far the greatest obstacle to a revival of economic life in the western zones. No progress has been made for a number of months; on the contrary, the grave food situation has brought on serious setbacks in production. The chances are slim that Germany could reach the levels of production set by the inter-Allied agreement before 1949.

But it is idle to speculate about the agreement since it has remained on paper. The Potsdam Declaration envisaged the introduction of central German economic agencies and the agreement of the Control Council of March 26 is unworkable without them. No export and import program of the type envisaged in the agreement could be operated. France, however, which had taken exception to some of the decisions made by the Potsdam Conference at an early time, objected in particular to the establishment of central economic agencies, and under the unanimity rule of the Allied Control Council has been able to block them, thereby making the realization of the whole March agreement impossible.[41]

France has been afraid that the introduction of German central agencies would militate against her desire for a separation of the Rhenish-Westphalian area, which includes both the Ruhr and Saar. She complained immediately after the Potsdam Conference, to which she was not invited, that the Conference had failed to pay attention to the western frontier of Germany. As General de Gaulle put it, the amputation of the eastern territories and the eviction of their German population would turn the Germans westward, and thus it was now more necessary than ever to make Western Europe secure against a potential renewal of German aggression. Whether or not this statement was correct in this form, nobody denied that the question of Germany's western boundaries would form the most important single problem of the conference which would draft a German peace treaty. Whatever decision such conference might reach there was no good reason why this settlement of the Rhine problem should precede the Allied Control Council period. The acceptance of the Oder–Neisse line by the Potsdam Conference could at least be defended by the necessity for enabling Poland to begin her reconstruction.

The French, however, pointed out that the creation of German central agencies would prejudice a future decision in favor of placing the Rhinelands under a special regime. In their opinion such a solution was necessary, both on account of the strategic importance of this region and of its crucial economic significance for Germany and Europe. They argued that the Rhinelands and Westphalia had produced more than two-thirds of the German coal and iron production on which German industrial and war making power had been built, and that Germany would be able to make use of these resources again once the occupation forces were withdrawn and inter-Allied controls were relaxed. The French demanded, therefore, the immediate establishment of international controls over this region. When the British military government authorities socialized the coal mines of the Ruhr, thus preparing the way for a control of the Ruhr industries through ownership rights, the French insisted that these economic controls would be inadequate if they were not accompanied by political separation.

The Allied Control Council was not in a position to settle the issues raised by the French stand. They went beyond its jurisdiction. The problem of the Rhinelands was, in the first place, one to be discussed by the governments of Britain and France as the two powers in actual control of the territory at the present moment and most vitally interested in its future status. The treatment of Germany's western frontier was closely linked up with the negotiations of an Anglo-French alliance which had been going on between London and Paris for more than a year. Little progress had been made in the Anglo-French discussions of the Rhine question by the time the Allied Control Council was about to reach agreement on the level of German industry, a plan which is incompatible with the French demands in the Rhine and Ruhr question. If the Rhinelands were politically separated from Germany, it is impossible to see how Germany could maintain even the low standard of living provided for in the plan for the level of German industries. The French have presented various proposals for using the profits from the Rhine and Ruhr for the benefit of all of Germany, but none of these proposals offered a solution that appeared workable in the eyes of the other powers.

The French attitude in these matters was apparently based on distrust of the four-power cooperation in Germany. The French were afraid of an early withdrawal of the United States from the Continent and a subsequent extension of direct or indirect influence of the Soviet Union in Central Europe. In the face of such potential dangers they wished to strengthen the eastern frontier of their own country. It may be doubted, however, that the security of France would be greatly enhanced by the accession of the Rhinelands. France's safety appears better protected by the cooperation of the four big powers and by active interest of the United States in the pacification of Europe.

France assumed a grave responsibility by blocking progress toward a fuller integration of the policies of the four powers in Germany. The Soviet government in the months after the Potsdam agreement was prepared to accept the economic unification of Germany not only in theory but also in practice. But Britain and the United States tolerated the French attitude, hoping, no doubt, it would change in time. As a matter of fact, owing to the long period needed to work out an Allied program on the level of industrial production, central German economic agencies could not have been established before March 1946. But new attempts made by America failed to change the French views on the Potsdam plan.

By that time it had become obvious that Russia had adopted a new policy in her zone and was apparently no longer ungrateful to France for sabotaging the central administration of Germany. German industries in the eastern zones were revived on a much larger scale than was possible in the West but their output went largely to Russia. This was a policy out of line with the Potsdam agreement. Reparations were not to come from current production but from the transfer of capital equipment. Exports were to be used to pay for imports. By abolishing zonal barriers a balanced economy was to be created which would minimize the need for imports and enable Germany to pay eventually the cost of occupation. The Potsdam Declaration had expressly stated that the returns from German exports were earmarked to pay for occupation costs. As long as Germany remained divided into zones, the plan for the revival of the German economy could not become operative. Both the United States and Britain were thus shouldered with heavy occupation costs. For the United States the bill for the first year ran to 200 million and for Britain, more than 160 million dollars, chiefly spent on food imports. This outlay, called by Hugh Dalton "our reparations to Germany," is a particularly great burden on Britain, because she has to employ her small foreign exchange reserves to purchase food. Russia, however, insisted on her reparations from the western zones while, in disregard of the Potsdam agreement, she took additional reparations from current production in her zone.

In the political field Russia was seemingly willing to fulfill the provisions of Potsdam. In contrast to the British zone, where political movements and even the activities of the German functionaries appointed by British military government have been hamstrung by close supervision of a huge corps of British officials, the Russians entered upon the administration of their zone with the declared aim of promoting indigenous political life. To them this meant, however, not merely the restoration of democratic processes, accompanied by denazification, but also an active reorganization of the social foundation of Germany by the dissolution of the large landed estates and the nationalization of industries. But soon they began to go one step further. By forcing the German Social Democrats into a union with the Communists they placed the largest political group practically under the control of a communist minority. This perversion of democracy jeopardized a future unification of the German zones, for there can be a wide variety of political forms in a democratic federal state, as is true in the United States, but it is inconceivable to combine states with opposed constitutional systems and practices into one federal state.

The attempt of Russia to secure control of the largest political party of Germany was not confined to her zone. By posing as the protector of German unity and as benefactor of the German masses through the successful achievement of industrial activity in her zone, Russia, it seems apparent, wanted to attract to the Socialist Unity Party a large following throughout Germany. Russian-inspired German propaganda spoke of the Western Allies as the advocates of the destruction of German industries and of German national unity. Through similar channels word was spread that only Russia had it in her power to fix a German-Polish frontier which would return to Germany at least some of the districts now under Polish administration.

With the stalling of the Allied Control Council by the French veto the German problem was thrown back into the lap of the four governments. Since the first Paris meeting of the four foreign secretaries in May 1946 the American government had tried to break the stalemate in the execution of the Potsdam agreement. But it became clear that Russia was not anxious to restore the Allied Control Council to effective leadership for the time being and preferred to have a situation continue in which Russia was more fortunately placed than the western powers. The Soviet Union avoided, however, taking an open stand against Potsdam. On the contrary, as Molotov stated in his Paris speech of July 10, 1946,[41a] the policy of demilitarization, denazification, democratization, and in addition the restoration of a unified Germany still constituted the official Russian aims with regard to Germany.

Molotov accused the other powers of harboring ideas to agrarianize Germany and destroy her industrial centers which he argued would undermine the European economy, dislocate world economy, and result "in a chronic political crisis in Germany that would spell a threat to peace and tranquillity." The same destructive designs, Molotov declared, were reflected in the talk about the construction of autonomous states and the separation of the Ruhr. Without the Ruhr no stable Germany could be created, for a general stimulation was essential to the expansion of peaceful German industries. The division of power between a future national German government and those of individual German states was in Russian eyes a decision to be taken by a democratic Germany and one not to be prejudiced by Allied ukases. As a first step toward the establishment of a future German government Molotov proposed the immediate creation of a German central administration.

This was a tone very different from that heard from Russia in 1945 and even as late as the spring of 1946, when Russia had not only defended the separation of Eastern Germany on strategic grounds but had insisted that even the production of peaceful German industries be reduced to an extremely low level. Economic and military disarmament now seemed to have lost some of its significance. Molotov, in his Paris speech, made the expansion of German production dependent upon the introduction of inter-Allied control of the Ruhr, a condition not in the Potsdam agreement.

It could be doubted for this and other reasons whether Russian policy was really desirous of seeing Allied cooperation and German unification realized. In any case the Russians did not consider the achievement of these objectives urgent enough to sit down with the other powers and discuss an immediate program of action. They were apparently well satisfied to have the impasse of inter-Allied cooperation linger on, which gave them reparation deliveries from the West under the terms of Potsdam and reparations from production in the eastern zone. And similarly they obviously hoped to make hay in the realm of German party politics by proclaiming themselves the friends of German national unity and high employment.

In these circumstances General Clay took action by suspending further assignment of industrial plants for Russian reparations. The Potsdam plan had been drafted not only for the benefit of the Russians, but with a view to making the Allied occupation a cooperative enterprise. If the zonal division was to last or even to become permanent, the economy of the western zones could be stabilized only by higher industrial productivity. It was certainly not the intention of the western Allies to finance German reparations out of their own pockets.

After the second (July, 1946) Paris Conference of the four foreign secretaries ended without practical results, the American Government announced that it was inviting the other occupying powers to set up at once the German central economic agencies as envisaged in the Potsdam agreement. And when the Soviet Union and France declined to participate, the American and British governors proceeded to begin the unification of the economic administrations and policies of the two zones.[41b] The American and British governments have stated continuously that they did not intend a separation of the four powers and that they wished for nothing better than the accession of the two other powers.

The economic unification of the two zones was not a simple process. As the result of a year in which the zones had become national compartments, even the American and British zones were mutually shut off. Trade between the two zones was small and the Germans were kept from circulating between the British and American zones. Moreover, the British worked their occupation on a different time-table and by a different system. The introduction of democratic representation was held to require a long period of time; and though British military government like the American was one of indirect rule, the German appointees of all ranks were strictly controlled by British superintendents. Very little administrative authority had been handed over to the Germans. In building up common German agencies for the two zones it was necessary first to adapt the organization of the British to that of the United States zone. Progress in unification was therefore slow in the beginning.

In Stuttgart, on September 6, Secretary Byrnes outlined American policy in Germany.[41c] He did not depart from the policy expressed in the Potsdam Declaration and though he defended not only disarmament and denazification but also the necessity of reparations and territorial cessions, he made it clear that American policy had always aimed at an early restoration of normal conditions in Germany. American policy had not merely tried to achieve those Potsdam aims bound to result in hardships for the German people but, equally, those designed to enable the Germans to rehabilitate the country. America wanted to see the promises made at Potsdam fulfilled, particularly with regard to the economic unification of Germany.

Secretary Byrnes pointed out that after more than a year of Allied occupation it was necessary to implement the policy of Potsdam. In this year disarmament, denazification, and the rebuilding of democratic institutions on the local and regional level had gone far enough to envisage turning over to the German people under proper safeguards "the preparations for setting up a democratic German government which can accept and observe" the Allied peace terms. Both with regard to the peace terms and the methods by which a German government could be rebuilt, Secretary Byrnes made concrete proposals. He told his audience that the United States had not created the present demarcation line between Poland and Germany, and though she was committed to support the transfer of the Koenigsberg area to the Soviet Union and a revision of the western boundary of Poland, she was not bound to support the present line at the peace conference. On her own part she favored the French claim to the Saar district. But with these exceptions America was opposed to encroachments on indisputably German territory and to any division of Germany not genuinely desired by the people concerned.

American policy thus was able to demonstrate that even within the framework of the Potsdam agreement it held out better prospects for a democratic Germany than those Molotov claimed Russia desired to extend. The political offensive launched by the Russians to rally German support for their controlled parties was now parried. The practical proposals made by the two foreign secretaries for the treatment of the German problem were not very far apart, and provided both governments had been equally anxious to make quick progress in the formulation of joint policies, it should not have been too difficult to reach a practical working agreement, preferably by first putting the unfulfilled provisions of the Potsdam agreement into operation and then by beginning the discussion of steps to be taken for a stabilization of German conditions. The Russians, however, declared that the introduction of a central economic administration without the simultaneous appointment of a German government would be impractical. On the other hand they showed no eagerness to enter upon official consultations for replacing these Potsdam provisions by a new inter-Allied control agreement. It appeared unlikely that the German problems could be taken up by the four foreign secretaries before January 1947.

But it may be doubted that the Russian position in these negotiations has been strengthened by the delay. The Russians have undoubtedly been too optimistic in their estimate of the German reaction to their policy. The 1946 elections in the Russian zone and in Berlin must have proved a disappointment to them. Even more important was the fact that Russia could hardly contemplate her complete exclusion from the rest of Germany with equanimity. She is fully aware of the tremendous impact of the economic resources and productivity of Germany on the recovery of Europe and even of Russia herself, and she will presumably want to retain an influential voice in moulding the future German economy. There were even signs that Russia, in her grave need for industrial goods, is herself interested in exports from the western zones of Germany and was therefore willing to revise the Control Council agreement of March 26, 1946 on the level of German industries. Both Britain and the United States could accept such a revision; provided it were done in a form that would not create a new German war potential nor interfere with the achievement of the German standard of living accepted at Potsdam, and that it would decrease the occupation cost of the Western Powers. Even then a new inter-Allied occupation scheme still requires agreement on the methods of creating a new German national government, on the stages by which it might receive growing authorities from the Allies, and on the forms which Allied supervision of Germany might take thereafter.

We can be accommodating in the negotiations of the details of such a program, but we cannot compromise on the basic principles. There is every good reason why we should make the strongest efforts to reach an agreement with the Russians. The American and British zones will gain by the tearing down of the existing barriers, but these zones can hardly be turned into a reasonably prosperous region without an expenditure which the British are not able to afford and we ourselves are probably unwilling to foot. The contribution which these zones could make to the rehabilitation of Europe would be much smaller if they were finally cut off from the central and eastern parts of Germany. Even worse than economic competition between the Anglo-American and the Russian zones would be the resulting political tension. Either or both groups would probably try to appear in the eyes of the Germans as the true advocate of German national interests and very probably Secretary Byrnes' warning against using Germany "as a pawn or partner" would soon be vindicated. And since Germany, even after her defeat remains in the very heart of Europe, the repercussions from a breakdown of the quadripartite government of Germany would be felt around the world.

FOOTNOTES, CHAPTER 8

[36]For the circumstances of the German surrender, see General Eisenhower's final report to the Combined Chiefs of Staff, published under the title *Eisenhower's Own Story of the War,* New York, 1946, pp. 118-120. A legal discussion of the surrender and of the establishment of Allied rule over Germany is found in H. Kelsen, "The Legal Status of Germany according to the Declaration of Berlin," *American Journal of International Law,* Vol. XXXIX (1945), pp. 518-526.

[37]Department of State, *Bulletin,* Vol. XII, 1945, pp. 1056 ff.

[38]Cf. also President Roosevelt's report to Congress of March 1, 1945 and Prime Minister Churchill's report to the House of Commons of February 27. Both reprinted in *International Conciliation,* No. 410, April 1945.

[39]See the statement by E. W. Pauley on "German Reparations" in Department of State, *Bulletin,* Vol. XIII (1945), pp. 308-309.

[40]See the transcript of the broadcast by Dean Acheson, J. J. McCloy, H. Parkman "Our Military Government Policy in Germany," Department of State, *Bulletin,* Vol. XIII (1945), pp. 310-318, and the address by J. Riddleberger, "U. S. Policy Towards Germany," *ibid.,* p. 841. See also the report published by the Economics Division, Office of Military Government, *A Year of Potsdam: The German Economy Since the Surrender.* (Berlin, 1946.)

[41]The most important official sources are the note of the Secretary of State, Mr. Byrnes, of February 1 and the reply of the French Foreign Minister, Mr. Bidault, of March 2, 1946. See Department of State, *Bulletin,* Vol. XIV, 1946, pp. 440-43.

[41a]Text in *New York Times,* July 11, 1946.

[41b]See the instructions to General McNarney and the British acceptance of the American proposal in Department of State *Bulletin,* Vol. XV (1946), pp. 227-228, 266.

[41c]Department of State *Bulletin,* Vol. XV (1946), pp. 496-501.

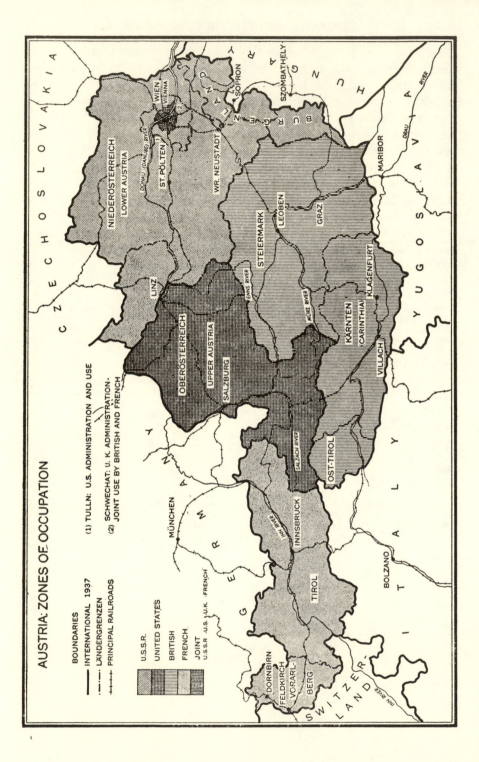

AUSTRIA: ZONES OF OCCUPATION

BOUNDARIES

INTERNATIONAL 1937
LÄNDERGRENZEN
PRINCIPAL RAILROADS

U.S.S.R.
UNITED STATES
BRITISH
FRENCH
JOINT
U.S.S.R U.S. U.K. FRENCH

(1) TULLN: U.S. ADMINISTRATION AND USE

(2) SCHWECHAT: U.K. ADMINISTRATION-
JOINT USE BY BRITISH AND FRENCH

CZECHOSLOVAKIA

NIEDERÖSTERREICH
LOWER AUSTRIA

WIEN
VIENNA

ST. PÖLTEN

WR. NEUSTADT

DONAU (DANUBE) RIVER

LINZ

OBERÖSTERREICH
UPPER AUSTRIA

SALZBURG

ENNS RIVER

STEIERMARK

LEOBEN

GRAZ

MÜR RIVER

KÄRNTEN
(CARINTHIA)

KLAGENFURT

VILLACH

OST-TIROL

SALZACH RIVER

INNSBRUCK

INN RIVER

TIROL

DORNBIRN

FELDKIRCH

VORARL-
BERG

SWITZER-
LAND

INN RIVER 8394 12

ITALY

BOLZANO

MARIBOR

DRAU RIVER

YUGOSLAVIA

SZOMBATHELY

SOPRON

BURGENLAND

GERMANY

MÜNCHEN

Chapter 9

The Planning and Establishment of Allied Military Government in Austria

IN THE Moscow Declaration of November 1, 1943 the United States, British, and Russian governments proclaimed that "Austria, the first free country to fall a victim to Hitlerite aggression, shall be liberated from German domination."* The German annexation of 1938 was declared void and the reestablishment of a free and independent Austria was considered the best method of assuring to the Austrian people and their neighbors an ultimate political and economic security. But at the same time, Austria was reminded that she had a responsibility for having participated in the war on the side of Germany and that "in the final settlement account will inevitably be taken of her own contribution to her liberation."

The crucial position of Austria in the European order was recognized in the Moscow Declaration. Austria was not only the first country that had been invaded by Hitler, but its annexation had placed Czechoslovakia in jeopardy and had made the German conquest of the whole Danube region possible. The German control of the Alpine passes had also weakened the position of Italy by actually turning the erstwhile ally into a virtual satellite of Germany. The lower Rhine, the lower Vistula, and Austria are probably the most important strategic areas of Europe, and by announcing the plan to restore Austrian independence the Moscow Conference of 1943 laid down a major principle for the future European order.

Austria was promised "liberation," although this pledge was qualified by the statement that the Allies would appraise her own contribution in the final settlement and there was also the threat that the Austrian participation in the war could not be completely forgotten. At the time, these statements were prompted by political warfare motives, but they injected a certain ambiguity into the Allied postwar program for Austria. Austria necessarily would be required to restore looted property to the United Nations and to cooperate in the restitution of damage done by Greater Germany to her unhappy victims. But if Austria was to be independent it was unwise to separate her from Germany without giving her the means to sustain herself economically. Her economic weakness had been one of the major causes of the downfall of the first Austrian Republic. The Moscow Declaration seemed to accept this by speaking of "political and economic se-

*Appendix IV.

75

curity" as two complementary aspects of the problem of Austrian statehood. This appeared to imply that Austrian resources could in the future be used for the recovery of the countries invaded by Hitler only to an extent compatible with the ultimate creation of a healthy Austrian economy.

Incidentally, the Allies never tried to evaluate the activities of the Austrian underground, and it would be very difficult to pass such a judgment. Undoubtedly the Nazis never succeeded in stamping out the Austrian opposition, which became more active in the final phase of the War. It was hardly decisive toward bringing the War to an earlier conclusion, and it could not have been since the Nazi police state wielded such tremendous power over the small country. Nor did the heterogeneous oppositional groups form strong nuclei for the revival of indigenous political life after the Nazi defeat. The collapse of the Nazi regime saw the old parties of pre-*Anschluss* days emerge again.

As mentioned before, the Tehran Conference had assigned the task of formulating a tripartite, and after Yalta a quadripartite, occupation scheme for Austria to the European Advisory Commission in London. The long discussions of the document of German surrender and of the other German papers made it impossible for the Commission to attack the Austrian problems before the winter of 1944. As in Germany, national zones were laid out, and Vienna was to become an inter-Allied zone. Again the creation of a zonal system was inevitable as the logical outcome of a coalition that invaded Austria from different directions. But it seemed rather extravagant to create in Vienna, as in Berlin, national zones under an Allied *Kommandatura*. Up to a point all the powers admitted this, insofar as the heart of Vienna, containing the chief administrative buildings of the city, was set up as an inter-Allied zone. But this final concession was bought at the price of establishing two Russian, two British, one American, and—after Yalta—one French section of Vienna, so that in the end Vienna was divided into seven sections. This solution was, however, coupled with the understanding that the inter-Allied administration of Vienna was to be much more closely integrated than that of Berlin. The police jeeps patrolling the city of Vienna, carrying military policemen from each of the four nations, each swinging into action in his particular zone, demonstrate this greater unity, but they are, at the same time, a curious illustration of the roundabout way in which agreement may be reached in international affairs.

The occupation of Austria presented a special problem to the United States. President Roosevelt maintained serious doubts about the commitment of American troops to the task. He was not willing in the beginning to consider more than an American representative on the Allied Commission in Vienna. But the Allied Commission was composed of military commanders, and it was difficult to claim a full vote on the Council without accepting the full responsibilities of an occupying power. Moreover the other governments without exception desired the United States to be an equal partner in the occupation. In view of the crucial character of the Austrian problem for the achievement of the aims of the United States in Germany and Europe, it could not be denied that American troops would have to be assigned to the occupation of Austria. This decision was facilitated by the definite selection of southern Germany as the American zone of occupation in Germany. Since Bavaria was contiguous to Austria, little had to be added to the military strength of the United States in the European Theater of Operations.

The United States received the whole province of Salzburg and most of Upper Austria to the southwest of the Danube as her zone of occupation; France, the province of Vorarlberg-Tyrol, with the exception of East-Tyrol which together with Carinthia and Styria came under British control. The Soviet Union had as its zone Lower Austria, the part of Upper Austria on the east bank of the Danube, and the *Burgenland,* a district which Austria annexed in 1919 from Hungary and Yugoslavia.[42]

The zonal system of Allied occupation, though inevitable, was not an ideal practical approach to the Austrian problem considering the political objectives of the Allied Powers. Their most immediate aim was the separation of Austria from Germany. But the Nazis had left no Austria at all. They had abolished the Austrian government altogether and maintained only the seven old provinces (*lands,* or as the Nazis called them *Reichsgaus*): Vienna, Upper Austria, Lower Austria, Salzburg, Styria, Carinthia, Tyrol-Vorarlberg. Each of these districts received its orders directly from Berlin, and Vienna had ceased to be an administrative center for the other six Austrian provinces.

The zonal system of occupation blunted the efficiency of the Allied military government in Germany, but the Allies wished to accomplish in Germany a large measure of decentralization. In Austria they wanted to attain unity among the seven provinces and the zonal division was, therefore, unappropriate for the attainment of this end. But it was considered only a temporary device "to secure the establishment, as soon as possible, of a central Austrian administrative machine" and "to prepare the way for the establishment of a freely elected Austrian government." Great emphasis was placed on the *joint* responsibility

of the Allied Control Council for the whole of Austria and particularly
upon its task of organizing central Austrian administrative departments, which were supposed to administer Austria after a short while
under the general supervision of the Allied Control Council. In contrast to the inter-Allied control machinery for Germany no elaborate
Allied Coordinating Commission was contemplated but only "an
executive committee and staffs."

In other words, the agreements on Austria achieved by the three
or, after Yalta, the four powers through the European Advisory Commission envisaged a relatively short phase in which the Allies would
act as an Austrian government. This was to be followed by a second,
and presumably somewhat longer, period during which the Allies
would turn over an increasing number of administrative functions to
the newly created indigenous central agencies and would assist in arranging for free elections of an Austrian parliament and government.
Thereafter the Allied Control Council was merely to act as a general
supervisory body, and in particular to assist Austria in developing her
economic life. Under this plan, Allied intervention in Austrian affairs
was held to a minimum, though everyone was agreed on the necessity
for taking vigorous action against the German influence in Austria.
Among the special duties of Allied control were the enforcement of
the German surrender with regard to German troops found in Austria,
the arrest of war criminals and dangerous Nazis, the restoration of
stolen property, and the repatriation of United Nations members.

The directives to the commander of the American occupation forces*
were drafted strictly in accordance with these principles, but before
they were finally issued on June 27, 1945, military and political events
created new and unexpected problems. Late in March 1945, Russian
troops crossed the Austrian frontier from Hungary, and the army of
Marshal Tolbukhin captured Vienna on April 13. It was Tolbukhin,
and not the Russian governor-designate Marshal Konev, who received
the inter-party committee which Karl Renner had formed and which
the Russian marshal then proceeded to recognize on April 29 as the
Provisional Government of Austria. This step was a clear departure
from the agreements reached by the European Advisory Commission
and caused uneasiness among the Allies, the more so since Russia had
installed governments in Rumania, Bulgaria, Hungary, which aroused
suspicions in the United States and Britain about all Russian plans in
South-East Europe. At first sight the creation of a Provisional Government of Austria appeared to be a Russian attempt to prejudice Austria's
future political development by one-sided dictation.

*Appendix XI.

The European Advisory Commission had aimed at achieving the closest cooperation of the four powers in all major political decisions concerning Austria. It had deliberately postponed the establishment of a provisional Austrian government, but had agreed on the introduction of central administrative agencies to function under the Allied Commission until elections could be held. It seemed futile to envisage the formation of a government immediately after the Nazi surrender, for no one was in a position to predict what political forces would emerge in Austria at that time. The restoration of the Austria of 1937, if taken literally, would have meant the revival of the authoritarian regime of the Dollfus-Schuschnigg era, which had struggled bravely against German National Socialism, but had actually suppressed the democratic movement in alliance with Italian fascism. A return to the Austria of 1937 was unfeasible and a new Austrian republic could only emerge from popular elections.

The Russian recognition of the Provisional Government, if analyzed more closely, had some good aspects. The lack of consultation, or rather the unwillingness of the Russians to wait for replies from the Allied governments, was inexcusable. But the Russians did not take the initiative in founding the Renner Cabinet and were apparently themselves surprised by its appearance. Karl Renner, who had been the first Chancellor of the first Austrian Republic and had represented his country at the Peace Conference of Paris, could not be suspected of Russian leanings. It was largely due to the Austrian Social Democratic Party, of which he had been one of the foremost leaders, that from 1919 to 1934, when Dollfus suppressed the Socialists, Communism had hardly been noticeable in the country. The list of Cabinet members he presented to the only Allied commander whom he could reach made fairly large concessions to the Communists and not many concessions to the Austrian People's Party, the more democratic wing of the old Christian Social Party. Under the conditions with which Renner had to wrestle this was probably unavoidable. The elections in November 1945 showed that the Christian Socials actually had the strongest popular support and that the Social Democrats were second, while the Communists comprised only a small minority. In spite of these later events the Provisional Government of Renner was a serious attempt of the popular groups to form an Austrian representation and was not a screen for unilateral Russian schemes.

The Russians were apparently tempted to accept it because it promised to facilitate considerably the problems of occupation. They could argue that their action was at least not a violation of the Moscow Declaration, and that the agreements of the European Advisory Com-

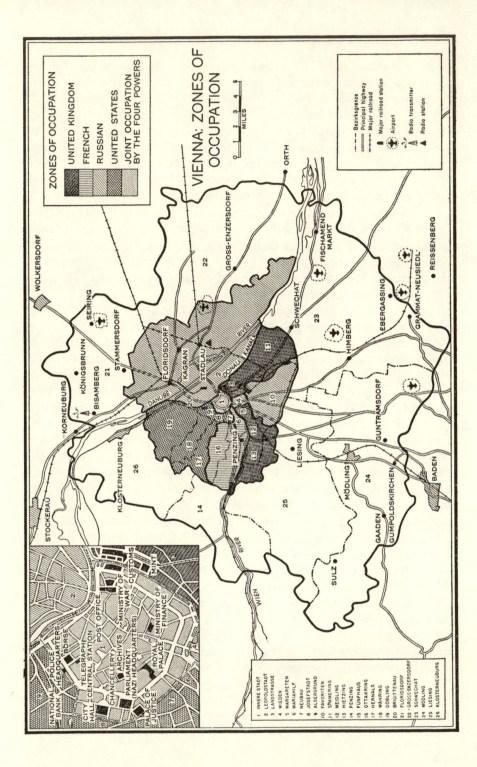

VIENNA: ZONES OF OCCUPATION

ZONES OF OCCUPATION

UNITED KINGDOM
FRENCH
RUSSIAN
UNITED STATES
JOINT OCCUPATION
BY THE FOUR POWERS

Bezirksgrenze
Principal highway
Major railroad
Major railroad station
Airport
Radio transmitter
Radio station

0 1 2 3 4 5
MILES

1 INNERE STADT
2 LEOPOLDSTADT
3 LANDSTRASSE
4 WIEDEN
5 MARGARETEN
6 MARIAHILF
7 NEUBAU
8 JOSEFSTADT
9 ALSERGRUND
10 FAVORITEN
11 SIMMERING
12 MEIDLING
13 HIETZING
14 PENZING
15 FÜNFHAUS
16 OTTAKRING
17 HERNALS
18 WÄHRING
19 DÖBLING
20 BRIGITTENAU
21 FLORIDSDORF
22 GROSS-ENZERSDORF
23 SCHWECHAT
24 MÖDLING
25 LIESING
26 KLOSTERNEUBURG

NATIONAL POLICE HEADQUARTERS
BANK
BÖRSE
TELEGRAPH CENTRAL STATION
CITY HALL
POST OFFICE
CHANCELLERY
ARCHIVES
PARLIAMENT (NAZI HEADQUARTERS)
MINISTRY OF WAR
CUSTOMS
MINISTRY OF FINANCE
ROYAL PALACE
PALACE OF JUSTICE
MINT

mission might have been drafted differently if its members had been in a position to learn more about the continued existence of democratic groups in Austria. The American Government was not unmindful of the advantages which the Allied occupation could derive from the existence of the provisional Austrian government and was willing to adjust the earlier plans accordingly. It was not prepared, however, to compromise the very character of the occupation as a joint enterprise of the four powers. If the Russians insisted on the confirmation of their decision by the other powers prior to the establishment of the Allied Control Council in Vienna, the role of the Western Powers in Austria would be affected in a manner that would have made equal and free cooperation difficult.

The negotiations among the Allies were time-consuming. The intervention of the Big Three was needed to break the stalemate. The Potsdam Declaration of August 2, 1945 announced that the Conference had examined a Soviet proposal on the extension of the authority of the Austrian Provisional Government to the zones occupied by the other three powers, but that the United States and Britain made the final settlement of the issue dependent on the entry of American and British forces into Vienna. The first troops arrived there a few days later, but the four Allied commanders, General Clark, Marshal Konev, General McCreery, and General Bethouart did not meet in Vienna at all until August 23. After a number of informal meetings, the Allied Control Council held its first official meeting on September 11.

Other unhappy circumstances interfered with the military government operations in the early period. The actual preparations had been made in the Mediterranean Theater, for the U.S. Fifth Army and the British Eighth Army were expected to invade Austria first. But it was the U.S. Seventh and Third Armies that did enter Austria from the north while the troops of the Mediterranean command were held up by the delay in the surrender of the German Army in Italy. The civil affairs personnel trained for Austria was with the forces in. Italy, and it was civil affairs officers briefed for German jobs not Austrian that established military government in Austria. Considerable confusion resulted from this. Some officers merely applied the German directives. Others in the desire to be kind to the Austrians were lenient towards Austrian Nazis. Some personnel was flown in from Italy by plane; but the reshuffling of officers, made more difficult by the general redeployment and demobilization, took considerable time. Early in August the military government in Germany was better in hand than that of Austria. But thereafter General Clark succeeded remarkably well in making the Austrian occupation effective.

Unfortunately the discussions about the recognition of the Renner government dragged on until October 20.[43] The British had strong objections about the representative character of the government. They maintained that it represented Vienna and Lower Austria rather than all the Austrian provinces and that it was also too leftist. This was true, but of no great consequence. Since at the time of its formation the other provinces had not been liberated, the Renner government could not add members from other parts of Austria. Its political composition did not matter much, either, for its political decisions were to be reviewed by the Allied Control Commission in any event. What was important in these circumstances was to make it generally understood that it was only a *provisional* government—to be superseded as soon as possible by a democratically elected national government. The solution finally agreed upon by the four powers on October 20 consisted of a minor reform of the Renner Cabinet by the admission of provincial representatives and by a slight shift towards the Austrian People's Party. In addition the Renner government was requested to arrange for elections before the end of the year.

The elections took place on November 25, 1945 and resulted in a majority for the Austrian People's Party. The Communists gained only 5 out of 165 seats in the new parliament. A new national coalition government was formed, this time under the leader of the Austrian People's Party, Mr. Figl, while Renner became the president of the new republic, which the four powers officially recognized in early January 1946.[44] Still, the Austrian situation remained under the shadow of dark political and economic issues—issues which the Austrians could not solve by themselves and which the four powers on their part were unable to settle for another seven months. As a matter of fact, the quadripartite occupation has acted often enough as a restraint on the Austrian Cabinet.

It is doubtful if the military occupation of Austria can be terminated in the near future. The Austrian administration is still gravely handicapped by the lack of the large number of democratic officials needed. Moreover, Austria does not yet have adequate police forces, able in particular to handle satisfactorily the denazification of Austria. If the peacemakers should in the end decide on frontier modifications, the presence of Allied troops would be even more urgently required. But it seems desirable to reduce the size of the occupation forces to the bare minimum compatible with the internal and external security of the country, for Austria with her small population and weak resources cannot stand the quartering of large forces of occupation. The Western Powers have made early efforts to withdraw troops, but though there have been Russian withdrawals, the Russians prior to May 1946 were slow to decrease the strength of their occupation forces. This was one of the major reasons for the serious food situation in Austria, since the Russians, like the French in Tyrol, have lived largely off the land.

The battles which the Russian armies fought in the region of Budapest, Bratislava, and Vienna were of the highest importance. This is rarely realized. Nor is it well remembered how bloody and devastating they were, with the Nazis themselves setting the torch to much of what they left behind in their retreat. Lower Austria suffered more than any other part of the country. Therefore the impact of large foreign armies was even more severely felt, and the food situation of Vienna and Lower Austria deteriorated to a lower standard than ever occurred in any part of Germany. After the establishment of the Allied Commission the food situation of Vienna was somewhat relieved, but the Austrian resources would not have sufficed to carry the Austrians through to the harvest of 1946 even on a near-starvation diet. The Allied Commission recommended that the feeding of Austria be turned over to the United Nations Relief and Rehabilitation Administration. As in Italy, special authorization was needed from the UNRRA Council, which was given at the fourth Council meeting in March 1946. Largely through American initiative it was, however, made clear that UNRRA was not supposed to operate in areas where occupation forces would contribute to the creation of scarcity by the requisitioning of food. It was on this basis that UNRRA, under the auspices of the Allied Commission in Vienna, assumed the administration of food imports and distribution on May 1, 1946.

The decision came too late to avoid great suffering in Austria and particularly in Vienna. UNRRA's shipping and food resources had been committed by then to other countries and the world food crisis made only minimum shipments possible. Even in June 1946 Austria existed only on a diet considered inferior to that of the British zone of Germany. But the food distribution was at least removed from interference by the military authorities in the zones, which continued to strangle the reconstruction of Austria most severely. The Moscow Declaration emphasized the need for the economic security of Austria, and indeed in the light of the history of the first Austrian Republic the wisdom of setting up an independent Austria is highly questionable if the state is not made economically stable. At present it would be impossible to formulate a long-range program for the economy of the small country, since it could only be part of a wider plan for the reconstruction of Central Europe. More specifically, such a program will have to wait till the trade relations between the Russian and western economic systems have been clarified. But it is desirable to prepare Austria's economic life, now paralyzed, for peaceful purposes, not only for her benefit but also for that of her neighbors. Apart from Czechoslovakia, Austria has more undamaged industries than any other Central European country. With the limitations placed on German industries, Austrian industries could play a relatively large part in the reconstruction of the devastated countries of eastern and southern Europe.

Allied Military Government has made some important contributions to the rehabilitation of Austria's economic life, in the first place by the restoration of communications. Still, the major prerequisite for a more definitive policy on the part of the Austrian government was not achieved before June 1946. Meanwhile the zonal division made the free flow of goods between the Austrian provinces extremely difficult. Price levels tended to become different, endangering effective anti-inflation measures. Nor could the rebuilding of economic activities be projected as a common Austrian effort. The chief obstacles which the members of the Allied Control Commission encountered in their attempts to make the zonal lines invisible and increase the actual power of the Austrian government were their disagreements on vital issues in the treatment of economic problems. The western Allies were ready to treat Austria as a liberated country except for disarmament and denazification. But the Soviet Union was apparently not yet satisfied with the purge of Austria and not willing to waive any possible title to reparations she might hold.

The reparations settlement of Potsdam renounced all American and British claims "in respect of reparations to shares of German enterprises which are located in the eastern zone of occupation in Germany, as well as to German foreign assets in Bulgaria, Finland, Hungary, Rumania, and Eastern Austria." This provision which failed to be accompanied by clear reservations protecting Austria's vital interests has led the Russians to demand even the appropriation of property which the Austrians were forced to hand over to the Nazis under duress. Since the penetration of Austrian industries by the Nazis was extensive, the Austrians would lose a substantial part of their industries and other resources to the Russians if these insisted upon a literal interpretation. The most important practical case is the Russian seizure of the oil of Zistersdorf. The development of these oil resources of Austria was probably the most significant event in Austrian economic history under the Nazis and German investment in them was heavy. On the other hand, the oil wells and refineries of Zistersdorf constitute one of the natural foundations of Austria's economic life, the more so since

Austria has hardly any coal resources. If Austria cannot maintain control over the output of the Zistersdorf region her economic independence, which never will be absolute, will be greatly crippled.

In the spring of 1946 the divergence of opinions was being expressed mostly in legalistic terms, but the conflict went deeper. The Moscow Declaration said that the Allies considered themselves "as in no way bound by any changes effected in Austria" since 1938. Behind this statement was the willingness of the Allies, including Russia, to build a politically and economically independent Austria. But Russia gave other interests at least temporarily higher priority. It seems that the Russians view the Cabinet of Figl with as much reserve as the British used to eye the provisional government under Renner. Russia clings more stubbornly to all the guarantees of control she has gained as a consequence of the War, and she is more interested in her own reconstruction and that of Yugoslavia and Czechoslovakia than in the future of Austria.

The slow progress of Allied Military Government in Austria is the result of these great political tensions between the big powers and Austria had to pay a heavy price for being the "turntable" of the Continent. Secretary Byrnes tried to solve the Austrian problem by proposing at the Paris Conference of foreign ministers in May 1946 the immediate negotiation of a peace treaty with Austria. The Russians refused to consider this proposal, but the Allied Commission in Vienna succeeded in working out a new Allied control plan for Austria which was finally accepted on June 28* and became effective immediately.

Under this plan the zonal boundaries were to become mere lines of demarcation for the occupation forces and no longer to serve as barriers for the movement of Austrian citizens and goods. Simultaneously the Austrian government received authority to pass domestic laws, other than constitutional provisions, and conclude international agreements. Such laws and agreements become automatically effective thirty-one days after being reported to the Allied Commission unless disapproved unanimously by the Commission. Austria has received, too, control of her customs and frontiers. The functions of the Allied Commission have thus become entirely supervisory rather than administrative while at the same time official contacts between zonal military authorities and Austrians cease. Logically the plan provides that the personnel of the Allied groups of the Commission may be either civilian or military, including their highest officers. It should be mentioned that the control of the city of Vienna is to be gradually turned over to the city council.

*Appendix XIX.

The new Allied control plan for Austria was an important achievement in Allied cooperation and would fulfill the major promises which the Allies made in the Moscow Declaration if it were given full play. Under the plan the Austrian government would be able to lay the foundations for a new Austrian economy. But Austria still remains dependent on the good will of the outside world for her most elementary needs. UNRRA has not been in a position to import more food than barely enough to keep the Austrians above a starvation level and the imminent discontinuation of UNRRA created an even more serious threat for the recovery of the country in 1947. It is probably true that the summer of 1946 saw even more hunger in Vienna and other urban centers of Austria than in the cities of the American zone of Germany which, too, were maintained only on a near-starvation diet.

Austria is now legally free to make bilateral agreements with foreign nations and she could conclude trade pacts with either the Soviet Union or the Western Powers. But Russia has not changed her attitude of claiming extraordinary rights on the basis of the Potsdam agreement and has continued to defy the Allied authority in matters which she chose to construe as being related to that issue. The Russian policy has not only again cast a shadow over the operations of the Allied Commission in Vienna but has kept the Austrian government from gaining actual control over the management of Austrian economic policy. It will have to be seen whether or not the situation will improve after international agreement has been reached on the peace treaties with Hungary, Rumania, Bulgaria, and Italy. It may not be impossible either to achieve a better interpretation of the "German assets in Eastern Austria" promised to Russia in the Potsdam agreement in connection with a new inter-Allied reparations program for Germany. Meanwhile the situation of Austria will remain precarious.

FOOTNOTES, CHAPTER 9

[42]See the article by L. A. Hoffmann, "Austria: Zones of Occupation," Department of State, *Bulletin,* Vol. XIV (1946), pp. 649-654.

[43]A good account of the initial stages of Allied Military Government in Austria up to October is to be found in the article "The Allied Commission for Austria" in *The World Today,* Vol. I, No. 5 (November 1945).

[44]See Department of State, *Bulletin,* Vol. XIII (1945), p. 612, Vol. XIV (1946), p. 81.

Chapter 10

American Military Government in the Far East

ILITARY GOVERNMENT operations in the Pacific areas prior to the surrender of Japan were of relatively small scope and raised no considerable political problems. The Central Pacific command of Admiral Nimitz—officially known as Pacific Ocean Area—was a United States theater and consequently under the Joint Chiefs of Staff, whereas the Southwest Pacific Theater under General MacArthur was under the Combined Chiefs of Staff. This made little difference in the military government and civil affairs practices. When the Gilbert Islands were taken by the U. S. Navy and Marines, British officers had been invited to accompany the landing forces in order to reestablish the British administration, and in Dutch Hollandia Dutch officers with the American troops exercised similar functions.

The Joint Chiefs of Staff had laid down the principle in 1943 that military government on the smaller islands like the Marianas, Carolines, Marshalls, Izu, Bonin, Volcanoes, Marcus, Ryukyu Islands was to be a responsibility of the Navy, while the larger land masses were to constitute a responsibility of the Army. But in Okinawa, which was invaded by the Tenth Army commanded by General Buckner, who in turn was under Admiral Nimitz, largely Army personnel operated military government in the combat period. A considerable number of Army officers was thus acquainted with the problems they were likely to encounter upon entering Japan. After Japan offered to surrender, military government in Okinawa and the other Ryukyus was taken over by the Navy, a move which freed Army personnel for service in Japan and Korea for which, under orders of the Joint Chiefs of Staff, it had been preparing for a long time. On May 1, 1945, a Joint Civil Affairs Committee was established to facilitate full unity of command in this field. In general the planning for Japan was benefited greatly by the operational and political lessons learned in the planning and conduct of American civil affairs in Europe. Still, there were unpredictable circumstances which no planning could solve beforehand.

The first invasion of one of the main islands of Japan, Kyushu, was planned for the fall of 1945, the invasion of Honshu for the spring of 1946. Whatever losses the Japanese suffered in the first half of the year 1945, "the Japanese defense grew more desperate as our advance moved towards the shores of the homeland."[45] Civil affairs preparations could not exclude the possibility of a lengthy period of military government under heavy combat conditions. In this situation the establishment of military government controls on the local and district level would have been as important as central supervision. But it was quite thinkable that if the Japanese government carried its resistance to the same suicidal length as the Nazis had done, American military government would have to rebuild the whole Japanese government structure after the final defeat of Japan. Such a system of direct military government had its weaknesses in Europe, but it would have had even greater difficulties in the Orient. For it would have called for a much larger group of men fully familiar with the civilization and administration of Japan than was available in the United States or could have been trained by experts at short notice. It would also have required far greater military forces for the occupation than were likely to exist after the close of the War.

Warnings were heard early against the danger of establishing a system of direct control by American military government. In the public mind the controversy is remembered as centering around the question of Emperor Hirohito. Should America and the United Nations make peace with him? Was not the monarchy one of the cornerstones of the aggressive militarism? Could it be separated from the militaristic forces and made a useful tool in the reconstruction of a liberal Japan? Once the problem was closely analyzed there appeared more than the mere alternative between retention and non-retention of the Emperor. It was certainly poor advice to plead for the continuation of imperial rule if this meant the acceptance of the Emperor as a sovereign ruler. But it was even more dangerous to argue merely for the removal of the upper crust of the militarists and recommend American cooperation with the so-called "liberal" industrialists. With the old social order of Japan undisturbed, and with the throne made safe by the victors, the future of democracy in Japan would have been hopeless. If Japan was to be disarmed, demilitarized, and set on the road to a peaceful democratic state, American military government needed control over the Emperor and a free hand to mould, not only the political, but the social and economic conditions of Japan as well. It could not become committed to guarantee the continued existence of an exalted monarchy and an antiquated social order unlikely to last after the War unless backed by strong force.

The Anglo-Sino-American Conference at Cairo of November 1943 had already proclaimed the restoration of Manchuria, Formosa, and the Pescadores to China as Allied war aims.* "Japan," the three statesmen added, "will also be expelled from all other territories which she has taken by violence or greed." The three Allies expressed specifically their determination "that in due course Korea shall become free and

---
*Appendix III.

independent." In other words, Japan was to be deprived of all she had conquered since 1894 and was to be confined to her four major islands with a few tiny adjacent islands. It may be assumed that under the Yalta accord of February 11, 1945 the Soviet Union received only Japanese territories which the other powers had long considered as likely to go back to Russia.[46]

By these political decisions Japan was reduced to an area which could not grow sufficient food for her seventy million people, while her industries were cut off from their sources of raw materials. It was unrealistic, therefore, to believe that Japan's economic and social order could be restored to a 1925 level, quite apart from the fact that such a policy was open to grave doubts with regard to Japan's future role in the community of nations. For Japan had turned towards expansionist imperialism, not by 1931, but forty years earlier. If the fundamental war aim of the United States, namely the destruction of Japan's ability to disturb the peace of the world, was to be achieved, the United States could not be tied to the monarchical institutions of Japan. Nor could she abstain from directing herself the reconstruction of Japan as a peaceful member in international affairs.

But this did not necessarily mean that, as in Germany, the central government and administration had to be liquidated. If the Emperor showed the strength to extricate himself from the dominating influence of the war lords and to surrender the armed forces of Japan to the Allies, no good reason existed to expend additional lives, provided the supreme authority of the American military governor was established beyond any doubt. Such an arrangement was also bound to simplify greatly the problems of the occupation and military government in Japan. In the spring of 1945 these ideas had become the guiding principles of official thinking in Washington through the deliberations of the State-War-Navy Coordinating Committee.

Inevitably they had to remain tentative, depending upon the course of the War and upon the internal development of Japan. After the invasion of the Philippines in the fall of 1944, the Pacific war moved much faster towards its final climax than was realized, even at the time of the Okinawa campaign. Still not even the most optimistic leaders, unaware of the full impact of air and naval destruction, could have hoped for a final decision before the winter of 1945. Only by then would the redeployment of the American forces from Europe to the Pacific have built up adequate military power to begin the invasions of the heartlands of Japan and would Russia have started her attack against the industries and resources on the Asiatic mainland.

The atomic bomb changed the timetable of subsequent political events. During the Conference of Potsdam President Truman received the report of the successful test in New Mexico and it was decided to use the weapon after August 3. But before Japan suffered the terrifying blows of Hiroshima and Nagasaki she had been informed by President Truman, Prime Minister Churchill and Generalissimo Chiang Kai-shek of the terms for a Japanese surrender.* Undoubtedly Generalissimo Stalin, through whom the Japanese had just tried to open negotiations with the Allies, was fully cognizant of the Potsdam Declaration of July 26, 1945, to which he publicly acceded on August 8, when the Soviet Union declared war upon Japan.

The political significance of the Declaration can be summarized in a few points. The Allies declined firmly a negotiated peace or even an armistice which would limit their freedom of action in dealing with the defeated country. They insisted upon the complete removal of all the militaristic forces from government and other influences in public life and the radical destruction of Japan's war-making power. The Allies announced their intention to occupy certain points of Japan until such objectives were accomplished and a "peacefully inclined and responsible government" had been established "in accordance with the freely expressed will of the Japanese people." On the other hand the Allies stated that they did not plan to enslave the Japanese people. In particular the Japanese military forces would be allowed to return home after disarmament, and Japan would be permitted to retain peaceful industries and for that purpose would be given access to raw materials.

The Declaration did not mention the Emperor directly, but said that the time had come to throw off "those self-willed militaristic advisers" who had brought "the Empire of Japan" to the brink of annihilation. But the document contained no promise with reference to the future of the Japanese monarchy and took an aloof attitude by emphasizing that Japan should develop a free, democratic and peaceful government.

On August 10, 1945 the new Japanese government indicated Japan's willingness to accept the terms of the Potsdam Declaration "with the understanding that the said declaration does not comprise any demand which prejudices the prerogatives of His Majesty as a Sovereign Ruler."** The note by Secretary of State Byrnes, made it clear that through the surrender the authority of the Emperor and of the Japanese government would become subject to the Supreme Commander of the Allied Powers, "who will take such steps as he deems proper to effectuate the surrender terms." The Secretary also reminded the Japanese

---

*Appendix XIII.
**Appendix XIV.

government that "the ultimate form of government of Japan shall, in accordance with the Potsdam Declaration, be established by the freely expressed will of the Japanese people." Three days later the Japanese government made known to the Allied governments its readiness to accept the terms of the Potsdam Declaration without stating any further qualifications. The Japanese Surrender of September 1, in the interpretation of the Joint Chiefs' directives to General MacArthur,[47] did not establish any contractual relationship between the United States and the Japanese government. General MacArthur was consequently directed not to entertain any question on the part of the Japanese as to the scope of his supreme authority in Japan. As far as the arrangement produced satisfactory results, he was advised to exercise his control through the Japanese government, though this was not to prejudice his right to act directly and use any measures he deemed wise.

The final offer by the Japanese to surrender of August 14 raised difficult problems of an operational nature. Events had moved so unexpectedly and swiftly that it was impossible to make landings in Japan at once. Large forces had to be brought to Japan and they had to be fully equipped for battle in case the Japanese army of two million men should show signs of disobeying the orders of the Emperor to hand over their arms. Hard thinking and quick action were needed during the next two weeks before American troops in sufficient strength could sail toward Tokyo Bay. The troops were under their tactical commanders. Once it became clear that no serious resistance would be encountered a radical reorganization had to be performed within a few days which would enable the vast combat machine to cope with the supervision of the Japanese administration. This most difficult and intricate task was accomplished with amazing smoothness and dispatch.

The civil affairs officers trained in the civil affairs training schools of the Army and Navy had begun to assemble in the Civil Affairs Staging Area (CASA) since the fall of 1944, reaching full strength in the subsequent spring. It was impossible to find space for them in the Pacific islands that were packed with troops and supplies for the final onslaught against Japan. The Civil Affairs Staging Area had to be placed on a California "beachhead" in Monterey. Here the military civil affairs personnel received its final training. It had been hoped to establish an advance area in Hawaii or in the Philippines in fall 1945, but the surrender of Japan happened too soon to start the movement of the civil affairs officers before the end of August. Shortly thereafter the first civilian experts followed. But it is easily forgotten how heavy the general military duty of General MacArthur's headquarters was during the early months of the occupation of Japan. On the American side they consisted of the direction of demobilization, on the Japanese of disarmament, and these two tasks were not simple to combine.

This also explains why General MacArthur had to move with great circumspection in the execution of the directives on the military government of Japan which he received from the Joint Chiefs of Staff on August 29, 1945.* The directives did not suggest in what order the various contemplated measures should be taken nor did they prescribe any time limit on their full realization. Such matters were left to the good judgment of the Supreme Commander who would be in a position to set his course according to the local conditions and reactions he would find. Today it is generally agreed that General MacArthur moved with the greatest possible speed and during the first year of the American occupation achieved more substantial results than even sanguine observers of the Japanese scene could have predicted. Still he himself believes that the directives have not been fully translated into action, and that further measures for their realization will need to be taken as conditions may warrant.

Although the sudden collapse of Japan caused some initial difficulties in civil affairs operations, the policy decisions had been made well in advance. The program for the future American occupation policy had grown steadily from the time when the State-War-Navy Coordinating Committee reached agreement on its basic principles, in the spring of 1945, to the days of the Potsdam Conference. Neither the surrender document nor a substantive policy of American military government had to be improvised when the Japanese offered surrender on August 12. The directives on the Military Government of Japan, issued to General MacArthur on August 29,[48] were the logical result of intensive study and discussion among the various agencies of the United States Government over a period of months. In this respect, too, the experiences gathered in the debates on the German problem proved most advantageous.

Broadly speaking the general objective of American military government of Japan and of Germany is identical: Neither country shall become a menace to world peace again. This major aim is approached not only through outward disarmament and demilitarization, but also through an active policy of democratization of the political, economic, social, and cultural life of the two countries. However, American occupation policies are built on the belief that democratic reform cannot be decreed from above, but can be made genuine only by the people themselves. The punitive and prohibitive measures enforced by military government have centered, therefore, around a few fundamental

---

*Appendix XV.

principles. Apart from the apprehension of war criminals and the arrest of dangerous war leaders, they include the removal of prominent militarists from positions of influence in government, business, and education. Beyond these negative steps there is to be the positive assertion of liberal and democratic rights—freedom of speech and assembly, of religion and press. Similarly, equality of race, nationality, creed and political opinion is being upheld and economic monopolies are dissolved.

Since, in the Pacific Theater, in contrast with the Southeast Asia Theater, mostly American forces were employed and were supposed to launch the invasion of Japan, the planning and organization of the military government of Japan was considered an American responsibility. But though the United States was to direct and operate military government, the United States Government was acting on behalf of the United Nations. This not only found expression in the formulation of policies in preparation for military government operations but it was always expected to be demonstrated, as soon as fighting ended, by the participation of Allied contingents in the occupation and by the creation of consultative inter-Allied bodies. If the American military government of Japan was to fulfill its mission of turning Japan into a peaceful member of the Pacific world, all the states around the Pacific not only had to be kept fully informed about its actual progress but also had to take counsel among themselves how to promote the realization of such aims.

The first opportunity for the discussion of Allied policies with regard to Japan was the Potsdam Conference. The Potsdam Declaration, defining terms for the Japanese surrender, was a full endorsement of the principal American occupation policies. The Japanese offer of surrender of August 10 and the full acceptance of the Potsdam Declaration of August 14 were both answered by Secretary of State Byrnes "on behalf of the Governments of the United States, the United Kingdom, the Union of Soviet Socialist Republics, and China." And in his second note he informed the Japanese that General MacArthur had been designated as the Supreme Commander for the Allied Powers. The instrument of surrender was signed by General MacArthur "for the United States, Republic of China, United Kingdom, and the Union of the Soviet Socialist Republics, and in the interest of the other United Nations at war with Japan." These other nations were Australia, New Zealand, Canada, France, and the Netherlands.

Even preceding the signing of the Japanese surrender the Joint Chiefs' directives of August 29 concerning the Military Government of Japan had informed General MacArthur that "the occupation shall have the character of an operation on behalf of the principal Allied powers acting in the interests of the United Nations at war with Japan. For that reason, participation of the forces of other nations that have taken a leading part in the war against Japan will be welcomed and expected. The occupation forces will be under the command of a Supreme Commander designated by the United States." And the directives added: "Although every effort will be made, by consultation and by constitution of appropriate advisory bodies, to establish policies for the conduct of the occupation and the control of Japan which will satisfy the principal Allied powers, in the event of any differences of opinion among them, the policies of the United States will govern."

Two major claims of the United States were asserted in these directives. First, all occupation forces in Japan, even those from other nations, would come under the command of General MacArthur and no combined command or zones under an Allied Control Council comparable to the German Control Council would be created. Second, inter-Allied consultation on policies was not to delay the operations of military government. In case of disagreement the United States point of view was to be carried into effect. Both these principles have since been accepted by our Allies.

The American Government, as mentioned before, was at the same time desirous of inviting the cooperation of the Allied Powers and the United Nations. Unhappily, the first American proposal made to achieve this objective through the establishment of an advisory council, fell short of this accomplishment. As early as August 21 the United States Government had proposed to China, Britain, and the Soviet Union the creation of a Far Eastern Advisory Commission.[49] Its functions were defined as making "recommendations to the participating Governments" on certain matters. In other words the Commission was patterned along the lines of the European Advisory Commission which had no authority to settle policy issues, but simply made recommendations to the three or four governments, which then had to reach a common decision with regard to the adoption of such plans through the usual diplomatic channels. Although the slow progress of the work of the European Advisory Commission, as we have seen, was largely due to the uncertainties of the political and military situation prevailing in 1944, its organizational structure already explained much of the resulting procrastination. The European Advisory Commission proved capable of producing the technical arrangements for the inter-Allied military government of Germany and Austria, but agreements on substantive occupation policies always issued from the meetings of the Big Three.

The proposed Far Eastern Advisory Commission would have started its deliberations under different conditions after VJ-day. The Big Four had already agreed at Potsdam both on the form and the general policies of the American military government of Japan. Still, the policies laid down in the Potsdam Declaration needed implementation and, as time would pass, considerable augmentation by new principles. The Far Eastern Advisory Commission, as proposed on August 21, 1945, was a rather weak instrument for reaching such political agreements, the more so since its establishment would not provide any clear system of regular information to its members by the United States Government. The proposed Far Eastern Advisory Commission would have contributed merely a forum for the exchange of views.

The American proposal aimed chiefly at the preservation of the unity of command over the actual operations of American military government in Japan. It was understandable that the United States Government did not wish to weaken the authority of General Mac-Arthur, who had just been accepted by the other Allied Powers as Supreme Commander of the Allied Forces. If General MacArthur was to be hampered in his actions by an Allied Control Council, or if the United States Government was to be kept by an inter-Allied agency from supplying him in time with adequate policy guidance, the gates would be opened to the same elements of political disunity and ensuing stagnation that had marred the occupations of Germany and Austria. But the proposed Far Eastern Advisory Commission was hardly a suitable instrument to keep the other powers interested in the progress of the American occupation of Japan and give it their full political support. If the other nations did not receive any more effective representation than this, they would watch American operations and policies merely from the sidelines and might become suspicious and critical. They might even voice disapproval and thus raise hopes in the hearts of those Japanese groups waiting to undo the order introduced by the Americans. At the very least, some Pacific powers could simply refuse to recognize the government of Japan to which the United States will eventually wish to turn over control. As Japan had surrendered to the four powers and the United Nations, peace will have to be made among all of them. The Far Eastern Advisory Commission did not provide adequate machinery of inter-Allied cooperation for the achievement of this long-term objective.

There were indications that China and Britain, who accepted the invitation of the United States to join the Far Eastern Advisory Commission, had their misgivings about its functions and hoped for changes in its character. The Soviet Union after first indicating its willingness to join the Advisory Commission, refused after September to cooperate in an agency which would lack all functions of control. But the United States Government, though not unwilling to discuss the terms of reference of the Commission, did not wish to postpone the beginnings of inter-Allied consultation on Japanese problems. Additional invitations were issued to Australia, Canada, France, India, the Netherlands, New Zealand, and the Philippines. On October 30, 1945 the first meeting of the Far Eastern Advisory Commission was held in Washington.[50] One of the main desires of the Commission was to form an opinion of Japanese conditions and of American military government through a visit to Japan. The members of the Commission left Washington on December 11, 1945.[51] But even before its arrival in Japan the Commission learned that it was to be replaced by a new agency as a consequence of the agreement reached at the Moscow Conference of Secretary Byrnes, Foreign Minister Molotov, and Foreign Secretary Bevin.

The Moscow Conference of December 1945 decided to replace the Far Eastern Advisory Commission by the Far Eastern Commission.* As the name indicates, it was to be a body of higher political standing than its predecessor, though it was not an Allied Control Council. As in the past the Supreme Commander would receive his directives exclusively from the United States Government through the established military channels. But the Commission was empowered not only, as the Far Eastern Advisory Commission had been, to make recommendations to the governments, but "to formulate the policies, principles, and standards in conformity with which the fulfillment by Japan of its obligations under the terms of surrender may be accomplished." As to procedure it was now stated that any member could demand the review of "any directive issued to the Supreme Commander for the Allied powers" or of "any action taken by the Supreme Commander involving policy decisions within the jurisdiction of the Commission." It was declared to be the function of the United States Government to "prepare directives in accordance with policy decisions of the Commission;" but if the Commission decided "that any directive or action reviewed. . . should be modified, its decision shall be regarded as a policy decision." There was no change in the rules on membership of the Commission; but in accordance with the document of Japanese surrender and perhaps in analogy to the voting procedures of the United Nations Security Council, greater power was given to the big four powers. In contrast to the Allied Control Councils in Berlin and Vienna the unanimity rule did not apply, but the majority was limited by the provision that it should include the big four Pacific

*Appendix XVII.

powers. Nothing was said about what would happen if the four powers failed to reach agreement, though it may be assumed that in this case an agreement among the four would have to be sought through diplomatic channels. Meanwhile, however, the United States could use its right to "issue interim directives to the Supreme Commander pending action by the Commission whenever urgent matters arise not covered by policies already formulated by the Commission; provided that any directive dealing with fundamental changes in the Japanese constitutional structure or in the regime of control, or dealing with a change in the Japanese government as a whole will be issued only following consultation and following the attainment of agreement in the Far Eastern Commission."

The Far Eastern Commission has been discussed in America almost exclusively in reference to the position of General MacArthur as military governor of Japan. Its creation had little bearing upon his role. It has to be appraised as an organizational method of maintaining effective unity among the signatories of the Potsdam Declaration on Japan and of the Japanese Surrender, thus to reach at an early moment a state of administration of Japan where its control could be turned over to the United Nations Organization. In fact the Far Eastern Commission could in many respects serve as a model for the regional councils contemplated by the United Nations Charter, though it should be understood that its jurisdiction is confined to Japan.[52] The Moscow Communiqué of December 28, 1945, did not speak of a future transfer of the Commission as a whole to the United Nations Organization, but laid down that the Commission would cease to function if a majority of its members, including the big four powers, should so decide. However, it was declared that the same majority of the Commission could pass on, prior to its termination, those functions which may appropriately be transferred to any interim or permanent security organization of which the participating governments are members.

In addition to the Far Eastern Commission, which was to have its regular seat in Washington, though it could hold meetings anywhere including Tokyo, the Moscow Conference established an Allied Council for Japan in Tokyo. Hereby the existing practice of American military government operations was taken into account. Directives on military government, and for that matter on any phase of military leadership, are confined to general principles. It is the task of the commander to implement these general policies by his own decisions. This organization of command responsibilities was expressly confirmed by the Moscow Communiqué in its statement that "the Supreme Commander shall be charged with the implementation of the directives."

He remained the "sole executive authority for the Allied Powers in Japan," but a council was created under his or his deputy's chairmanship "for the purpose of consulting with and advising the Supreme Commander in regard to the implementation of the terms of surrender, the occupation and control of Japan, and of directives supplementary thereto." With few exceptions the Allied Council for Japan was thought of exclusively as an advisory and consultative body. It should prove useful to General MacArthur if its members make it their chief duty to acquaint him with their national interpretation of the directives emanating from Washington after having been passed on by the Far Eastern Commission. It is not the function of the Allied Council in Tokyo to produce policies, but only to advise on their implementation. However, even in this respect the Council has no controlling authority. The rule requesting the Supreme Commander to "consult and advise with the Council in advance of the issuance of orders on matters of substance, the exigencies of the situation permitting," is not to be construed as limiting his authority to make his own decisions upon all these matters.

In a few cases the members of the Allied Council can insist upon a delay of the actions of the Supreme Commander till the Far Eastern Commission has had time to clarify its intentions. The Moscow Communiqué said that "if regarding the implementation of policy decisions of the Far Eastern Commission on questions concerning a change in the regime of control, fundamental changes in the Japanese constitutional structure, and a change in the Japanese government as a whole, a member of the Council disagrees with the Supreme Commander, the Supreme Commander will withhold the issuance of orders on these questions pending agreement thereon in the Far Eastern Commission."

It is in this connection that the Allied Council is most closely linked up with the Far Eastern Commission. As to membership the Council is a representation of the big four powers only, though the fourth member represents not Britain but the British Commonwealth. The role of the four powers in winning the War is once more demonstrated to the Japanese people in the composition of the Tokyo Council. Similarly the structure of the Council enhances once more the position of the big powers in the Far Eastern Commission where they already enjoy special voting privileges.

The Far Eastern Commission held its first meeting in Washington on February 26, 1946. Represented were the big four powers, the United States, Great Britain, China, and the Soviet Union, and also Australia, Canada, France, India, the Netherlands, New Zealand, the Philippines. The Commission elected General Frank R. McCoy, who had formerly served as chairman of the Far Eastern Advisory Commission, permanent chairman.[53] Secretary Byrnes welcomed the new "policy-making group," saying that its major responsibility was to guide Japan to a position of peaceful association with other nations.[54] A general idea of the new methods by which the Commission is attempting to fulfill its mission can be gleaned from a list of committees it has approved in addition to the Steering Committee. Seven of them have come into existence: (1) Reparations; (2) Economic and Financial Affairs; (3) Constitutional and Legal Reform; (4) Strengthening of Democratic Tendencies; (5) War Criminals; (6) Aliens in Japan; (7) Disarmament of Japan.[55]

The Allied Council in Tokyo convened for the first time on April 4, when General MacArthur addressed its members. He proposed that "all formal sessions" be open to public and press. "There is nothing in its deliberations to conceal even from the eyes and ears of our alien adversary."[56] This hope was not immediately realized and informal meetings were needed to reach a better understanding among the members about the functions of the Allied Council which is presided over by General MacArthur's deputy and political adviser, Mr. George Atcheson.

It is too early to appraise the work of the Allied Council for Japan and of the Far Eastern Commission. It can be stated, however, that at least the organization of inter-Allied cooperation in the control of Japan would augur well both for the untrammeled progress of the actual American operations in Japan[57] and for the eventual disestablishment of military government through a final peace settlement. This may be preceded by a preliminary arrangement under which remaining control functions would be exercised by the United Nations.

While in Japan both the actual operations of military government and the formulation of occupation policies have kept pace with the existing needs, the evolution of the military government in Korea has been arrested by the division of Korea in an American and Russian zone of occupation and by the inability of the two powers to agree on a workable administrative system and to adopt common policies. The developments of Allied control over Korea are the more deplorable since they have inflicted serious hardships on a nation which was promised liberation by the Allies. Through the Cairo Declaration of December 1, 1943 President Roosevelt, Prime Minister Churchill, and Generalissimo Chiang Kai-shek announced that the Korean people would "in due course" receive freedom and independence, and the Potsdam Declaration defining terms of a Japanese surrender tacitly confirmed this earlier pledge. But the Potsdam Conference did not take the time to draft an agreement on the methods by which the goal was to be reached or on what forms an interim regime of the American and Russian armies was to assume.

When after the surrender of Japan American and Russian troops moved into Korea from the north and south to disarm the Japanese army and remove the Japanese from the country which they had ruled for forty years, the local commanders fixed a line of demarkation for purposes of military occupation. Since they met north of Seoul on the 38th parallel this line was chosen. The line was considered to have only a temporary character, like the Elbe–Mulde line in Germany in the summer of 1945. But latitude 38 has continued since September 1945 as a wall separating two entirely different political regimes. The American zone of occupation covers the larger area and contains about 17 million of the 25 million Koreans.[58] But with the exception of the national capital, Seoul, it is a predominantly agricultural region though it contains also a substantial part of the industrial processing plants. The Russian sphere includes all the major industrial resources. Hence, the economic life of the country has been paralyzed by the unnatural division. Though communications were found in fair condition they do not carry traffic between the two Koreas.

The stagnation of economic activities has made the economic position of the Koreans probably more precarious than it was under the Japanese, though these had exploited Korean economy as much as possible for their own benefit. Without the creation of a healthy economic system the foundation of a democratic government cannot be laid. Still, the economic problems are only one of the aspects created by the virtual partition of Korea. The political issues are equally grave.

The removal of the Japanese rulers who occupied all higher positions in public administration and economic enterprise will leave Korea in need of foreign advisers and teachers for a long time to come. The Japanese made every effort to deny Koreans access to higher skills and professions. Korean personnel is consequently scarce and as far as it exists often trained in foreign schools. Similarly, the political movements in Korea had been suppressed and therefore it was not surprising that after VJ-day only small parties were found. By October 1945 more than fifty different political organizations were registered with the American military government and their number increased thereafter. This situation was natural in a country in which political organizations could grow only around some local leaders.

Trained and skilled Koreans could acquire their education abroad, which meant chiefly in the United States, the Soviet Union and China.

From these countries Korean exiles had tried to create organizations to keep resistance against the domination by Japan alive and to build up potential governments. One group located in Shanghai, and since 1940 in Chungking, has always looked to Chiang Kai-shek and the United States for support, others have placed their trust in cooperation with the Russians and the Red Chinese groups. It is unlikely that the latter group commands anything remotely approaching a majority in Korea, but its leaders have been in closer contact with the conditions of the country and have lived in the midst of the large emigrant population which had settled in Russia's Pacific provinces. A great number of political organizers, trained by the Communist Party in Russia, accompanied the Russian army into Korea and it seems that the Russians also used large military units composed of Koreans in their invasion from the north.

The political situation of Korea could hardly be more perplexing than it was found after American troops had entered.[59] The confusing variety of internal political groups and the foreign ramifications of the national movement made it extremely difficult to devise a coalition of forces that would be acceptable both domestically and diplomatically. This was at least true if one wanted to avoid intervention in matters which were considered fundamental issues of national life by the Americans, settlement of which should be reserved to a national government of Korea. The American military government therefore has used Koreans individually in the administration and has been making every effort to increase their number, but has abstained from turning over large responsibilities to Korean groups. American administrators have been careful not to take decisions which would prejudice the future political and social life of Korea such as the disposition of former Japanese-owned property or a land reform. The Russians, on their part, have given the Koreans in the northern section a great amount of self-government which, however, is dominated by indigenous and returning Korean Communists. Meanwhile in the Russian zone a far-reaching social revolution has taken place chiefly through a radical redistribution of land.

The divergent policies of the two occupation regimes are not likely to make the political problems of a future independent government of Korea easier to solve. Still, as long as there is hope that the conflict between the struggling factions and sections will be carried on by democratic processes Korea could emerge as a unified national state. The question is whether the United States and the Soviet Union keep their determination to combine in nursing a national government of Korea on a democratic basis.

At the time of the Moscow Conference of the three foreign ministers of December 1945 the two governments seemed bent upon such cooperation. The Moscow decisions provided an immediate measure for the meeting of members of the American and Russian commands to consider urgent problems affecting North and South Korea and achieve better liaison. With regard to the fundamental problems of Korean independence the Moscow Conference decided that a "provisional Korean democratic government" should be established which should take "all the necessary steps for developing the industry, transport and agriculture of Korea and the national culture of the Korean people."

In order to establish such a provisional government a Joint American-Soviet Commission was to be convened, composed of representatives of the two commands, which in consultation with Korean democratic parties and social organizations was to make recommendations concerning the formation of a Korean provisional government. The recommendations were to be presented for the consideration of the governments of Russia, China, Britain, and the United States and to be finally approved by the United States and Russia. The Joint Commission was also expected to work out, together with the Provisional Government, measures "for helping and assisting (trusteeship) the political, economic, and social progress of the Korean people, the development of democratic self-government and the establishment of the national independence of Korea." In other words, the Joint Commission was to make recommendations with regard to a possible trusteeship of Korea and the forms which such trusteeship might take if agreed upon.

Meetings between representatives of the two commands were held between January 15 and May 8 with only brief intermissions. No agreement was achieved. The Soviet representatives were inclined to insist on the exclusion of all Korean groups which had criticized the results of the Moscow Conference and attacked the establishment of a trusteeship over Korea. This would eliminate most groups of a democratic complexion in addition to some admittedly less democratic elements whose cause the Americans were not championing. But it is not wise to consider the issue only in terms of the principle of the democratic freedom of speech and expression. Obviously the Moscow Communiqué did not request the Joint Commission to make proposals for an ideal or final Korean government. It stated expressly that it should propose a "provisional" government and also assumed that this was to be a government with limited powers to work with, and possibly under, the two military governors and later under four-power supervision. Naturally then its members should inspire confidence among the two powers.

On the other hand, the Moscow Communiqué placed equal emphasis on the democratic nature of the provisional government. The United States cannot accept a government that would not in its composition demonstrate its willingness to protect freedom of political life and accept the verdict of the people. This would not necessarily mean that all parties should be represented in the provisional government. If the Russians would broaden their interpretation of the meaning of a democratic government of Korea, as envisaged in the Moscow Communiqué, and the Americans lay greater stress on the provisional character of this government, agreement may still be achieved.

The importance of cooperation in Korea is of the first order. The interest of the Soviet Union in Korea is most urgent on account of the security of her Far Eastern provinces. Both her maritime provinces and her influence in Manchuria depend on the Korean settlement. The whole future of the Far East is affected by the fate of Korea, a country of the size of Spain, which was the natural stepping stone for Japan for removing Russia as a major power in the Far East and starting her own conquest of the Asiatic mainland. The largely unexploited natural resources of Korea will play a great part in the expansion of the industries of the whole Far East. The problem of finding a solution of the conflict between liberal and communist ideas which is the great challenge to Chinese unity is posed in Korea as well. If we fail to achieve in time a practical form of cooperation in Korea, the repercussions upon the whole Far East will be most disturbing.

FOOTNOTES, CHAPTER 10

[45]General Marshall's Report, *The Winning of the War in Europe and the Pacific*, p. 80.

[46]The Yalta agreement concerning the future position of the Soviet Union in the Far East was published a year later. See Department of State, *Bulletin*, Vol. XIV (1946), p. 282. The ensuing treaty of friendship and alliance between Russia and China, *Ibidem*, pp. 201-08.

[47]Department of State, *Bulletin*, Vol. XIII, (1945), p. 480.

[48]Appendix, No. XV. An authoritative interpretation of American military government policies in Japan was given by J. C. Vincent, J. H. Hilldring, R. L. Dennison, "Our Occupation Policy for Japan," Department of State, *Bulletin*, Vol. XIII (1945), pp. 538-545.

[49]Department of State, *Bulletin*, Vol. XIII (1945), pp. 545, 561, 580.

[50]See Department of State, *Bulletin*, Vol. XIII (1945), pp. 728 f.

[51]See the summary report in Department of State, *Bulletin*, Vol. XIV (1946), pp. 370-374.

[52]See Department of State, *Bulletin*, Vol. XIV (1946), pp. 375-76.

[53]Department of State, *Bulletin*, Vol. XIV (1946), pp. 375-76.

[54]Department of State, *Bulletin*, Vol. XIV (1946), p. 378.

[55]Department of State, *Bulletin*, Vol. XIV (1946), p. 477 and 655.

[56]*New York Times*, April 5, 1946.

[57]The official summation for the month of February by General MacArthur was reproduced in Department of State, *Bulletin*, Vol. XIV (1946) pp. 749-751; 805-812. For

the early stage of the American operations see General C. A. Willoughby's article "Occupation of Japan and Japanese Reaction," *Military Review,* Vol. XXVI (June 1946), also Department of State, *Occupation of Japan: Policy and Progress,* 1946 (Publication 2671).

[58]For a description of the two zones of Korea see A. J. Grajdanzer, "Korea Divided," *Far Eastern Survey,* October 10, 1945. Cf. also "Korea Past and Present" in *The World Today,* April 1946.

[59]See the radio transcript "Korea and the Far East" by J. C. Vincent, E. M. Martin, B. E. Prescott, Department of State, *Bulletin,* Vol. XIV (1946), pp. 104-110.

Chapter 11
Lessons of the Occupation

AMERICAN MILITARY GOVERNMENT operations have been in existence for more than three years. From 1943 to 1945 these operations were undertaken chiefly to assist American forces in achieving their military objectives without being distracted by the problems posed by the civilian population of the invaded countries. But the creation of a special branch of service made it also possible to organize the civil administration of foreign territories from the outset with a view to the ultimate war and peace aims of the United States and of the United Nations. As a matter of fact, many shortcomings of American military government—shortcomings for which it has frequently been castigated—were due to the lack of a clear definition of American foreign policies. Delays were often unavoidable in the face of an international situation charged with uncertainties. But waiting is not necessarily a good strategy with which to meet such situations. It is better to have in hand a plan of action, even though it may be found necessary later to adapt that plan to different circumstances. And especially, a country that has both the power and responsibility of the United States in shaping world conditions should not find itself without a concrete policy.

On the other hand, it should not be denied that American civil affairs officers have often failed to understand the political function of civil affairs and military government operations, shielding themselves by the assertion that the exigencies of military or non-military local conditions made the realization of political aims unfeasible. It is impossible to say without a very close study of the actual overseas operations how wide-spread such failures were. To some extent they were to be expected in a new branch of service which had to be quickly improvised and hastily trained. Novices in the domestic civil service have the advantage of moving in a community in which they have grown up, and which even in extraordinary conditions does not entirely lose its familiar contours. Moreover, they are normally placed within a group in which they can consult with the more experienced administrators. But civil affairs officers were usually soon sent to lonely posts where they found themselves in a world they had studied academically but which looked very unfamiliar under the impact of war and revolution that had changed it. Small wonder that some of them chose the way of least resistance to discharge their duties.

But we cannot pass judgment on the efficiency of American military government merely on the basis of such considerations. The decisive question is whether the directors of American military government operations were able to weed out unsuitable personnel and enforce adherence to the general policy of the United States before serious damage had been done. On the whole this was accomplished, even in the most difficult circumstances.

Probably the greatest crisis of this type experienced by American military government operations occurred after VJ-day. It will be remembered that shortly before that date the administration of the American zone of Germany had been established, and that American military government was still wrestling at that time to introduce, mostly on a local basis, a rudimentary order into the wreckage of German life. The American press, always free to study and criticize civil affairs operations, at no other time indulged so freely in criticism while neglecting any real study, thus contributing to a slump in American morale. To the military government personnel the future seemed uncertain. The Army had never wanted to administer foreign territories beyond the period of combat and the immediate post-hostilities period. Now there seemed to be a lively demand in the United States to replace military government by a civilian administration, though no one was able to say where such a civilian force should be raised. In this situation many military government officers decided to make use of their rights under the Army's plan of demobilization. Then, almost immediately, the Army was taken to task by certain critics for releasing civil affairs officers at a time when they were most needed.

The Army could do no more than declare military government personnel essential, a ruling that delayed the demobilization of civil affairs officers for a period of six months. The Army could not possibly have placed this group under a law different from the one applying to other members of the armed forces. If any criticism was to be levelled against any agency of the Government, it should have been directed against those who failed to prepare in time an organization capable of supplanting the military administration by a civilian agency and overseas staff. As things worked out it did fall to the Army to manage American overseas administration far beyond the immediate post-hostilities period and to foster its own civilian successors.

It is greatly to the credit of the Army that it did succeed in maintaining at all times an adequate corps of foreign administrators overseas, and that thereby the realization of American political objectives was carried forward without interruption, though it was sometimes slowed up by the necessity of reorganization and replacement. It is equally impressive to see the Army function as the tutor of a new group of American overseas administrators. Since VE- and VJ-days, an ever increasing number of civilians has been selected for service with military government. By July 1, 1946 two thirds of the personnel of the American Military Government of Germany consisted of civilians. Similar progress was made in Austria, Japan, and Korea, and even in the composition of the Civil Affairs Division of the War Department in Washington. Thus a gradual transition from military government by military officers to a civilian overseas administration has been taking place, though it remained under the direction of the War Department and the commanders of the theaters. The separation of the American administration of occupied areas from the Army would require only a few administrative steps.

Considering the history of American military government during World War II, it is not surprising that the Army is managing the administration of occupied areas far beyond the period which everyone, including the Army, had envisaged as the period of military administration. There were important international and national reasons for an extension of the military period. From the international viewpoint, it was unfeasible to replace the military governors by civilian high commissioners so long as the other powers had their military chiefs act as governors. The plan of June 28, 1946 for a new Allied regime of Austria for the first time envisaged the "civilianization" of one of the highest Allied control organs. Moreover, as long as fairly large forces of occupation have to be kept abroad and overseas transportation remains largely an Army responsibility, it is practical to leave both military and civilian supplies in the hands of the Army.

But conditions at home made it equally desirable not to exclude the Army from military government at too early a date. The contrast between military and civilian administration has often been exaggerated. Most of the American civil affairs officers were civilians in the sense that their professional peacetime pursuits constituted their chief qualification for their wartime jobs with the Army. Even on higher staff levels, where the direction of civil affairs operations had to be fitted into the general military plans, and where consequently a general military education was most advantageous, by no means were regular officers only employed. In the recruitment of civilian personnel for military government, many former civil affairs officers are the best qualified candidates for appointment. It would have gravely weakened the efficiency of the American overseas administration if its continuity had been broken by the sudden replacement of the military personnel by a completely new corps of civilian administrators. A slow process of "civilianization" both with regard to personnel and to administrative channels was greatly preferable.

The threat that the United States would be left without a staff of foreign administrators after VJ-day was obviated, and simultaneously a way was found to achieve the eventual transfer of all administrative responsibilities to civilian agencies. At present the commanders of American troops still act as military governors, but everywhere their military government staffs are separated from the military staffs of the occupation forces. Within the Government the War Department has remained responsible for the administration of American policies, but in the formulation of these policies the State Department has assumed full leadership. In April 1946 General Hilldring was appointed Assistant Secretary of State and charged by the Secretary with the coordination and formulation of American policies in occupied areas.

With the creation of a single office for occupied territories, the State Department has recognized the important role of American military government in the international relations of the United States and in the process of peacemaking in which we are engaged. In the present stage of American foreign policy the policies of military government should form a continuous concern of American diplomacy, and it is imperative to integrate the policies of the political, economic, and information branches of the State Department into one single policy. This was often difficult for the State Department to achieve, the more so since it was too remote from the actual operations of military government and therefore inclined to disregard its time-table and other practical needs. The selection of the new Assistant Secretary, who, as the former military director of the Civil Affairs Division since its inception, has been familiar with all the problems connected with the execution of military government and civil affairs operations, was by itself a guarantee that American policy would be closely linked to operations. This contact is further strengthened by the continuation of the State-War-Navy Coordinating Committee over which General Hilldring now presides. It is to this committee that State Department policies are presented and through which they are passed on to the theaters.[60]

American military government has thus found a machinery capable of issuing policies and executing them, and at the same time fully adaptable to a future period of complete civilian responsibility. Of course, this organization and all the work that thousands of Americans have devoted since 1942 to building an effective arm of national policy would be lost if Congress refused to provide the men needed for occupation duty. What was true during the War is perhaps even more true in the post-surrender period. Without an able group of military government officials, much larger forces of occupation would be required. But we shall need occupation forces for a long time to come if we want to see those aims for which the War was fought made secure. A retreat from these obligations would be taken by the world as a sign of America's unwillingness to shoulder its part of the burden in the building of a stable international order.

Obviously, we have already aroused suspicion among our Allies, who accuse American military government of being hasty and superficial in its policies and operations. If these accusations are examined they stem mostly from the bad impression created by the American demobilization rush in the fall of 1945. But this hectic demobilization never blocked the work of American military government completely and slowed its progress only temporarily. More to the point is the criticism levelled by our Allies, the British, French, Russians, and Australians against what they call America's unholy zeal to arrange for early elections in the occupied countries. This American policy is considered a sure symptom of American willingness to accept a semblance of democratic activity as the realization of democracy in order to be excused from further tedious duties overseas. The policy of American military government to hold elections at the earliest possible moment has been motivated exclusively by the well founded American belief that democracy can only grow among people who are free to practice it and that a paternal regime is incapable of producing these results. American military government has acted on the assumption that an elected government, even if its character was open to some doubts, was preferable to one that continued the older authoritarian pattern or to one that was hand-picked by military government.

There is no good reason to justify the criticism of our Allies of our efforts to reestablish political parties and trade unions and arrange for early elections so long as we ourselves do not lose sight of the real purpose of these elections. They are to be judged at the present moment as a means of launching democracy. They are not by themselves to be considered the achievement of the ultimate democratic objectives of American military government. It may be necessary, as General MacArthur admitted,[61] to hold elections from time to time, and the military governors have the power to dissolve parliaments and other representative bodies and call new elections. General Hilldring called the German elections "a part of our training program for democracy."[64]

Elections are a useful method of starting democratic life. But the granting of votes and rights of political organization and assembly by itself does not make a nation peaceful and democratic. By that token the Weimar Republic should have proved the safest guarantee against militarism and aggression. Why should the Germans and Japanese not find it profitable to act democratically if such an attitude would contribute to an early removal of the occupation by foreigners and the reestablishment of their own sovereignty? Obviously, even the militaristic forces will not disturb a process that will eventually work in their favor. Democracy is unlikely to take firm roots if the social and economic organization of a country is dominated by forces of a feudal and anti-democratic past. The removal of the militaristic leaders of Germany and Japan gives the democratic groups of these countries only a temporary breathing spell. Unless the social and economic obstacles to full equality of opportunity are removed, the mere introduction of the forms of democratic life cannot produce a democratic state and the recrudescence of authoritarian forces can be expected.

American military government has been conscious of these objectives and has even been aware of the natural handicaps of military government in achieving these ends. Maintenance of order is habitual with any military regime and the security of the military forces in enemy countries seems to make it imperative. It is very difficult for military government to tolerate riots and revolutions, though these have proved in the history of most nations the crises through which people proceeded from a feudal and authoritarian order to a democratic social order. The directive on the military government of Japan* attempts to draw practical conclusions from such experiences. It contains the remarkable statement: "Changes in the form of government initiated by the Japanese people or government in the direction of modifying its feudal and authoritarian tendencies are to be permitted and favored. In the event that the effectuation of such changes involves the use of force by the Japanese people or government against persons opposed thereto, the Supreme Commander should intervene only where necessary to ensure the security of his forces and the attainment of all other objectives of the occupation."

But any violent solution of such constitutional ills by the action of people living under military government has not occurred, and it is unlikely to happen for a long time to come. In the defeated countries people are not primarily interested in politics. They are preoccupied, rather, with the primitive problems of individual survival, such as finding food, shelter and heat. They have not been accustomed to solve their political problems by group action through voluntary and free associations, but by currying favors with the existing authorities. It is a sad spectacle to see to what extent the political movements in Europe conform again to the real or supposed political predilections of the powers that happen to occupy a country. There is no strong up-

___
*Appendix XV.

surge of popular energy behind the new parties nor any fierce determination for the realization of new political programs. The new parties feed largely on the programs of an unreal past.

Little else could be expected in the present circumstances. In a
democracy parties gain their vitality by taking a position on the great
issues of national and international life. These major decisions, both
in Germany and in Japan, remain by necessity in the hands of the
governments of the occupying powers. Therefore it will be practically
impossible for the new parties to develop ideas which would command enthusiastic support of the masses. For example, the relative per-
suasiveness of a program for a free-enterprise or government-controlled
system of German economy will entirely depend on the agreement
which the Allies may reach with regard to German reparations, industrial disarmament, future industrial production, and German exports
and imports. Closely connected with these problems are the stability
of a German currency and of the German budget. These questions
are among the most crucial issues around which popular parties group
and struggle in free and prosperous democratic countries. At present
German parties face them helplessly, not so much on account of the
existence of military government, but because the occupying powers
alone hold the key to a solution to these problems. Until they have
reached an understanding on the fundamentals of a German settlement and have given the Germans clearer ideas about their future,
German political life will remain shadowy and listless.

American military government, in order to democratize the defeated
nations, may still have to assume tasks of social and economic reform
which it was originally hoped would be accomplished by domestic
forces. Initiative in legislation will still be preferable to the one-sided
support of individual parties which has been frequently advocated in
recent times. Military government should, of course, never be objective
in the distorted sense of being equally considerate to both democratic
and undemocratic groups. But if American military government should
throw its support behind a single party, it would stigmatize that party
as an "American" group. We do not intend to Americanize but only
to democratize the occupied country, and we are not planning to create
conditions which could only endure if the countries of occupation were
to become permanent American protectorates. American policy can
take the lead in suggesting, and even in imposing, legislative measures.
But it should shun full identification with distinct political organizations in the occupied countries.

A beginning has been made in the democratic reform of the defeated
nations by the suppression of cartels and monopolies. And in Japan

a land reform is being prepared by the Far Eastern Commission. As these actions become effective the internal balance of power in Germany and Japan will begin to shift from the groups that enjoyed unusual privileges in the past to all those groups which will form the productive society of the future. Only by such measures can true democratization be achieved. Progress will be slow, for in Germany even more than in Japan such reforms depend on international negotiations, and it will take additional time before the less privileged groups of the past can gain strength and confident leadership.

While these social and economic reforms are carried forward the reorganization of education and intellectual life cannot be neglected. In the final analysis the chances for a survival of a future German and Japanese democracy rest upon a successful reorientation of the German and Japanese mind. It would be futile to hope for the growth of a democratic spirit in the defeated countries unless they can expect to regain in due course a stable, if modest, way of life. To that extent an intellectual rebirth of these nations hinges upon the general policies of American and Allied military government. But educational and social reforms are also connected by the role of education in the training of competent popular leaders for a democratic society and the spread of a sense of civic responsibility through all classes.

American military government is not a short-range responsibility. We cannot expect to reap in the fall what we have sown in the spring. As in forestry results will appear only after a period of years. Even then the trees may still be small and tender. It is only the next generation that will benefit by the work extended. The democratization of Germany and Japan calls for similar patience and labor. Whether the present generation will make the necessary effort to secure a durable peace will decide whether the next generation will die or live. American military government is a crucial part in the process of peacemaking and no easy victories can be gained. Only a sober enthusiasm can meet the challenge.

FOOTNOTES, CHAPTER 11

[60]A brief description of the new organization was presented in the radio discussion of May 18, 1946 "Germany and the Occupation," in which General Hilldring and Assistant Secretary of War H. C. Petersen participated. Department of State, *Bulletin,* Vol. XIV (1946), pp. 910-914. Cf. also V. H. Cassidy, *Ibid.,* Vol. XV (1946), pp. 291-296.

[61]See the discussion on the Japanese General Elections between General MacArthur and the Far Eastern Commission in Department of State, *Bulletin,* Vol. XIV (1946), pp. 639-641.

[62]*Ibidem,* p. 913.

APPENDIX

Documents on Civil Affairs
1943-1946

I

COMBINED DIRECTIVE ON
MILITARY GOVERNMENT IN SICILY

May 31, 1943[1]

Forwarded for your information in the setting up and functioning of Military Government in the Sicilian operations is this directive which has been satisfactorily agreed to by Great Britain and the United States. The CCS will furnish you with information and directives which will guide you in all policies regarding political, fiscal or economic matters. You will act in accordance with the following guides:

A. *Political:* (a) A military administration as an Allied undertaking will be set up with identical administrative procedures throughout the entire area. The MG Headquarters and Posts will display both U.S. and U.K. flags.

(b) In dealing with the civilian populace the administration acting within limits of military regulations will maintain a benevolent attitude. An efficient and fair administration will be favorably received by the war-weary civilian population which has been oppressed by the corrupt Fascist Regime and German overlordship. The local population should be told that military occupation intends to free the Italian people who have been led into war by the corrupt party, and to make Italy a free country.

(c) Neither British nor American Government political agencies or political representatives shall be members of the prospective military administration (Sicily).

(d) Participation by civilian representatives of either government will be permitted in the early stages. At a future date the CCS will control their participation.

(e) Holders of prominent posts, government officials and employees shall be clearly instructed that the continuance of their jobs will be based entirely upon their behavior, satisfactory cooperation and performance of duty.

It will be the military commander's responsibility to replace any mayors or prefects who may be removed from prominent communities. It will be decided by the commander whether the operation of military government is better handled by using Italian officials or the appointment of occupation forces officers. No permanent appointment of Italians to important posts will be made until approval by the two governments through the CCS has been obtained.

(f) The Fascist party will be liquidated immediately and the continuation of any political activity will absolutely be prohibited. All Fascist leaders and pro-Nazi partisans will be arrested and the entire Fascist Youth Organizations and militia will be done away with. Personnel from the highest party leadership, the Hierarchy, to the local secretary of any post will be cast out. All propaganda and Fascist doctrines are forbidden.

The initial goal will be to organize and maintain a smooth-working local government so that the Commander-in-Chief may be relieved of all problems

---

[1]This is an official transcription of the directives transmitted by the Combined Chiefs of Staff to the Supreme Allied Commander, Mediterranean Theater, in two parts: the basic directive of May 31, 1943, and an additional one of June 10.

connected with the civilian populace. As a guide the following may be of assistance:

A line of distinction should be made between (a) organizations of a nature that do not function for the security and benefit of the populace, that is, the party organization itself, and all solely Fascist units which have become part of local government, and (b) organizations directly benefiting the populace removal of which would have an adverse effect on the administration's efficiency. Suppression should be made of the former, while there is an apparent case for the latter's maintenance.

(g) Regardless of how convincing they appear in sentiment, neither local personalities nor political groups will be permitted to take part in determining administration policies. It is absolutely necessary to refrain from any deals with political groups in the local population. The Administration will not tolerate participation of exiled political leaders.

(h) All war criminals who have been charged with war crimes by the United Nations shall be imprisoned, and retained pending future instructions. (A list of names will be forwarded you.)

(i) The freedom of press, and speech shall be restored insofar as it does not impair the interest of Allied Forces. Any law which shows a decided partiality in reference to race, creed or color will be abolished immediately. The rights of religious worship will be made known.

(j) Action will be taken to release all political prisoners immediately. When released, they will be notified that for the duration of military government they will not be allowed to participate in political activities. You will abolish the special tribunal for the defense of the state.

(k) Suspension of the Crown's powers shall be enforced for the duration of military occupation.

(l) You are to prepare a plan to halt transfers of title of valuable personal and real property, intending to evade, defeat, or avoid the punishments, responsibilities or fines placed, or to be placed, on the national government or on present owners.

(m) Special efforts will be put forth for preserving monumental and historical art objects and due respect shall be shown to all churches and religious institutions.

(n) The Combined Chiefs of Staff will issue directives on propaganda and you will act accordingly.

B. *Fiscal and Monetary:* (a) The task forces of the U.S. will use regular U.S. coins and yellow seal dollars in the first phase of operations. The military forces of Great Britain will use British coins and British Military Authority Notes (BMA) and also any local currency possessed by them. NATOUSA has available BMA notes and yellow seal dollars and additional quantities can be obtained from the British Treasury or the U.S. Treasury. The total currencies used by the British and U.S. Forces shall be recorded.

(b) Allied Military (AM) lire will be used as soon as it becomes available, for local procurement and for Army payments to troops, instead of the yellow seal dollars and BMA notes, unless the Military Government deems it unfavorable to make such a change at this time. The Treasury Department of the U.S.

will have available AM lire currency for consignment to any given location within four days after the zero hour. Keep records of the total issuance of AM lire.

(c) It is not intended that the AM lire currency replace the local lire currency now in use, but rather its purpose will be supplementary.

(d) As quickly as it can be accomplished satisfactorily, the United States yellow seal currency and BMA notes shall be taken out of circulation. After operation has begun the Military Government shall decide date of withdrawal.

(e) Four dollars to one pound shall be the exchange rate between the United States dollar and the BMA notes, both currencies interchangeable at that rate. The U.S. Treasury Department will negotiate with British Treasury regarding arrangements necessary.

(f) Four hundred lire to the pound sterling and one hundred lire to the dollar shall be the exchange rate decreed on D-day. An order shall be issued making it a requirement that all persons accept the BMA notes and the yellow seal dollars at the above rate. You shall prohibit transactions at any other rate. Anyone who has in his possession AM or local lire notes or deposits must have special permission before obtaining pound or dollar notes. In order to secure pound notes, dollars, foreign exchange credits or any other foreign currency it will be necessary to comply with Military Government exchange regulations.

(g) All imports and exports of currency and all foreign trade and financial exchanges will not be permitted with the exceptions listed in Military Government regulations which are to be issued.

(h) An Allied Military Financial Agency under control of the Military Government shall be established with such sub-agencies as considered necessary.

The Bank of Sicily under immediate control of the Military Governor will be named as agent for the AM Financial Agency, if desirable and practicable. After decision is made that the Bank of Sicily is adequately controlled, the Military Governor and other authorities of the Allied Military may utilize this Bank for official business by making credits available to it by the provision of AM lire notes, placing the Bank in a position to finance other banks and branches for carrying on business as approved by the military government. Loans may be made by the AM Financial Agency when other effective facilities for banking are not obtainable. Restriction shall be made to lire loans except in very unusual conditions.

Insofar as the operations of the AM Financial Agency relate to providing of currencies for the payment and monetary requirements of the military forces of either army it shall draw on the currency reserve of the military government and a debit will be recorded against the army affected in terms of the currency of issue. Deposits may be accepted from the military personnel of Allied Armies and from finance officers. In its operations pertaining to civil administration the AM Financial Agency shall draw on the currency reserve and the military government will be debited.

Control and direction of all disbursements and receipts for civil administration purposes made by U.K. or U.S. Civil Affairs Officers will rest with the military government which will advance funds and receive all cash receipts and revenues through the AM Financial Agency.

In all instances, records shall be kept in the AM Financial Agency as to in what currency disbursements were made or receipts obtained.

(i) Military authorities on occupying an area shall immediately take the following steps:

(1) All financial institutions and banks shall be closed and put under the custody of the military forces.

(2) A general moratorium shall be declared.

(3) The funds of Axis Government Agencies as well as Government banks shall be blocked or impounded for future disposition.

(4) All safety deposit boxes and vaults are to be sealed.

(5) As soon as possible an inventory of assets shall be secured.

(j) When such action seems advisable to the Military Government, banks should be encouraged to reopen for business. Lire currency or bank notes shall not be an authorized issue by private banks, agencies or government banks. Only after a proper supervised method has been put into effect will the access to vaults and safety deposit boxes be permitted. All papers of value, foreign securities, gold and foreign currencies shall be impounded with receipts granted to the recognized owners.

(k) The Allied Military Financial Agency or any appointed agency by the MG will take into immediate custody all foreign securities and currencies, holdings of gold, national funds and holdings of Fascist organizations for deposit.

(l) Prior to the reopening of banks, provisions should be made for the banks to negotiate loans from banks or agencies named by the military government. The bank making the loan may demand as collateral any or all of the assets of the bank seeking the loan or of its directors and may take as collateral national government obligations or those of its subdivisions.

(m) Lire accounts only shall be permitted in local banks unless otherwise granted special permission; however, these banks may take BMA notes and yellow seal dollars at the established exchange rate, and they shall receive in exchange for those they turn in local or Allied Military lire.

(n) All government monopolies, including telephone and telegraph services, postal, radio and the railways will be placed under military jurisdiction and the revenues from each shall be at the disposal of the MG.

(o) Authority will be invested in the military government for the maintenance of present tax laws and to collect such contributions for the administration of the country as are in conformity with usage and custom. Deposits of all national tax receipts shall be made to banks acceptable to the military government or in the Allied Military Financial Agency.

(p) Military control shall be obtained over the National Insurance Institute and all its branches, and all revenues therefrom will be made accessible to the MG.

(q) Utilization shall not be made of the tax or other revenues for the payment of interest or principal on obligations of the national government.

C. *Economic:* (a) You are to be responsible for procuring supplies necessary for the maintenance of agricultural production and the reestablishment of the many utilities. In addition, you will be responsible for procuring for export such materials of a strategic nature as the United Nations may need. No materials for these purposes will be provided except upon requisition from Allied Force Headquarters.

(b) Steps should be taken immediately for the providing of local residents from indigenous supply and production. Authorization is given you to furnish such supplies to the local residents as may be expedient in light of requirements for the military. These stocks shall, as far as possible, be sold through commercial channels already in existence and under strict control of the military. Employment of direct relief will take place only in instances where it is deemed most necessary.

(c) Severe punishment should be effected in cases of hoarding and the practicing of black market activities. The establishment of rationing and maximum prices of staple commodities of an important nature shall be put into effect immediately.

(d) If the military authorities find it necessary in order to prevent the immediate disruption of internal economy, provincial and interprovincial relations of employees and employers may be continued temporarily. However, Fascists or officers of an objectionable nature shall be removed and objectionable characters eliminated. Authorities shall abolish Fascist corporations and their councils. Due consideration shall be given by the military government to the matter of fair, sound and voluntary labor relations and it shall fix wages and hours of labor if it is found necessary.

(e) Measures shall be taken without delay for the setting up of a system to control the export and import of materials by local business concerns and licencing for such shipments shall be required. Permission shall be given for exports only to countries of a friendly nature. Utmost consideration should be given to the requirements of the local residents and the military forces when determining permitted exports.

II

DOCUMENTS RELATING TO ITALIAN ARMISTICE

A. ITALIAN MILITARY ARMISTICE

September 3, 1943[1]

The following conditions of an Armistice are presented by General Dwight D. Eisenhower, Commander-in-Chief of the Allied Forces, acting by authority of the Governments of the United States and Great Britain and in the interest of the United Nations, and are accepted by Marshal Pietro Badoglio, Head of the Italian Government.

1. Immediate cessation of all hostile activity by the Italian armed forces.

2. Italy will use its best endeavors to deny, to the Germans, facilities that might be used against the United Nations.

3. All prisoners or internees of the United Nations to be immediately turned over to the Allied Commander-in-Chief, and none of these may now or at any time be evacuated to Germany.

4. Immediate transfer of the Italian Fleet and Italian aircraft to such points as may be designated by the Allied Commander-in-Chief, with details of disarmament to be prescribed by him.

5. Italian merchant shipping may be requisitioned by the Allied Commander-in-Chief to meet the needs of his military-naval program.

6. Immediate surrender of Corsica and of all Italian territory, both islands

---

[1]This and the following documents were published for the first time in November 1945, Department of State, *Bulletin,* Vol. XIII (1945), pp. 748-760.

and mainland, to the Allies, for such use as operational bases and other purposes as the Allies may see fit.

7. Immediate guarantee of the free use by the Allies of all airfields and naval ports in Italian territory, regardless of the rate of evacuation of the Italian territory by the German forces. These ports and fields to be protected by Italian armed forces until this function is taken over by the Allies.

8. Immediate withdrawal to Italy of Italian armed forces from all participation in the current war from whatever areas in which they may now be engaged.

9. Guarantee by the Italian Government that if necessary it will employ all its available armed forces to insure prompt and exact compliance with all the provisions of this armistice.

10. The Commander-in-Chief of the Allied Forces reserves to himself the right to take any measure which in his opinion may be necessary for the protection of the interests of the Allied Forces for the prosecution of the war, and the Italian Government binds itself to such administrative or other action as the Commander-in-Chief may require, and in particular the Commander-in-Chief will establish Allied Military Government over such parts of Italian territory as he may deem necessary in the military interests of the Allied Nations.

11. The Commander-in-Chief of the Allied Forces will have a full right to impose measures of disarmament, demobilization and demilitarization.

12. Other conditions of a political, economic and financial nature with which Italy will be bound to comply will be transmitted at later date.

The conditions of the present Armistice will not be made public without prior approval of the Allied Commander-in-Chief. The English will be considered the official text.

B. ADDITIONAL CONDITIONS OF ARMISTICE WITH ITALY

(As modified by the protocol signed Nov. 9, 1943.)

Whereas in consequence of an Armistice dated September 3, 1943 between the United States and United Kingdom Governments acting in the interests of all the United Nations on the one hand, and the Italian Government on the other hand, hostilities were suspended between Italy and United Nations on certain terms of a military nature.

And whereas in addition to those terms it was also provided in the said Armistice that the Italian Government bound themselves to comply with other conditions of a political, economic and financial nature to be transmitted later;

And whereas it is convenient that the terms of a military nature and the said other conditions of a political, economic and financial nature should without prejudice to the continued validity of the terms of the said Armistice of September 3d, 1943, be comprised in a further instrument;

The following, together with the terms of the Armistice of September 3, 1943, are the terms on which the United States, United Kingdom and Soviet Governments, acting on behalf of the United Nations, are prepared to suspend hostilities against Italy so long as their military operations against Germany and the Allies are not obstructed and Italy does not assist these powers in any way and complies with the requirements of these governments.

These terms have been presented by General Dwight D. Eisenhower, Commander-in-Chief, Allied Forces, duly authorized to that effect; and have been accepted unconditionally by Marshal Pietro Badoglio, Head of the Italian Government representing the Supreme Command of the Italian land, sea and air forces and duly authorized to that effect by the Italian Government.

1. (A) The Italian land, sea and air forces wherever located hereby surrender. Italian participation in the war in all Theaters will cease immediately. There will be no opposition to landings, movements or other operations of the Land, Sea and Air Forces of the United Nations. Accordingly, the Italian Supreme Command will order the immediate cessation of hostilities of any kind against the Forces of the United Nations and will direct the Italian Navy, Military and Air Force authorities in all Theaters to issue forthwith the approximate instructions to those under their Command.

(B) The Italian Supreme Command will further order all Italian Naval, Military and Air Forces or authorities and personnel to refrain immediately from destruction of or damage to any real or personal property, whether public or private.

2. The Italian Supreme Command will give full information concerning the disposition and condition of all Italian Land, Sea and Air Forces, wherever they are situated and of all such forces of Italy's Allies as are situated in Italian or Italian occupied territory.

3. The Italian Supreme Command will take the necessary measures to secure airfields, port facilities, and all other installations against seizure or attack by any of Italy's Allies. The Italian Supreme Command will take the necessary measures to insure Law and Order and to use its available armed forces to insure prompt and exact compliance with all the provisions of the present instrument. Subject to such use of Italian troops for the above purposes, as may be sanctioned by the Allied Commander-in-Chief, all other Italian Land, Sea and Air Forces will proceed to and remain in their barracks, camps or ships pending directions from the United Nations as to their future status and disposal. Exceptionally such Naval personnel shall proceed to shore establishments as the United Nations may direct.

4. Italian Land, Sea and Air Forces will within the periods to be laid down by the United Nations withdraw from all areas outside Italian territory notified to the Italian Government by the United Nations and proceed to areas to be specified by the United Nations. Such movement of Italian Land, Sea and Air Forces will be carried out in conditions to be laid down by the United Nations and in accordance with the orders to be issued by them. All Italian officials will similarly leave the areas notified except any who may be permitted to remain by the United Nations. Those permitted to remain will comply with the instructions of the Allied Commander-in-Chief.

5. No requisitioning, seizures or other coercive measures shall be effected by Italian Land, Sea and Air Forces or officials in regard to persons or property in the areas notified under Article 4.

6. The demobilization of Italian Land, Sea and Air Forces in excess of such establishments as shall be notified will take place as prescribed by the Allied Commander-in-Chief.

7. Italian warships of all descriptions, auxiliaries and transports will be assembled as directed in ports to be specified by the Allied Commander-in-Chief and will be dealt with as prescribed by the Allied Commander-in-Chief. (Note. If at the date of the Armistice the whole of the Italian Fleet has been assembled in Allied ports, this article would run—"Italian warships of all descriptions, auxiliaries, and transports will remain until further notice in the ports where

they are at present assembled, and will be dealt with as prescribed by the Allied Commander-in-Chief.")

8. Italian aircraft of all kinds will not leave the ground or water or ships, except as directed by the Allied Commander-in-Chief.

9. Without prejudice to the provisions 14, 15 and 28 (A) and (D) below, all merchant ships, fishing or other craft of whatever flag, all aircraft and inland transport of whatever nationality in Italian or Italian-occupied territory or waters will, pending verification of their identity and status, be prevented from leaving.

10. The Italian Supreme Command will make available all information about naval, military and air devices, installations, and defenses, about all transport and inter-communication systems established by Italy or her allies on Italian territory or in the approaches thereto, about minefields or other obstacles to movement by land, sea or air and such other particulars as the United Nations may require in connection with the use of Italian bases, or with the operations, security, or welfare of the United Nations Land, Sea or Air Forces. Italian forces and equipment will be made available as required by the United Nations for the removal of the above mentioned obstacles.

11. The Italian Government will furnish forthwith lists of quantities of all war material showing the location of the same. Subject to such use as the Allied Commander-in-Chief may make of it, the war material will be placed in store under such control as he may direct. The ultimate disposal of war material will be prescribed by the United Nations.

12. There will be no destruction of nor damage to nor except as authorized or directed by the United Nations any removal of war material, wireless, radio location or meteorological stations, railroad, port or other installations or in general, public or private utilities or property of any kind, wherever situated, and the necessary maintenance and repair will be the responsibility of the Italian authorities.

13. The manufacture, production and construction of war material and its import, export and transit is prohibited, except as directed by the United Nations. The Italian Government will comply with any directions given by the United Nations for the manufacture, production or construction and the import, export or transit of war material.

14. (A) All Italian merchant shipping and fishing and other craft, wherever they may be, and any constructed or completed during the period of the present instrument will be made available in good repair and in seaworthy condition by the competent Italian authorities at such places and for such purposes and periods as the United Nations may prescribe. Transfer to enemy or neutral flags is prohibited. Crews will remain on board pending further instructions regarding their continued employment or dispersal. Any existing options to re-purchase or re-acquire or to resume control of Italian or former Italian vessels sold or otherwise transferred or chartered during the war will forthwith be exercised and the above provisions will apply to all such vessels and their crews.

(B) All Italian inland transport and all port equipment will be held at the disposal of the United Nations for such purposes as they may direct.

15. United Nations merchant ships, fishing and other craft in Italian hands wherever they may be (including for this purpose those of any country which has broken off diplomatic relations with Italy) whether or not the title has been transferred as the result of prize court proceedings or otherwise, will be sur-

rendered to the United Nations and will be assembled in ports to be specified by the United Nations for disposal as directed by them. The Italian Government will take all such steps as may be required to secure any necessary transfers of title. Any neutral merchant ship, fishing or other craft under Italian operation or control will be assembled in the same manner pending arrangements for their ultimate disposal. Any necessary repairs to any of the above mentioned vessels will be effected by the Italian Government, if required, at their expense. The Italian Government will take the necessary measures to insure that the vessels and their cargo are not damaged.

16. No radio or telecommunication installations or other forms of inter-communication, ashore or afloat, under Italian control whether belonging to Italy or any nation other than the United Nations will transmit until directions for the control of these installations have been prescribed by the Allied Commander-in-Chief. The Italian authorities will conform to such measures for control and censorship of press and of other publications, of theatrical and cinematograph performances, of broadcasting, and also of all forms of inter-communication as the Allied Commander-in-Chief may direct. The Allied Commander-in-Chief may, at his discretion, take over radio, cable and other communication stations.

17. The warships, auxiliaries, transports and merchant and other vessels and aircraft in the service of the United Nations will have the right freely to use the territorial waters around and the air over Italian territory.

18. The forces of the United Nations will require to occupy certain parts of Italian territory. The territories or areas concerned will from time to time be notified by the United Nations and all Italian Land, Sea and Air Forces will thereupon withdraw from such territories or areas in accordance with the instructions issued by the Allied Commander-in-Chief. The provisions of this article are without prejudice to those of article 4 above. The Italian Supreme Command will guarantee immediate use and access to the Allies of all airfields and Naval ports in Italy under their control.

19. In the territories or areas referred to in article 18 all Naval, Military and Air installations, power stations, oil refineries, public utility services, all ports and harbors, all transport and all inter-communication installations, facilities and equipment and such other installations or facilities and all such stocks as may be required by the United Nations will be made available in good condition by the competent Italian authorities with the personnel required for working them. The Italian Government will make available such other local resources or services as the United Nations may require.

20. Without prejudice to the provisions of the present instrument the United Nations will exercise all the rights of an occupying power throughout the territories or areas referred to in article 18, the administration of which will be provided for by the issue of proclamations, orders or regulations. Personnel of the Italian administrative, judicial and public services will carry out their functions under the control of the Allied Commander-in-Chief unless otherwise directed.

21. In addition to the rights in respect of occupied Italian territories described in articles 18 to 20,

(A) Members of the Land, Sea or Air Forces and officials of the United Nations will have the right of passage in or over non-occupied Italian territory and will be afforded all the necessary facilities and assistance in performing their functions.

(B) The Italian authorities will make available on non-occupied Italian territory all transport facilities required by the United Nations including free transit for their war material and supplies, and will comply with instructions issued by the Allied Commander-in-Chief regarding the use and control of airfields, ports, shipping, inland transport systems and vehicles, intercommunication systems, power stations and public utility services, oil refineries, stocks and such other fuel and power supplies and means of producing same, as United Nations may specify, together with connected repair and construction facilities.

22. The Italian Government and people will abstain from all action detrimental to the interests of the United Nations and will carry out promptly and efficiently all orders given by the United Nations.

23. The Italian Government will make available such Italian currency as the United Nations may require. The Italian Government will withdraw and redeem in Italian currency within such time limits and on such terms as the United Nations may specify all holdings in Italian territory of currencies issued by the United Nations during military operations or occupation and will hand over the currencies withdrawn free of cost to the United Nations. The Italian Government will take such measures as may be required by the United Nations for the control of banks and business in Italian territory, for the control of foreign exchange and foreign commercial and financial transactions and for the regulation of trade and production and will comply with any instructions issued by the United Nations regarding these and similar matters.

24. There shall be no financial, commercial or other intercourse with or dealings with or for the benefit of countries at war with any of the United Nations or territories occupied by such countries or any other foreign country except under authorization of the Allied Commander-in-Chief or designated officials.

25. (A) Relations with countries at war with any of the United Nations, or occupied by any such country, will be broken off. Italian diplomatic, consular and other officials and members of the Italian Land, Sea and Air Forces accredited to or serving on missions with any such country or in any other territory specified by the United Nations will be recalled. Diplomatic and consular officials of such countries will be dealt with as the United Nations may prescribe.

(B) The United Nations reserve the right to require the withdrawal of neutral diplomatic and consular officers from occupied Italian territory and to prescribe and lay down regulations governing the procedure for the methods of communication between the Italian Government and its representatives in neutral countries and regarding communications emanating from or destined for the representatives of neutral countries in Italian territory.

26. Italian subjects will pending further instructions be prevented from leaving Italian territory except as authorized by the Allied Commander-in-Chief and will not in any event take service with any of the countries or in any of the territories referred to in article 25 (A) nor will they proceed to any place for the purpose of undertaking work for any such country. Those at present so serving or working will be recalled as directed by the Allied Commander-in-Chief.

27. The Military, Naval and Air personnel and material and the merchant shipping, fishing and other craft and the aircraft, vehicles and other transport equipment of any country against which any of the United Nations is carrying on hostilities or which is occupied by any such country, remain liable to attack or seizure wherever found in or over Italian territory or waters.

28. (A) The warships, auxiliaries and transports of any such country or occupied country referred to in article 27 in Italian or Italian-occupied ports and waters and the aircraft, vehicles and other transport equipment of such countries in or over Italian or Italian-occupied ports and waters and the aircraft, vehicles and other transport equipment of such countries in or over Italian or Italian-occupied territory will, pending further instructions, be prevented from leaving.

(B) The Military, Naval and Air personnel and the civilian nationals of any such country or occupied country in Italian or Italian-occupied territory will be prevented from leaving and will be interned pending further instructions.

(C) All property in Italian territory belonging to any such country or occupied country or its nationals will be impounded and kept in custody pending further instructions.

(D) The Italian Government will comply with any instructions given by the Allied Commander-in-Chief concerning the internment, custody or subsequent disposal, utilization or employment of any of the above mentioned persons, vessels, aircraft, material or property.

29. Benito Mussolini, his chief Fascist associates, and all persons suspected of having committed war crimes or analogous offences whose names appear on lists to be communicated by the United Nations and who now or in the future are on territory controlled by the Allied Military Command or by the Italian Government, will forthwith be apprehended and surrendered into the hands of the United Nations. Any instructions given by the United Nations to this purpose will be complied with.

30. All Fascist organizations, including all branches of the Fascist Militia (MVSN), the Secret Police (OVRA), all Fascist youth organizations will insofar as this is not already accomplished be disbanded in accordance with the directions of the Allied Commander-in-Chief. The Italian Government will comply with all such further directions as the United Nations may give for abolition of Fascist institutions, the dismissal and internment of Fascist personnel, the control of Fascist funds, the suppression of Fascist ideology and teaching.

31. All Italian laws involving discrimination on grounds of race, color, creed or political opinions will insofar as this is not already accomplished be rescinded, and persons detained on such grounds will, as directed by the United Nations, be released and relieved from all legal disabilities to which they have been subjected. The Italian Government will comply with all such further directions as the Allied Commander-in-Chief may give for repeal of Fascist legislation and removal of any disabilities or prohibitions resulting therefrom.

32. (A) Prisoners of war belonging to the forces of or specified by the United Nations and any Nationals of the United Nations, including Abyssinian subjects, confined, interned, or otherwise under restraint in Italian or Italian-occupied territory will not be removed and will forthwith be handed over to representatives of the United Nations or otherwise dealt with as the United

Nations may direct. Any removal during the period between the presentation and the signature of the present instrument will be regarded as a breach of its terms.

(B) Persons of whatever nationality who have been placed under restriction, detention or sentence (including sentences in absentia) on account of their dealings or sympathies with the United Nations will be released under the direction of the United Nations and relieved from all legal disabilities to which they have been subjected.

(C) The Italian Government will take such steps as the United Nations may direct to safeguard the persons of foreign nationals and property of foreign nationals and property of foreign states and nationals.

33. (A) The Italian Government will comply with such directions as the United Nations may prescribe regarding restitution, deliveries, services or payments by way of reparation and payment of the costs of occupation during the period of the present instrument.

(B) The Italian Government will give to the Allied Commander-in-Chief such information as may be prescribed regarding the assets, whether inside or outside Italian territory, of the Italian state, the Bank of Italy, any Italian state or semi-state institutions or Fascist organizations or residents in Italian territory and will not dispose or allow the disposal, outside Italian territory of any such assets except with the permission of the United Nations.

34. The Italian Government will carry out during the period of the present instrument such measures of disarmament, demobilization and demilitarization as may be prescribed by the Allied Commander-in-Chief.

35. The Italian Government will supply all information and provide all documents required by the United Nations. There shall be no destruction or concealment of archives, records, plans or any other documents or information.

36. The Italian Government will take and enforce such legislative and other measures as may be necessary for the execution of the present instrument. Italian military and civil authorities will comply with any instructions issued by the Allied Commander-in-Chief for the same purpose.

37. There will be appointed a Control Commission representative of the United Nations charged with regulating and executing this instrument under the orders and general directions of the Allied Commander-in-Chief.

38. (A) The term "United Nations" in the present instrument includes the Allied Commander-in-Chief, the Control Commission and any other authority which the United Nations may designate.

(B) The term "Allied Commander-in-Chief" in the present instrument includes the Control Commission and such other officers and representatives as the Commander-in-Chief may designate.

39. Reference to Italian Land, Sea and Air Forces in the present instrument shall be deemed to include Fascist Militia and all such other military or paramilitary units, formations or bodies as the Allied Commander-in-Chief may prescribe.

40. The term "War Material" in the present instrument denotes all material specified in such lists or definitions as may from time to time be issued by the Control Commission.

41. The term "Italian Territory" includes all Italian colonies and dependencies and shall for the purposes of the present instrument (but without

prejudice to the question of sovereignty) be deemed to include Albania. Provided however that except in such cases and to such extent as the United Nations may direct the provisions of the present instrument shall not apply in or affect the administration of any Italian colony or dependency already occupied by the United Nations or the rights or powers therein possessed or exercised by them.

42. The Italian Government will send a delegation to the Headquarters of the Control Commission to represent Italian interests and to transmit the orders of the Control Commission to the competent Italian authorities.

43. The present instrument shall enter into force at once. It will remain in operation until superseded by any other arrangements or until the voting into force of the peace treaty with Italy.

44. The present instrument may be denounced by the United Nations with immediate effect if Italian obligations thereunder are not fulfilled or, as an alternative, the United Nations may penalize contravention of it by measures appropriate to the circumstances such as the extension of the areas of military occupation or air or other punitive action.

The present instrument is drawn up in English and Italian, the English text being authentic, and in case of any dispute regarding its interpretation, the decision of the Control Commission will prevail.

Signed at Malta on the 29 day of September, 1943.

Marshal Pietro Badoglio
Head of the Italian Government

Dwight D. Eisenhower
General, United States Army
Commander-in-Chief, Allied Force.

C. LETTER FROM GENERAL EISENHOWER TO MARSHAL BADOGLIO ON OCCASION OF SIGNING ARMISTICE DOCUMENT

29th September, 1943.

My Dear Marshal Badoglio,

The terms of the armistice to which we have just appended our signatures are supplementary to the short military armistice signed by your representative and mine on September 3d, 1943. They are based upon the situation obtaining prior to the cessation of hostilities. Developments since that time have altered considerably the status of Italy, which has become in effect a co-operator with the United Nations.

It is fully recognized by the Governments on whose behalf I am acting that these terms are in some respects superseded by subsequent events and that several of the clauses have become obsolescent or have already been put into execution. We also recognize that it is not at this time in the power of the Italian Government to carry out certain of the terms. Failure to do so because of existing conditions will not be regarded as a breach of good faith on the part of Italy. However, this document represents the requirements with which the Italian Government can be expected to comply when in a position to do so.

It is to be understood that the terms both of this document and of the short military armistice of September 3d may be modified from time to time if military necessity or the extent of co-operation by the Italian Government indicates this as desirable.

D. AIDE-MÉMOIRE TO THE ITALIAN GOVERNMENT FROM PRESIDENT, ALLIED COMMISSION

February 24, 1945

In accordance with the declaration of the President of the United States of America and the Prime Minister of the United Kingdom of Great Britain, the Allied Governments propose to relax the control of the Italian Government under the armistice in the matter of day-to-day administration and only to exercise such control when Allied military interests require.

2. The Political Section of the Allied Commission is being abolished as of the 1st March, 1945. The Italian Ministry for Foreign Affairs will deal with the Chief Commissioner on matters of major policy, and on matters of minor policy and routine business it will address itself to whatever section (economic or civil affairs) of the commission may be appropriate to the subject involved. Matters involving the travel of diplomatic and other public officials will hereafter be dealt with on behalf of the commission by the office of the Executive Commissioner.

3. The Italian Government will continue, as at present, to have direct relations with foreign diplomatic representatives accredited to the Quirinal. The Allied Commission should be kept generally informed by the Italian Government of any negotiations in which they engage with other Governments. Facilities for the use of secret bags will be granted to the Italian Government for use in correspondence with their diplomatic representatives abroad. Undeposited cypher facilities cannot be allowed for the present.

In so far as these negotiations have to do with economic and financial matters, the Economic Section and its Finance Sub-Commission should be kept informed of their progress.

It would be convenient if the Italian Government would furnish a periodic summary of all negotiations completed or pending with other Governments.

4. The Allied Commission will limit its dealings with respect to territory under the jurisdiction of the Italian Government to consultation with and advice to the Ministers of the Italian Government.

5. The advisory functions of the Sub-Commissions of Education, Monuments and Fine Arts, Local Government, Legal and Labour in territory under the jurisdiction of the Italian Government will be performed only when requested by the Italian Government.

6. It will no longer be necessary for the Italian Government to obtain the approval of the Allied Commission for decrees and other legislation enacted by the Italian Government in the territory under the jurisdiction of the Italian Government.

Nevertheless the Allied Commission should be informed of proposed decrees some time before their enactment, in order to enable the Chief Commissioner to consult with the Italian Government as to their application to territory under the jurisdiction of Allied Military Government (A.M.G.), and to lay plans for their effective implementation in such territory when appropriate.

7. It will no longer be necessary for the Italian Government to obtain approval of the Allied Commission for Italian appointments, whether to national or local offices, in territory under the jurisdiction of the Italian Government except with regard to the attached list of positions having military significance.

The Italian Government will have the right to alter appointments made previously by A.M.G. authorities.

8. The Allied Commission officers stationed in the field in the territory under the jurisdiction of the Italian Government will be withdrawn. As a first step it is intended to abolish by the 1st April, 1945, the Regional Offices of the Allied Commission for Sicilia, Sardegna, Southern and Lazio-Umbria Regions. Representatives of the Allied Commission will, however, be sent into territory under the jurisdiction of the Italian Government when necessary, and certain specialist officers with economic functions will remain in such territory for a limited period.

9. It is the desire of the Allies to encourage free trade in knowledge and learning with the Italian people. Arrangements will be facilitated for the flow between Italy and the United Nations of books and other publications of a scientific, political, philosophical and artistic nature, and for the movement of scholars, artists and professional men between Italy and the United Nations.

10. The Allies welcome the decision to hold local elections in territory under the jurisdiction of the Italian Government as soon as may be.

11. The Allied nations desire to make concessions with regard to Italian prisoners of war now or hereafter held in Italy, other than those captured since the armistice was signed. Provided that arrangements can be made for the services of such persons to continue to be made available on terms satisfactory to the Supreme Allied Commander, their status as prisoners of war will be terminated.

12. It is essential that the Italian Government formulate and implement appropriate economic controls and take all other steps possible both in order to ensure that maximum production and effective and equitable distribution and control of consumption of local resources possible under existing conditions be secured and as a prerequisite to increased economic assistance.

13. In the joint programme of essential Italian imports, now being prepared by the Inter-Ministerial Committee for Reconstruction and the Economic Section of this commission, there will be some supplies for which the combined United States-United Kingdom military authorities will assume responsibility for procurement (Category "A") and other supplies for which they will not assume responsibility (Category "B"). A definition of the supplies which fall into Category "A" follows:

(a) Those quantities of agreed essential supplies necessary to prevent disease and unrest prejudicial to military operations, such as food, fuel, clothing, medical and sanitary supplies.

(b) Those supplies, the importation of which will reduce military requirements for the import of essential civilian supplies for the purposes referred to in this paragraph, such as fertilizer, raw materials, machinery and equipment.

(c) Those materials essential for the rehabilitation of such of the Italian communication facilities, power systems and transportation facilities as will directly further the Allied military effort.

14. The programme for which the military authorities assume responsibility will be maintained for the duration of combined (United States-United Kingdom) operations in Italy. For this period, and within the limits defined in paragraph 13, Italy will be treated as a whole. The date of the termination of military responsibility will be fixed by the Allied Nations.

15. In addition to the programme of supplies for which the military assume responsibility for procurement (Category "A") the Allied Commission will assist

the Italian Government in the preparation of programmes of supplies designed to rehabilitate Italian industry. Such programmes, referred to as Category "B," will be handled under procedures already notified. The purchasing of supplies in Category "B" programmes will be undertaken immediately without reference to the present difficult shipping position in order that the supplies so purchased may be called forward as and when shipping space becomes available.

16. The Allies desire that industrial rehabilitation in Italy be carried out by the Italian Government to the fullest extent permitted by Italian resources and such supplies as it may be possible to import under the terms of paragraphs 13, 14 and 15 above, and subject to the limitation in paragraph 19 below. The sole exception to this principle is to be made in the case of industries involving the production or repair of munitions or other implements of war, which will be rehabilitated only to the extent required by the Supreme Allied Commander in the discharge of his military mission, and to the extent necessary to further the Allied military effort in other theaters. The priority order in which Italian industry will be rehabilitated (after the rehabilitation of industries essential for Allied Military purposes) will be determined by the Italian Government, with the assistance and advice of the Allied Commission.

17. The prime responsibility for the control of inflation in Italy, including the imposition and administration of the appropriate financial controls and economic controls, and appropriate utilization of supplies, rests with the Italian Government. In this connexion, as in others, the Allied Commission stands ready to advise and assist.

18. The extent to which exports are to be stimulated and the development of machinery to handle export trade are for determination by the Italian Government. For the time being, the Italian export programme will necessarily be limited by certain shipping, military, financial and supply factors. The applicability of these factors to individual programmes will be worked out between the Italian Government and the Economic Section of the Allied Commission along the lines already discussed by the Economic Section with the Inter-Ministerial Committee for Reconstruction.

19. Nothing contained in the above should be taken as constituting a commitment by the Allied Nations with respect to shipping. Any supplies to be imported into Italy must be transported within such shipping as may be allocated from time to time by the Allied Nations.

24th February, 1945   Harold Macmillan

E. COMMENTARY ON THE ADDITIONAL CONDITIONS OF THE ARMISTICE WITH ITALY

The extent to which certain articles of the agreement have been implemented or modified is indicated in the following comment. The remaining articles, on which no comment is given, have either been superseded by events and are therefore dormant, or are still in force.

Articles 1 to 5 were complied with.

Articles 6 to 12: With the cooperation of the Italian Government, the Italian armed forces have been used to the maximum useful extent in the service of the United Nations and have contributed materially towards the liberation of Italy and final victory. The Italian Navy has operated with Allied warships in the

Mediterranean and elsewhere, and since the cessation of hostilities has largely been employed in the Italian interest in minesweeping and the transport of displaced persons.

The Army fought alongside Allied formations during the campaign in Italy and the Air Force took its place with the Allied Air Forces.

Article 14: While Italian merchant ships have been employed in the general interests of the United Nations they have been primarily employed in the Italian interest. Italian inland transport and ports have now been largely returned to Italian administration except insofar as redeployment and maintenance of Allied Forces has had to be effected.

Article 15: The provisions of this clause, as regards small vessels and craft, have not been fully satisfied owing to the difficulty of locating and identifying the vessels and craft concerned.

Article 16: Control of radio has been returned to the Italian Government. All military and rehabilitated civilian telecommunications are being handed over to the Italians as military requirements decrease. Internal censorship has been abolished in the areas under Italian Government control.

Article 18: The second sentence of this clause has never been invoked, except in two frontier areas, i.e., on the France-Italian frontier and in Venezia Giulia.

Article 19: Care has been taken to conserve wherever possible Italian resources for the use of the civil economy and to utilize local goods and services only when military necessity demanded. The Allied Forces Local Resources Board, on the Committees of which Italian representatives have sat, was established as the allocation agency.

While the legal rights of the Allied Forces under this article have not been modified, in practice it has been administered with as much regard as possible for Italian needs.

With the redeployment of Allied troops from Italy, the utilization of local resources and facilities is diminishing rapidly. In addition, large quantities of food, coal, clothing and other commodities have been imported into Italy by the United Nations largely in United Nations ships to supplement local resources and to alleviate distress.

Article 20: Allied Military Government was rigorously enforced in combat zones for obvious operational reasons. This was progressively relaxed as the battle moved forward until territories were handed over wholly to Italian administration.

Article 21: As Allied Forces are redeployed, facilities are progressively being handed back to Italian control.

Article 22: With the declaration of war upon the Germans by the Italian Government in October 1943, and the cooperation and loyalty of the Italian people to the Allied cause, there has never been any necessity to invoke this article.

Article 23: The Italian Government has been informed that the Allied Commission will no longer intervene in Italian internal financial affairs (except in cases of Allied military necessity) and that, with certain exceptions in Italy's own interest, the Italian Government need no longer obtain the approval of the Allied Commission prior to the execution of external financial transactions. The Italian Government is now free to fix or negotiate exchange rates for the lira without prior consultation with the Allied Commission.

Article 24: Private export trade may now be resumed and all types of commercial and financial correspondence may now go forward from Italy to the non-enemy world, subject to the Italian Government putting into force certain trade control measures similar to those employed by the United Nations against enemy interests.

Article 26: This article is no longer enforced, and provided an individual has the necessary civil documents, such as passport, visas, et cetera, there is nothing to prevent him from leaving Italian territory, subject, of course, to the immigration laws and regulations of the countries of intended destination.

Aricles 30 and 31: The Italian Government has of its own volition done all that would have been required.

Article 32: This article has been complied with and is, in the case of Clauses A and B, no longer applicable. As regards Clause C the Italian Government has cooperated loyally in carrying out such instructions as have been given concerning the preservation and administration of United Nations property in Italy, previously sequestered by the Italian Government.

Article 33: The part of Clause B that deals with the disposal of foreign assets has been modified in favor of the Italian Government (see under Article 23).

Articles 36 and 37: The execution of these articles has been modified by the Macmillan aide mémoire of February 24, 1945.

Article 41: In practice the Armistice conditions have not been applied to Albania or to any former Italian territories overseas.

III

THE CAIRO DECLARATION

December 1, 1943[1]

The several military missions have agreed upon future military operations against Japan. The Three Great Allies expressed their resolve to bring unrelenting pressure against their brutal enemies by sea, land, and air. This pressure is already rising.

The Three Great Allies are fighting this war to restrain and punish the aggression of Japan. They covet no gain for themselves and have no thought of territorial expansion. It is their purpose that Japan shall be stripped of all the islands in the Pacific which she has seized or occupied since the beginning of the first World War in 1914, and that all the territories Japan has stolen from the Chinese, such as Manchuria, Formosa, and the Pescadores, shall be restored to the Republic of China. Japan will also be expelled from all other territories which she has taken by violence and greed. The aforesaid three great powers, mindful of the enslavement of the people of Korea, are determined that in due course Korea shall become free and independent.

With these objects in view the three Allies, in harmony with those of the United Nations at war with Japan, will continue to persevere in the serious and prolonged operations necessary to procure the unconditional surrender of Japan.

[1]This statement was released by the White House on December 1, 1943, following the conference of President Roosevelt, Generalissimo Chiang Kai-shek and Prime Minister Churchill at Cairo, November 22-26, 1943. Department of State, *Bulletin*, Vol. IX (1943), p. 393. *Documents on American Foreign Relations*, edited by L. M. Goodrich and M. J. Carroll, Vol. VI, Boston, 1945, pp. 232-33.

IV

THE MOSCOW DECLARATIONS

November 1, 1943[1]

A. ANGLO-SOVIET-AMERICAN COMMUNIQUÉ

The conference of Foreign Secretaries of the United States of America, Mr. Cordell Hull, of the United Kingdom, Mr. Anthony Eden, and of the Soviet Union, Mr. V. M. Molotov, took place at Moscow from the 19th to the 30th of October 1943. There were twelve meetings.

[A list of participants in addition to the Foreign Secretaries follows here in the original.]

The agenda included all the questions submitted for discussion by the three Governments. Some of the questions called for final decisions and these were taken. On other questions, after discussion, decisions of principle were taken: these questions were referred for detailed consideration to commissions specially set up for the purpose, or reserved for treatment through diplomatic channels. Other questions again were disposed of by an exchange of views.

The Governments of the United States, the United Kingdom and the Soviet Union have been in close cooperation in all matters concerning the common war effort. But this is the first time that the Foreign Secretaries of the three Governments have been able to meet together in conference.

In the first place there were frank and exhaustive discussions of measures to be taken to shorten the war against Germany and her satellites in Europe. Advantage was taken of the presence of military advisers, representing the respective Chiefs of Staff, in order to discuss definite military operations, with regard to which decisions had been taken and which are already being prepared, and in order to create a basis for the closest military cooperation in the future between the three countries.

Second only to the importance of hastening the end of the war was the unanimous recognition by the three Governments that it was essential in their own national interests and in the interest of all peace-loving nations to continue the present close collaboration and cooperation in the conduct of the war into the period following the end of hostilities, and that only in this way could peace be maintained and the political, economic and social welfare of their peoples fully promoted.

This conviction is expressed in a declaration in which the Chinese Government joined during the Conference and which was signed by the three Foreign Secretaries and the Chinese Ambassador at Moscow on behalf of their governments. This declaration, published today, provides for even closer collaboration in the prosecution of the war and in all matters pertaining to the surrender and disarmament of the enemies with which the four countries are respectively at war. It sets forth the principles upon which the four governments agree that a broad system of international cooperation and security should be based. Provision is made for the inclusion of all other peace-loving nations, great and small, in this system.

---

[1]The three governments issued the following declarations on October 30 and November 1, 1943. Department of State, *Bulletin*, Vol. IX (1943), pp. 307 ff. *Documents on American Foreign Relations*, Vol. VI, pp. 226-232. There was in addition to the tripartite declarations, the Declaration of Four Nations on General Security, that is not reproduced here.

The Conference agreed to set up machinery for ensuring the closest coopera-tion between the three Governments in the examination of European questions arising as the war develops. For this purpose the Conference decided to estab-lish in London a European Advisory Commission to study these questions and to make joint recommendations to the three Governments.

Provision was made for continuing, when necessary, tripartite consultations of representatives of the three Governments in the respective capitals through the existing diplomatic channels.

The Conference also agreed to establish an Advisory Council for matters re-lating to Italy, to be composed in the first instance of representatives of their three governments and of the French Committee of National Liberation. Pro-vision is made for the addition to this council of representatives of Greece and Yugoslavia in view of their special interests arising out of the aggressions of Fascist Italy upon their territory during the present war. This Council will deal with day-to-day questions, other than military operations, and will make recom-mendations designed to coordinate Allied policy with regard to Italy.

The three Foreign Secretaries considered it appropriate to reaffirm, by a dec-laration published today, the attitude of their Governments in favor of restora-tion of democracy in Italy.

The three Foreign Secretaries declared it to be the purpose of their Govern-ments to restore the independence of Austria. At the same time they reminded Austria that in the final settlement account will be taken of efforts that Austria may make towards its own liberation. The declaration on Austria is published today.

The Foreign Secretaries issued at the Conference a declaration by President Roosevelt, Prime Minister Churchill and Premier Stalin containing a solemn warning that at the time of granting any armistice to any German Government those German officers and men and members of the Nazi party who have had any connection with atrocities and executions in countries overrun by German forces will be taken back to the countries in which their abominable crimes were committed to be charged and punished according to the laws of those countries.

In the atmosphere of mutual confidence and understanding which character-ized all the work of the Conference, consideration was also given to other im-portant questions. These included not only questions of a current nature, but also questions concerning the treatment of Hitlerite Germany and its satellites, economic cooperation and the assurance of general peace.

B. DECLARATION REGARDING ITALY

The Foreign Secretaries of the United States of America, the United Kingdom and the Soviet Union have established that their three Governments are in com-plete agreement that Allied policy towards Italy must be based upon the fun-damental principle that Fascism and all its evil influences and emanations shall be utterly destroyed and that the Italian people shall be given every opportunity to establish governmental and other institutions based upon democratic prin-ciples.

The Foreign Secretaries of the United States of America and the United King-dom declare that the action of their Governments from the inception of the invasion of Italian territory, insofar as paramount military requirements have permitted, has been based upon this policy.

In the furtherance of this policy in the future the Foreign Secretaries of the three Governments are agreed that the following measures are important and should be put into effect:

1. It is essential that the Italian Government should be made more democratic by the introduction of representatives of those sections of the Italian people who have always opposed Fascism.

2. Freedom of speech, of religious worship, of political belief of the press and of public meeting shall be restored in full measure to the Italian people, who shall also be entitled to form anti-Fascist political groups.

3. All institutions and organizations created by the Fascist regime shall be suppressed.

4. All Fascist or pro-Fascist elements shall be removed from the administration and from the institutions and organizations of a public character.

5. All political prisoners of the Fascist regime shall be released and accorded a full amnesty.

6. Democratic organs of local government shall be created.

7. Fascist chiefs and other persons known or suspected to be war criminals shall be arrested and handed over to justice.

In making this declaration the three Foreign Secretaries recognize that as long as active military operations continue in Italy the time at which it is possible to give full effect to the principles set out above will be determined by the Commander-in-Chief on the basis of instructions received through the Combined Chiefs of Staff. The three Governments parties to this declaration will at the request of any one of them consult on this matter.

It is further understood that nothing in this resolution is to operate against the right of the Italian people ultimately to choose their own form of government.

C. DECLARATION ON AUSTRIA

The Governments of the United Kingdom, the Soviet Union and the United States of America are agreed that Austria, the first free country to fall a victim to Hitlerite aggression, shall be liberated from German domination.

They regard the annexation imposed upon Austria by Germany on March 15, 1938, as null and void. They consider themselves as in no way bound by any changes effected in Austria since that date. They declare that they wish to see reestablished a free and independent Austria, and thereby to open the way for the Austrian people themselves, as well as those neighboring states which will be faced with similar problems, to find that political and economic security which is the only basis for lasting peace.

Austria is reminded, however, that she has a responsibility which she cannot evade for participation in the war on the side of Hitlerite Germany, and that in the final settlement account will inevitably be taken of her own contribution to her liberation.

D. DECLARATION ON GERMAN ATROCITIES

The United Kingdom, the United States and the Soviet Union have received from many quarters evidence of atrocities, massacres and cold-blooded mass executions which are being perpetrated by the Hitlerite forces in the many countries they have overrun and from which they are now being steadily expelled. The brutalities of Hitlerite domination are no new thing and all the peoples or territories in their grip have suffered from the worst form of government by terror. What is new is that many of these territories are now being redeemed by the advancing armies of the liberating Powers and that in their desperation, the recoiling Hitlerite Huns are redoubling their ruthless cruelties. This is now evidenced with particular clearness by monstrous crimes of the Hitlerites on the territory of the Soviet Union which is being liberated from the Hitlerites, and on French and Italian territory.

Accordingly, the aforesaid three Allied Powers, speaking in the interests of the thirty-two [thirty-three] United Nations, hereby solemnly declare and give full warning of their declaration as follows:

At the time of the granting of any armistice to any government which may be set up in Germany, those German officers and men and members of the Nazi party who have been responsible for, or have taken a consenting part in the above atrocities, massacres and executions, will be sent back to the countries in which their abominable deeds were done in order that they may be judged and punished according to the laws of these liberated countries and of the free governments which will be created therein. Lists will be compiled in all possible detail from all these countries having regard especially to the invaded parts of the Soviet Union, to Poland and Czechoslovakia, to Yugoslavia and Greece, including Crete and other islands, to Norway, Denmark, the Netherlands, Belgium, Luxemburg, France and Italy.

Thus, the Germans who take part in wholesale shootings of Italian officers or in the execution of French, Dutch, Belgium or Norwegian or of Cretan peasants, or who have shared in the slaughters inflicted on the people of Poland or in territories of the Soviet Union which are now being swept clear of the enemy, will know that they will be brought back to the scene of their crimes and judged on the spot by the peoples whom they have outraged. Let those who have hitherto not imbrued their hands with innocent blood beware lest they join the ranks of the guilty, for most assuredly the three Allied Powers will pursue them to the uttermost ends of the earth and will deliver them to their accusers in order that justice may be done.

The above declaration is without prejudice to the case of the major criminals, whose offences have no particular geographical localisation and who will be punished by the joint decision of the Governments of the Allies.

V

COMBINED DIRECTIVE FOR MILITARY GOVERNMENT IN GERMANY PRIOR TO DEFEAT OR SURRENDER
April 28, 1944[1]

1. This directive is subject to such alteration as may be necessary to meet joint recommendations of the European Advisory Commission in regard to the post-surrender period. It relates to the period before defeat or surrender of

---

[1]The directive was approved by the Combined Chiefs of Staff and transmitted by them to the Supreme Commander, Allied Expeditionary Force, on April 28, 1944. But it consisted then only of the basic and political directive and included only the political guides for Germany and Austria. As the text (par. 7, p. 136) indicated Appendices C, D, E were not yet ready. They were transmitted on May 31, 1944. However, the economic and relief guides were merged into Appendix D. The financial guide (Appendix C) was revised in August and a program adopted that envisaged to impose only a minimum of new financial controls and regulations. It was felt largely on the basis of the Italian experiences that a comprehensive anti-inflationary and control program could be formulated only after a practical observation of the financial and economic factors appearing in Germany during the post-hostilities period. Appendix C is published here in its revised form.

Germany and to such parts of Germany and Austria as are overrun by the forces under your command during such period. The same policy will be applied to occupied parts of Austria as to occupied parts of Germany except where different treatment is required for Austria to meet the provision of the Political Guide at Appendix B or other paragraphs dealing specifically with Austria.

2. Military government will be established and will extend over all parts of Germany, including Austria, progressively as the forces under your command capture German territory. Your rights in Germany prior to unconditional surrender or German defeat will be those of an occupying power.

3. a. By virtue of your position you are clothed with supreme legislative, executive, and judicial authority and power in the areas occupied by forces under your command. This authority will be broadly construed and includes authority to take all measures deemed by you necessary, desirable or appropriate in relation to the exigencies of military operations and the objectives of a firm military government.

b. You are authorized at your discretion, to delegate the authority herein granted to you in whole or in part to members of your command, and further to authorize them at their discretion to make appropriate subdelegations. You are further authorized to appoint members of your command as Military Governors of such territory or areas as you may determine.

c. You are authorized to establish such military courts for the control of the population of the occupied areas as may seem to you desirable, and to establish appropriate regulations regarding their jurisdiction and powers.

d. The military government shall be a military administration which will show every characteristic of an Allied undertaking, acting in the interests of the United Nations. Whether or not U. S. and U. K. civil affairs personnel will be integrated other than at your headquarters will be a matter for your decision.

4. The U. S. and British flags shall be displayed at headquarters and posts of the military government. The administration shall be identical throughout those parts of Germany occupied by forces under your command, subject to any special requirements due to local circumstances.

5. The military administration shall contain no political agencies or political representatives of the U. S. and U. K. U. S. and U. K. political officers appointed at your headquarters will continue in office.

6. Representatives of civilian agencies of the U.S.-U.K. Governments or of UNRRA shall not participate unless and until you consider such participation desirable when it will be subject, as to time and extent, to decision by the Combined Chiefs of Staff on your recommendation.

7. Appendix A, Political Guide for Germany; Appendix B, Political Guide for Austria, are attached hereto. Appendix C, Financial Guide; Appendix D, Economic Guide; and Appendix E, Relief Guide; will be transmitted at a later date.

Appendix A

POLITICAL GUIDE

1. The administration shall be firm. It will at the same time be just and humane with respect to the civilian population so far as consistent with strict military requirements. You will strongly discourage fraternization between Allied troops and the German officials and population. It should be made clear to the local population that military occupation is intended; (1) to aid military

operations; (2) to destroy Nazism-Fascism and the Nazi Hierarchy; (3) to maintain and preserve law and order; and (4) to restore normal conditions among the civilian population as soon as possible, insofar as such conditions will not interfere with military operations.

2. a. Adolf Hitler, his chief Nazi associates, and all persons suspected of having committed war crimes will be arrested and held for investigation and subsequent disposition, including those who appear on lists drawn up by the United Nations which will be communicated to you. The heads of all ministries and other high political functionaries of the German Reich and those Germans who have held high positions in occupied Allied countries found within occupied territory will be interned and held pending further instructions.

b. The same shall apply in the case of any national of any of the United Nations who is alleged to have committed offenses against his national law and of any other person whose name or designation appears on lists to be similarly communicated.

3. The intention is to dissolve the Nazi Party throughout Germany as soon as possible. In furtherance of this object, you should: (1) take possession of offices and records of all Party organizations and make lists of them; (2) suspend activities of all Party organizations except those which you may require to continue to function for administrative convenience; (3) arrest and imprison high Party officials; (4) take Party property into custody, except for those organizations specially directed by you in (2) above. A special effort should be made to seize and preserve all records and plans of the German military organizations and of the Nazi Party, and of the Security, Criminal, and Ordinary Police, and records of Nazi economic organizations and industrial establishments.

4. You will take steps to prevent the operation of all Nazi laws which discriminate on the basis of race, color, or creed or political opinions. All persons who were detained or placed in custody by the Nazis on such grounds should be released subject to requirements of security and interests of the individual concerned.

5. a. The operation of the criminal and civil courts of the German Reich will be suspended. However, at the earliest possible moment you should permit their functioning under such regulation, supervision, and control as you may determine. The operation of politically objectionable courts, e.g., People's courts, will be permanently suspended with a view to eventual abolition. All Nazi elements will be eliminated from the judiciary.

b. Security Police, excluding Criminal Police, but including Gestapo and Sicherheitsdienst, should be disarmed, disbanded and imprisoned. Criminal and Ordinary Police should be retained subject to the removal of Nazi or otherwise undesirable elements.

6. The replacement of local Government officials who may be removed will rest with the Supreme Commander who will decide whether the functioning of the military government is better served by the appointment of officers of the occupation forces or by the use of the services of Germans. Military Government will be effected as a general principle through indirect rule. The principal link for this indirect rule should be at the Bezirk or Kreis level; controls at higher levels will be inserted at your discretion. Subject to any necessary dismissals, local officials should be instructed to continue to carry out their duties. No actual appointment of Germans to important posts will be made until it has been approved by the Combined Chiefs of Staff. It should be made clear

to any German, after eventual appointment to an important post, and to all other Governmental officials and employees, that their continued employment is solely on the basis of satisfactory performance and behavior. In general the entire Nazi leadership will be removed from any post of authority and no permanent member of the German General Staff nor of the Nazi Hierarchy will occupy any important Governmental or Civil position. The German Supreme Command and General Staff will be disbanded in such a way as will insure that its possible resuscitation later will be made as difficult as possible.

7. Subject to the provisions of paragraph 10, and to the extent that military interests are not prejudiced, freedom of speech and press, and of religious worship should be permitted. Consistent with military necessity, all religious institutions shall be respected and all efforts will be made to preserve historical archives, classical monuments, and objects of art.

8. Diplomatic and consular officials of countries at war with any of the United Nations and of neutrals will be dealt with in accordance with instructions to be issued by the Combined Chiefs of Staff.

9. a. Prisoners of war belonging to the forces of the United Nations and associated nations and their nationals confined, interned or otherwise under restraint by German authorities will be freed from confinement and placed under military control or restriction as may be appropriate pending other disposition.

b. So far as practicable after identification and examination, Allied nationals should be given opportunity to join the armed forces of their country if represented by units in the theater, or to serve in labor battalions organized by the military or in other approved civilian work, provided their loyalties to the Allies have been determined and they qualify physically and otherwise. All practical measures should be taken to insure health and welfare of Allied nationals. They should not be allowed to disperse until plans are made for their employment or other disposition. Former prisoners of war released by the Axis may be found. They should be identified and requests addressed to their respective military commands for instructions as to their disposition.

c. Allied and neutral civilian internees found in the territory should be placed in restricted residence with provision being made for their care until they show that they can provide for themselves. Work should be provided when practicable. They should be identified as to nationality in order that their presence in the territory may be communicated to their respective governments.

d. If feasible and practicable, enemy nationals, other than nationals of the country under occupation, will be identified and registered and those whose freedom of movement would endanger the security of the armed forces or be otherwise undesirable will be interned or their activities curtailed as may be necessary under the circumstances.

10. a. The propagation of Nazi doctrines and propaganda in any form shall be prohibited. Guidance on German education and schools will be given to you in a separate directive.

b. No political activity of any kind shall be countenanced unless authorized by you. Unless you deem otherwise, it is desirable that neither political personalities nor organized political groups, shall have any part in determining the policies of the military administration. It is essential to avoid any commitments to, or negotiations with, any political elements. German political leaders in exile shall have no part in the administration.

c. You will institute such censorship and control of press, printing, publications, and the dissemination of news or information by the above means and by mail, radio, telephone, and cable or other means as you consider necessary in the interests of military security and intelligence of all kinds and to carry out the principles laid down in this directive.

11. A plan should be prepared by you to prevent transfers of title of real and personal property intended to defeat, evade, or avoid the orders, proclamations, or decrees of the military government or the decision of the courts established by it.

12. a. All property in the German territory belonging to the German Reich or to any country with which any of the United Nations are at war will be controlled directly or indirectly pending further instructions, subject to such use thereof as you may direct.

b. Your responsibility for the property of the United Nations other than U. K. and U. S. and their nationals in areas to be liberated or occupied by Allied Forces shall be the same as for the property of U. K. and U. S. and their nationals except where a distinction is expressly provided by treaty or agreement. Within such limits as are imposed by the military situation you should take all reasonable steps necessary to preserve and protect such property.

Appendix B

POLITICAL GUIDE FOR AUSTRIA

1. The political aims of the occupation of Austria will differ fundamentally from those of the occupation of Germany in that their primary purpose will be that of liberation. Though it will be of great importance that the occupying forces in Germany should make a good impression on the inhabitants, this will be of even more importance in Austria and the impression to be aimed at is of a different kind. You should try to insure that occupation by Allied Forces in no way suffers by comparison with occupation by Germans.

2. In applying the political guide at Appendix A to Austria you should bear in mind the following points:

a. Paragraph 1. The attitude to the Austrian population should be more friendly than in Germany. There will be no need to discourage some degree of fraternization. In addition to the four points enumerated in the last sentence in this paragraph the following should be added: "To liberate Austria from German domination and pave the way for a free and independent Austria."

b. Paragraph 6. A large proportion of the administrative posts in Austria have been filled by Reich Germans and the replacement of local government officials may therefore have to be more complete than in Germany. Their replacement should proceed as rapidly as practicable having regard to the requirements of military security and administrative possibilities. Every encouragement should be given to Austrians untainted by Nazi sympathies to fill the vacated posts. Only the highest appointments will require the prior approval of the Combined Chiefs of Staff.

c. In Austria there is no intermediate administrative unit between the Reichsgaue and the Kreise and the principal link for civil affairs must therefore be the former until it is possible to restore the old Austrian länder.

d. Paragraph 10 a. In addition to Nazi doctrines and propaganda, it will be necessary to prohibit propaganda for pan-Germanism and renewal of association with Germany.

e. Paragraph 10 b. You should be prepared to give more latitude to political activity in Austria than in Germany.

Appendix C
REVISED* FINANCIAL GUIDE FOR GERMANY

1. United States, British and other Allied forces will use Allied Military marks and Reichsmark currency or coins in their possession. Allied Military Marks and Reichsmark currency and coin now in circulation in Germany will be legal tender without distinction and will be interchangeable at a rate of—— Allied Military mark for —— Reichsmark. Records will be kept of the amounts of the German marks used by the forces of each nation. *Reichskreditkassenscheine* and other German Military currency will not be legal tender in Germany.

2. In the event, however, that for any reason adequate supplies of Allied Military marks and/or Reichsmarks are not available, the United States forces will use yellow seal dollars and regular United States coins and the British forces will use British Military Authority (BMA) notes and regular British coins. Records will be kept of the amounts of currencies used by the United States and British forces.

3. If it is found necessary to use US yellow seal dollars and BMA notes, the following provisions will apply to such use:

a. The rate of exchange between the U.S. yellow seal dollar and the BMA notes will be —— dollars to one pound, and the two currencies will be interchangeable at that rate. The United States Treasury will make the necessary arrangements with the British Treasury.

b. You will issue a proclamation, if necessary, requiring all persons to accept U.S. yellow seal dollars and BMA notes at the decreed rates. Transactions at any other rates will be prohibited.

c. The issuance of yellow seal dollars and BMA notes will cease and Allied Military mark and/or Reichsmark currency will be used in their place as soon as available.

d. U.S. yellow seal dollars and BMA notes will be withdrawn from circulation as soon as such withdrawal can be satisfactorily accomplished.

e. Records will be kept of the amounts of such currencies used by the United States, British and other Allied forces.

4. The rate of exchange to be decreed on your entry into the area will be —— marks to the dollar and —— marks to the pound sterling. Transactions at any other rates will be prohibited. Holders of mark currency or deposits will not be entitled to purchase foreign exchange without special permission. They will obtain dollars or pounds, or any other foreign currency or foreign exchange credits, only in accordance with exchange regulations issued by you.

5. The Financial Division of the Civil Affairs Section for Germany will include in its functions the control of all funds to be used by the Allied Military forces within the area, except yellow seal dollars and BMA notes which will be under the control of U.S. and British forces respectively. It will maintain all the accounts and records necessary to indicate the supply, control, and movement of these currencies including yellow seal dollars and BMA notes, and other funds, as well as financial data required for the determination of

*See p. 135, footnote.

expenditures arising out of operations or activities involving participation of Allied Military forces.

a. Insofar as operations relate to the provisions of currencies for the pay and other cash requirements of military components of the Allied forces, the Financial Division will supply Allied military marks from currency on hand and will record the debit against the military force concerned.

b. Insofar as operations relate to the provision of currencies for civil administration, the Financial Division will supply Allied Military marks from currency on hand and will record the debit against the Allied Military Government.

c. If found practicable and desirable, you will designate, under direct military control and supervision, the Reichsbank, or any branch thereof, or any other bank satisfactory to you, as agent for the Financial Division of Civil Affairs Sections. When satisfied that the Reichsbank, or any branch thereof, or other designated bank, is under adequate military control and supervision, you may use that bank for official business, and, if necessary, by making credits available, place such bank or banks in a position to finance other banks and branches thereof, for the conduct of their business as approved by the Allied military authorities.

d. The records of the Financial Division of the Civil Affairs Section established within the area will indicate in all cases in what currency receipts were obtained or disbursements made by the Financial Division.

6. Upon entering the area, you will take the following steps and will put into effect only such further financial measures as you may deem to be necessary from a strictly military standpoint:

a. You will declare a general or limited moratorium if you deem such measure to be necessary. In particular, it may prove desirable to prevent foreclosures of mortgages and the exercise of similar remedies by creditors against individuals and small business enterprises.

b. Banks should be placed under such control as deemed necessary by you in order that adequate facilities for military needs may be provided and to insure that instructions and regulations issued by military authorities will be fully complied with. Banks should be closed only long enough to introduce satisfactory control, to remove objectionable personnel, and to issue instructions for the determination of accounts to be blocked under paragraph e below. As soon as practicable banks should be required to file reports listing assets, liabilities, and all accounts in excess of 25,000 marks.

c. You will issue regulations prescribing the purposes for which credit may be extended and the terms and conditions governing the extension of credit. If banking facilities are not available you may establish such credits or make such loans as you deem necessary for essential economic activities. These will be restricted to mark credits and loans.

d. You will close all stock exchanges and similar financial institutions.

e. Pending determination of future disposition, all gold, foreign currencies, foreign securities, accounts in financial institutions, credits, valuable papers and all similar assets held by or on behalf of the following, will be impounded or blocked and will be used or otherwise dealt with only as permitted under licenses or other instructions which you may issue:

(1) German national, state, provincial, and local governments, and agencies and instrumentalities thereof.

(2) Other enemy governments, the agencies and instrumentalities thereof and their Nationals.

(3) Owners and holders, including neutral and United Nations Governments or national authorities, absent from the areas of Germany under your control.

(4) Nazi party organizations, including the party formations, affiliates, and supervised associations, and the officials, leading members, and supporters thereof.

(5) Persons under detention or other types of custody by Allied Military authorities and other persons whose activities are hostile to the interests of the military government.

f. No governmental or private bank or agency will be authorized to issue banknotes or currency except that, if found practicable and desirable, you may so authorize the Reichsbank and the Rentenbank when they are under adequate military control and supervision.

g. You will issue immediately a proclamation prohibiting all transfers of or other dealings in real estate and securities, other than central government securities. You may, however, prohibit or limit dealings in central government securities, but only pending resumption of service on the public debt.

7. All dealings in gold and foreign exchange and all foreign financial and foreign trade transactions of any kind, including all exports and imports of currency, will be prohibited except as permitted under such regulations as you may issue relative thereto. Except as you may otherwise authorize, local banks will be permitted to open and operate only mark accounts, but if yellow seal dollars and BMA notes are legal tender, they may be accepted at the decreed rate of exchange and will be turned in as directed by you in exchange for mark currency at the decreed rate of exchange.

8. Non-yellow seal U.S. dollar notes and regular British pound notes will not be legal tender. No person, agency or bank engaged in the exchange of money will acquire or otherwise deal in these notes except as you may so authorize. U. S. Army and Navy Finance Officers and British Paymasters may, however, be authorized to accept non-yellow seal U.S. dollar notes and regular British pound notes from United States and British Military or authorized personnel for conversion into Allied Military mark or Reichsmark currency at the decreed rate of exchange, after satisfying themselves as to the source of the notes.

9. All bona fide government pensions, allowances, and social security payments will continue to be paid, but steps will be taken as soon as practicable for a study of pensioners' records with a view to nullifying all unnecessary and undesirable pensions and bonuses of Nazi inception.

10. The railways, postal, telegraph and telephone service, radio and all government monopolies will be placed under your control and their revenues made available to the military government.

11. You will, consistent with international custom and usage, maintain existing tax laws, except that discriminatory taxes introduced under the Nazi regime will be abolished. Prompt action should be taken to maintain the inflow of revenue at the highest possible level. You will resume service on the public debt as soon as military and financial conditions permit.

Appendix D

ECONOMIC AND RELIEF GUIDE FOR GERMANY

The following directive relates to the period before the surrender of Germany. In areas where there are no military operations in progress, when practicable and consistent with military necessity you should:

(a) see that the systems of production, control, collection and distribution of food and agricultural produce are maintained, that food processing factories continue in operation and that the necessary labor and transport are provided to insure maximum production. German food and other supplies will be utilized for the German population to the minimum extent required to prevent disease and unrest. You will report on any surpluses that may be available as regards which separate instructions will be issued to you;

(b) instruct the German authorities to restore the various utilities to full working order, and to maintain coal mines in working condition and in full operation so far as transport will permit. Except insofar as their production is needed to meet your requirements, or as you may be instructed in subsequent directives, munitions factories will be closed pending further instructions. You will be responsible for procuring such goods and materials for export as you may from time to time be directed to obtain for the use of the United Nations. You will take steps to insure that no sabotage or destruction is carried out by the Germans of any industrial plant, equipment or stocks, or of any books or records relating thereto. Pending the issue of further directives you will take such steps as you think desirable to preserve intact all such plant, equipment, books and records, paying particular attention to research and experimental establishment;

(c) exercise control over German shipping, inland transport and communications primarily in the interests of the Allied military effort and see that they are maintained in a full state of efficiency;

(d) establish a system of control over export and import trade. In determining what exports shall be permitted, paramount consideration shall be granted to your military needs. Records will be kept of all import and export transactions;

(e) instruct the German authorities to maintain the limits on prices and wages in force under the most recent German regulations. The rationing system for important staple commodities shall be retained or reestablished. Black market activities and hoarding will be severely punished. Generally you will take all possible steps to prevent inflation;

(f) where possible, work through the existing German administrative and economic machinery in carrying out the above program, bearing in mind the principles as regards removal of Nazi personnel contained in paragraph 6 of the political guide at Appendix A;

(g) permit the formation of a democratic trade union movement and other forms of free economic association.

VI

DIRECTIVES AND AGREEMENTS ON CIVIL AFFAIRS IN FRANCE

August 25, 1944[1]

A. DIRECTIVE TO SCAEF FROM TNE COMBINED CHIEFS OF STAFF FOR CIVIL AFFAIRS ADMINISTRATION IN CONTINENTAL FRANCE

1. As a result of the discussions between American, British and French representatives, agreement has been reached on the practical arrangements for civil affairs administration in Continental France.

2. This agreement is recorded in Memoranda Nos. 1 to 5, inclusive:

No. I   Relating to Administrative and Jurisdictional Questions

No. II   Relating to Currency

No. III   Relating to Property in Continental France

No. IV   Relating to Publicity Arrangements

No. V   Relating to the Distribution of Relief Supplies for the Civil Population in Continental France.

These memoranda are being forwarded by air courier.

3. You should act in accordance with the terms of these memoranda in all matters which concern the civil administration of France. The designation "Supreme Allied Commander" used in these memoranda refers to the Supreme Commander, Allied Expeditionary Force (SCAEF). Memoranda I, III, IV and V become operative when put into effect for the British by the Foreign Secretary and when transmitted for the United States by the CG, USAF, ETO to the Chief of the French Military Mission. Memorandum II becomes operative when put into effect for the British by the Foreign Secretary and when transmitted by SCAEF to the Chief of the French Military Mission.[1]

4. In connection with your rights and powers to use or requisition war materials and other property, information has come to hand indicating that the Germans customarily requisition all usable supplies in any area before abandoning it. In exercising your right to use such supplies you should, so far as military necessity permits, give the greatest consideration to the economic interests of the civilian population and, where possible, leave at the disposal of the French authorities such transport material, food supplies and building materials as have been requisitioned by the German armies or handed over to them under duress, and which are not needed by you in connection with military operations.

B. DIRECTIVE TO COMMANDING GENERAL, U.S. ARMY FORCES, EUROPEAN THEATER OF OPERATIONS

You are directed to address the following letter in your capacity as Commanding General, U.S. Army Forces, European Theater of Operations, to General Koenig, as Chief of the French Military Mission.

It is understood that the memoranda referred to therein will also be put into

---

[1] The Supreme Commander transmitted the Memorandum II to General Koenig, Chief of the French Military Mission, with the following letter: "My dear General: This will confirm the fact that the arrangements between the French and Allied authorities concerning the issuance and use of currency in France, which are embodied in the attached memorandum, are approved, and the understanding that such arrangements are effective as of today."

effect for the British by Foreign Secretary Anthony Eden. Text of letter to General Koenig:

My dear General:

Pursuant to instructions I have received from the United States Chiefs of Staff, I am transmitting herewith four memoranda of arrangements with respect to civil affairs administration in France which have been agreed to between the French and American representatives in Washington.

I have been authorized to deal with the French Committee of National Liberation as the de facto authority in France, which will assume the leadership of and responsibility for the administration of the liberated areas of France. This action is taken on the understanding that the Supreme Commander, Allied Expeditionary Force must possess whatever authority he may need for the unimpeded conduct of military operations as well as in recognition of the fact that the civil administration in France, pending the full liberation of the country, should be exercised, insofar as it is practicable, by Frenchmen.

In authorizing me to take this action, my government also understands that it is the intention of the Committee that as soon as the military situation permits, the French people will be given an opportunity to select a government of their own free choice. My dealing with the Committee as above outlined is based upon the support which the Committee continues to receive from the majority of Frenchmen who are fighting for the defeat of Germany and the liberation of France.

I shall be happy to carry out the arrangements contained in the enclosed memoranda in the spirit of fullest cooperation with the French Committee and its representatives in dealing with civil affairs administration during the period of military operations in France against the common enemy.

C. MEMORANDUM NO. 1 RELATING TO ADMINISTRATIVE AND JURISDICTIONAL QUESTIONS

The present agreement, relating to the administrative and jurisdictional questions which will arise in the course of military operations of liberation on continental French territory, is intended to be essentially temporary and practical. It is designed to facilitate, as far as possible, the accomplishment of the following common objectives:

a. The speedy, total and final defeat of the common enemy, the liberation of French soil, and the resumption by France of her historic place among the nations of the world.

b. The direction and coordination of the assistance which the French authorities and people will be able to render to the Allied expeditionary forces on the territory of continental France.

c. The adoption in that territory of all measures deemed necessary by the Supreme Allied Commander for the successful conduct of his operations.

1. In areas in which military operations take place the Supreme Allied Commander will possess the necessary authority to ensure that all measures are taken which in his judgment are essential for the successful conduct of his operations. Arrangements designed to carry out this purpose are set forth in the following Articles.

2. (i) Liberated French Continental territory will be divided into two zones: a forward zone and an interior zone.

(ii) The forward zone will consist of the areas affected by active military operations; the boundary between the forward zone and the interior zone will be fixed in accordance with the provisions of paragraph (iv) below.

(iii) The interior zone will include all other regions in the liberated territory, whether or not they have previously formed part of the forward zone. In certain cases, having regard to the exigencies of operations, military zones may be created within the interior zone in accordance with the provisions of Article 5 (ii) below.

(iv) The Delegate referred to in Article 3 below will effect delimitation of the zones in accordance with French law in such a manner as to meet the requirements stated by the Supreme Allied Commander.

3. (i) In accordance with Article 1 of the ordinance made by the French Committee of National Liberation on March 14, 1944 a Delegate will be appointed for the present theater of operations. Other Delegates may be appointed in accordance with the development of operations.

(ii) The Delegate will have at his disposal an administrative organization, a Military Delegate and liaison officers for administrative duties. The Delegate's task will be in particular to centralize and facilitate relations between the Allied Military Command and the French authorities.

(iii) When the powers conferred on the Delegate by French law are transferred to higher French authorities, it will be for those authorities to execute the obligations of the Delegate under this agreement.

4. In the forward zone: (i) The Delegate will take, in accordance with French law, the measures deemed necessary by the Supreme Allied Commander to give effect to the provisions of Article 1, and in particular will issue regulations and make appointments in and removals from the public services.

(ii) In emergencies affecting military operations or where no French authority is in a position to put into effect the measures deemed necessary by the Supreme Allied Commander under paragraph (i) of this Article, the latter may, as a temporary and exceptional measure, take such measures as are required by military necessity.

(iii) At the request of the Supreme Allied Commander, the French Military Delegate will take such action under his powers under the state of siege in accordance with French law as may be necessary.

5. (i) In the interior zone the conduct of the administration of the territory and responsibility therefor including the powers under the state of siege, will be entirely a matter for the French authorities. Special arrangements will be made between the competent French authorities and the Supreme Allied Commander at the latter's request in order that all measures may be taken which the latter considers necessary for the conduct of military operations.

(ii) Moreover, in accordance with Article 2 (iii) and (iv), certain portions of the interior zone (known as military zones) may be subjected to a special regime on account of their vital military importance; for example, ports, fortified naval areas, aerodromes, and troop concentration areas. In such zones, the Supreme Allied Commander is given the right to take, or to cause the services in charge of installations of military importance to take, all measures considered by him to be necessary for the conduct of operations, and, in particular, to assure the security and efficient operation of such installations. Consistent with these provisions, the conduct of the territorial administration and the responsibility therefor will nevertheless be solely a matter for the French authorities.

6. The liaison officers referred to in Article 3 (ii), placed by the Military Delegate at the disposal of the French administration, will insure liaison between the said administration and the Allied Forces.

7. (i) Members of the French Armed Forces serving in French units with the Allied Forces in French territory will come under the exclusive jurisdiction of the French courts.

(ii) Persons who are subject to the exclusive jurisdiction of the French authorities may, in the absence of such authorities, be arrested by the Allied Military Police and detained by them until they can be handed over to the competent French authorities.

8. (i) In the exercise of jurisdiction over civilians, the Delegate will make the necessary arrangements for ensuring the speedy trial, in competent French courts in the vicinity, of such civilians as are alleged to have committed offenses against the persons, property or security of the Allied Forces.

(ii) For this purpose the Military Delegate will establish military tribunals as laid down in the ordinance of June 6, 1944 and ensure their effective operation. The Supreme Allied Commander will designate the military formations to which he wishes a military tribunal to be attached. The Military Delegate will immediately take the necessary measures to allocate these tribunals accordingly. The Supreme Allied Commander will be kept informed of the result of the proceedings.

9. (i) Without prejudice to the provisions of Article 13, Allied service courts and authorities will have exclusive jurisdiction over all members of their respective forces.

(ii) British or American nationals not belonging to such forces who are employed by or who accompany those forces, and are subject to Allied Naval, Military, or Air Force law, will for this purpose be regarded as members of the Allied Forces. The same will apply to such persons, if possessing the nationality of another Allied state provided that they were not first recruited in any French territory. If they were so recruited they will be subject to French jurisdiction in the absence of other arrangements between the authorities of their state and the French authorities.

(iii) The Allied military authorities will keep the French authorities informed of the result of proceedings taken against members of the Allied Forces charged with offenses against persons subject to the ordinary jurisdiction of the French courts.

(iv) The question of jurisdiction over such merchant seamen of non-French nationality as are not subject to Allied service law will require special treatment and should form the subject of separate arrangements.

10. Persons who, in accordance with Article 9, are subject to the exclusive jurisdiction of Allied service courts and authorities may however be arrested by the French Police for offenses against French law, and detained until they can be handed over for disposal to the appropriate Allied service authority. The procedure for handing over such persons will be a matter for local arrangements.

11. A certificate signed by an Allied officer of field rank or its equivalent that the person to whom it refers belongs to one of the classes mentioned in Article 9 shall be conclusive.

12. The necessary arrangements will be made between the Allied military authorities and the competent French authorities to provide machinery for such

mutual assistance as may be required in making investigations, collecting evidence, and ensuring the attendance of witnesses in relation to cases triable under Allied or French jurisdiction.

13. Should circumstances require provision to be made for the exercise of jurisdiction in civil matters over non-French members of the Allied Forces present in France, the Allied Governments concerned and the competent French authorities will consult together as to the measures to be adopted.

14. (i) The Allied Forces, their members and organizations attached to them, will be exempt from all direct taxes, whether levied for the state or local authorities. This provision does not apply to French nationals, nor, subject to the provisions of paragraph (iii) below to foreigners whatsoever their nationality, resident in France and recruited by the Allied Forces on the spot.

(ii) Articles imported by the Allied Forces or for their account, or by members of those forces within the limit of their personal needs, or imported by Allied Forces or agencies for the purpose of free relief, will be exempt from customs duties and from all internal dues levied by the customs administration, subject to the provisions of paragraph (iii) below.

(iii) The application of the above provisions, including any questions relating to the sale to the civilian population of imported articles referred to in paragraph (ii) above, will form the subject of later negotiations, which, at the request of either party, may be extended to cover taxes which are not referred to in this article.

15. The immunity from French jurisdiction and taxation resulting from Articles 9 and 14 will extend to such selected civilian officials and employees of the Allied Governments, present in France in furtherance of the purposes of the Allied Forces, as may from time to time be notified by the Allied military authorities to the competent French authority.

16. (i) The respective Allied authorities will establish claims commissions to examine and dispose of any claims for compensation for damage or injury preferred in Continental France against members of the Allied Forces concerned (other than members of the French Forces), exclusive of claims for damage or injury resulting from enemy action or operations against the enemy. These claims commissions will, to the greatest extent possible, deal with these claims in the same way and to the same extent as the competent French authorities would deal with claims growing out of damages or injury caused in similar circumstances by members of the French Armed Forces.

(ii) The competent Allied and French authorities will later discuss and determine the detailed arrangements necessary for examining and disposing of the claims referred to in this Article.

(iii) Nothing in this Article contained shall be deemed to prejudice any right which the French authorities, acting on behalf of French claimants, may have, under the relevant rules of international law, to present a claim through diplomatic channels in a case which has been dealt with in accordance with the foregoing provisions of this Article.

17. (i) The Allied Forces may obtain, within the limits of what is available, the supplies, facilities and services which they need for the common war effort.

(ii) At the request of the Supreme Allied Commander, the French authorities will requisition, in accordance with French law (in particular as regards prices, wages, and forms of payment) supplies, facilities and services which the Supreme Allied Commander determines are necessary for the military needs of his command. However, in the exceptional cases provided for in Article 4 (ii) above, the right of requisition is delegated to the Supreme Allied Commander, who will exercise it in accordance with current French prices and wages.

(iii) In order that the satisfaction of the local requirements of the Allied Armed Forces may have least possible disruptive effect on the economy of France, the Allied military authorities and the French authorities will consult together, whenever operations permit, as to the stores, supplies and labor which procurement agencies and individual officers and men of the Allied Forces are permitted by the Supreme Allied Commander to obtain locally by requisition, purchase or hire. The Allied military authorities will place such restrictions as are agreed to be necessary on purchases whether by agencies or troops.

(iv) The French and Allied military authorities shall jointly take the measures necessary to ensure that the provisions of this Article are carried out.

18. Other questions arising as a result of the liberation of continental French territory which are not dealt with in this memorandum shall form the subject of separate arrangements. Special arrangements will be made to secure the observation by the Allied Forces of the French regulations concerning the exchange of currency and export of capital and will be set out in an Appendix which will be attached to this memorandum.

D. MEMORANDUM NO. 2 RELATING TO CURRENCY

1. The notes denominated in francs which have been printed for the needs of Allied forces in continental France, as well as the notes denominated in francs which will be printed in the future for the same purpose, will be issued by the Trésor Central Français.

2. The notes denominated in francs which have been printed for the requirements of the Allied forces in continental France and which have been placed at their disposal before the signature of this memorandum, will be considered as having been issued by the Trésor Central Français.

3. The Allied forces will retain in their possession the notes denominated in francs which have been placed at their disposal prior to the signature of this memorandum.

4. The notes denominated in francs which have not actually been placed in circulation, or which have not yet been placed at the disposal of the Allied forces, will in the future be placed in circulation or placed at the disposal of these forces only by the Trésor Central Français. The necessary arrangements will be made to place these notes at the disposal of the Trésor Central Français, who subject to the provisions of Article 5 below, will be free to use these notes at their convenience.

5. The Trésor Central Français will place at the disposal of the Allied forces at the request of the Supreme Allied Commander such amounts of French franc currency as the Commander declares necessary for the use of Allied forces in continental France in such denominations, such types, and at such places as the Commander shall request.

6. Allied military authorities shall keep a record of use of franc notes placed at their disposal. French authorities shall be kept fully informed, and as regularly as practical, of all expenditures in these notes. A representative shall be specially appointed for this purpose by the Trésor Central Français.

7. The Allied forces will not introduce into continental France notes other than those which have been made available to them by the Trésor Central Français. The notes of the Bank of France used in continental France by the Allied forces will also be subject to the provisions of this memorandum. However, if it should become essential in the conduct of military operations to cause notes other than the French franc notes furnished hereunder to be used, such notes shall only be used by the Commander as an exceptional and temporary measure and after consultation with the French authorities.

8. The foregoing dispositions will also apply to franc coins manufactured or to be manufactured for the requirements in continental France for the Allied forces.

9. The financial arrangements which will be made with the French authorities in connection with the notes and coins dealt with in this memorandum and with the other costs arising out of operations or activities in continental France shall be negotiated between the U.S. and French authorities on the one hand, and between the British and French authorities on the other.

E. MEMORANDUM NO. 3 RELATING TO PROPERTY IN CONTINENTAL FRANCE

1. (i) War material falling into the hands of forces operating under the command of the Supreme Allied Commander shall be excluded from the operation of the succeeding articles of this Memorandum.

(ii) The term "war material" means any arms, equipment or other property whatsoever belonging to, used by, or intended for use by any enemy military or para-military formations or any members thereof in connection with their operation.

(iii) The Supreme Allied Commander shall have the right to retain any war material falling into the hands of forces operating under his command, subject to the provisions of paragraphs (iv), (v) and (vi) below.

(iv) Where the Supreme Allied Commander requires any material which prima facie appears to the French authorities prior to its acquisition by the enemy to have been in French ownership and not to have been produced or constructed by order of the enemy, such material shall be:

(a) If private property, requisitioned in accordance with Article 17 of Memorandum No. I, except in the cases in which military operations will not permit the immediate execution of the formalities of requisition.

(b) If public property used in accordance with the provisions of reciprocal aid agreements.

(v) The provisions of the preceding paragraph do not apply to war material produced or constructed in France by order of the enemy. However, when the Allied forces will no longer need such material that portion which will not have been either consumed or destroyed shall be dealt with in accordance with succeeding articles of this memorandum.

(vi) (a) The war material referred to in paragraph (iv) above not required by the Supreme Allied Commander shall be released directly to the French authorities.

(b) Any other war material not required by the Supreme Allied Commander which may be released by him to the French authorities operating through the procedures established by the Combined Chiefs of Staff shall be treated in accordance with the succeeding Articles of this Memorandum. The French authorities will be responsible for accounting as may be necessary to the other United Nations for all war material handed over to them under such conditions by the Supreme Allied Commander.

2. Subject to the provisions of Article 1, the Supreme Allied Commander shall, as soon as practicable, release all property which comes into the hands of the forces operating under his command in Continental France. The competent French authorities shall, in respect of such property, resume their normal administrative functions and powers.

3. The French authorities will accept responsibility for the protection and, in the event of the owner or his accredited agent not being present, the administration of any property referred to in Article 2 above which is not in public or private French ownership, and does not belong to any state or national of a state with which any of the United Nations has been at war at any time since September 1, 1939.

4. The French authorities will assume responsibility for the custody, in accordance with French law, of any property referred to in Article 2 above, which belongs to any state or national of a state with which any of the United Nations has been at war at any time since September 1, 1939. It is understood that the French authorities will be responsible for accounting, as may be necessary, to the other United Nations for all property referred to in this Article.

5. Nothing in this Memorandum shall affect the exercise of the right of the Supreme Allied Commander to requisition any property in accordance with the provisions of Article 17 of Memorandum No. I.

6. Nothing in this Memorandum shall affect the arrangements which have been or may be agreed between the competent Allied and French authorities concerning the use and disposal of vessels captured or found by Allied Forces in the course of operations for the liberation of Europe.

The United States representatives in initialing this document make it clear that it cannot come into force and effect unless and until the Combined Chiefs of Staff issue an appropriate directive to the London Munitions Assignment Board implementing paragraphs (v) and (vi) of Article I.

F. MEMORANDUM NO. 4 RELATING TO PUBLICITY ARRANGEMENTS

1. (i) In the forward zone the Supreme Allied Commander will exercise the right of strictly military censorship of the press, radio, cinema, news agencies and in general all publications. It is contemplated that this right will be exercised insofar as possible through a tripartite organization.

(ii) In the interior zone the French Services will consult the censorship authorities of the Supreme Allied Commander on all matters relating to military operations and will carry out the military censorship instructions communicated by him.

2. Newspapers and publications intended for Allied troops other than French and not for distribution or sale to the French public shall not be subject to any control from French authorities. The same provision will apply to the dispatches of press representatives intended for publication outside of France.

3. Equipment used or intended for use by the various organs of publicity enumerated in Article 1 above, e.g., premises, plant, supplies, will not be requisitioned by the Supreme Allied Commander except on ground of urgent military necessity or by agreement in each case between the Delegate and the Supreme Allied Commander or their representatives.

4. The French Services responsible for publicity will facilitate in every possible manner the task of the Supreme Allied Commander. They will be instructed to collaborate with him in regard to the issue of notices to the population necessitated by the conduct of operations or by the security requirements of the Allied Forces or of the population itself.

G. MEMORANDUM NO. 5 RELATING TO THE DISTRIBUTION OF RELIEF SUPPLIES FOR THE CIVIL POPULATION IN CONTINENTAL FRANCE

1. The places where the French authorities take over supplies imported for the civil population, and the arrangements for this purpose, shall be determined by agreement between the Supreme Allied Commander and the Delegate.

2. Save in the exceptional cases referred to in Article 4 (ii) of Memorandum No. I, the French authorities shall be responsible for the distribution of these supplies to the civil population.

H. MEMORANDUM RELATING TO LEND-LEASE AND RECIPROCAL AID[2]

1. The appropriate United States and French authorities will continue negotiations immediately on the basis of this memorandum with a view to concluding as soon as possible, in accordance with the general principles governing lend-lease aid, a lend-lease and reciprocal aid agreement applicable to continental France, which, when and as concluded, shall be deemed to have been in effect on and after June 6, 1944.

2. (a) The agreement contemplated in Article 1 above will determine the aid which the United States will furnish to France and, in particular, to the French armed forces (including the French forces of the interior) under the provisions of the Lend-Lease Act, including credit arrangements under Section 3 (c) of that Act.

(b) The contemplated agreement will also determine the aid which the French authorities will furnish to the United States and, in particular, to the United States forces in continental France in the way of supplies, materials, facilities and services.

(c) The contemplated agreement will provide that while each party retains the right of final decision, in the light of its own potentialities and responsibilities, decisions as to the most effective use of resources shall, as far as possible, be made in common, in pursuance of the common plans for winning the war.

3. The contemplated agreement will also be based on the following principles:

(a) The United States will make current payments in dollars to the French authorities for the equivalent of the amount of French francs used for the expenditures of the United States forces in continental France for purposes other than those treated as reciprocal aid under 2(b) above; in particular, for the net

---

[2]This memorandum was formally accepted by an exchange of communications between the Department of State and the French Delegation in Washington. The Department of State in accepting the memorandum stressed its understanding "that it is the intention of the Committee that the French people will be given an opportunity to select a government of their own free choice as soon as the military situation permits." It added: "The Department also understands that when the authority now exercised by the Committee is transferred to higher French authorities, the undertakings accepted by the French in the attached memorandum, to the extent not at that time already performed, will be assumed by such higher French authorities."

pay, allowances and other emoluments of the United States troops in continental France and for the cost of any articles requisitioned which are not supplied under 2(b) above.

(b) The French authorities will make current payments in dollars for civilian supplies furnished to continental France by the United States other than those furnished under the Lend-Lease Act pursuant to 2(a) above, and will use for this purpose French public dollar and gold assets including the holdings of the Bank of France.

4. Pending the conclusion of and without prejudice to the contemplated agreement:

(a) The United States will make current payments in dollars to the French authorities for the net amount of French franc currency used for the pay, allowances, or other emoluments of the United States troops in France, on or since June 6, 1944. Whenever it is mutually ascertained that supplies purchased with francs or requisitioned shall not be supplied under 2(b) above and will not be repaid in kind, payment in dollars will be made.

(b) The French authorities will make current payments in dollars to the United States for supplies furnished to continental France on or since June 6, 1944, by the United States under the agreed procedure under Plan A and Plan B. If the amount of dollars acquired by the French authorities on account of troop pay or from other sources is inadequate to make current payments for such supplies, the French authorities will use for this purpose other French public dollar and gold assets including the holdings of the Bank of France.

MINUTES WITH RESPECT TO ATTACHED MEMORANDUM AGREED TO AT THE MEETING OF UNITED STATES AND FRENCH DELEGATIONS ON JULY 28, 1944

As regards the provisions of articles 3(a) and 4(a) of the memorandum relating to Lend-Lease and reciprocal aid, the French Delegation makes the following statement:

For the reasons set forth in article 17 (iii) of Memorandum No. I,[3] it is not the intention of the French authorities to furnish in reciprocal aid the supplies and materials which are in France in short supply for the civilian population and which, if consumed by the United States forces, have to be replaced by imports by means of dollar purchases. If such goods are requisitioned or purchased, they should be therefore either replaced in kind or paid for in dollars by the competent American authorities.

However, the French Delegation indicates that this will not apply to unimportant quantities of supplies nor to component parts or component materials.

The American Delegation acquiesces to the above statement, which will govern the application of articles 3(a) and 4(a) of the memorandum relating to Lend-Lease and reciprocal aid.

With respect to Article 3, it is understood between the American authorities and the French authorities that in the negotiations respecting Lend-Lease and reciprocal aid referred to in Articles 1 and 2, the reciprocal aid to be furnished by the French authorities will be considered as a benefit under Section 3(b) of the Lend-Lease Act in the final settlement for the military aid furnished under the Act by the United States.

---

[3]See p. 148.

VII
REPORT OF CRIMEA CONFERENCE
February 11, 1945[1]

For the past eight days, Winston S. Churchill, Prime Minister of Great Britain, Franklin D. Roosevelt, President of the United States of America, and Marshal J. V. Stalin, Chairman of the Council of People's Commissars of the Union of Soviet Socialist Republics, have met with the Foreign Secretaries, Chiefs of Staff, and other advisors in the Crimea.

[A list of participants in addition to the three heads of governments follows here in the original.]

The following statement is made by the Prime Minister of Great Britain, the President of the United States of America, and the Chairman of the Council of People's Commissars of the Union of Soviet Socialist Republics on the results of the Crimean Conference:

The Defeat of Germany

We have considered and determined the military plans of the three Allied powers for the final defeat of the common enemy. The military staffs of the three Allied nations have met in daily meetings throughout the Conference. These meetings have been most satisfactory from every point of view and have resulted in closer coordination of the military effort of the three Allies than ever before. The fullest information has been interchanged. The timing, scope and coordination of new and even more powerful blows to be launched by our armies and air forces into the heart of Germany from the East, West, North and South have been fully agreed and planned in detail.

Our combined military plans will be made known only as we execute them, but we believe that the very close working partnership among the three staffs attained at this Conference will result in shortening the War. Meetings of the three staffs will be continued in the future whenever the need arises.

Nazi Germany is doomed. The German people will only make the cost of their defeat heavier to themselves by attempting to continue a hopeless resistance.

The Occupation and Control of Germany

We have agreed on common policies and plans for enforcing the unconditional surrender terms which we shall impose together on Nazi Germany after German armed resistance has been finally crushed. These terms will not be made known until the final defeat of Germany has been accomplished. Under the agreed plan, the forces of the three powers will each occupy a separate zone of Germany. Coordinated administration and control has been provided for under the plan through a central control commission consisting of the Supreme Commanders of the three powers with headquarters in Berlin. It has been agreed that France should be invited by the three powers, if she should so desire, to take over a zone of occupation, and to participate as a fourth member of the control commission. The limits of the French zone will be agreed by the four governments concerned through their representatives on the European Advisory Commission.

It is our inflexible purpose to destroy German militarism and Nazism and to ensure that Germany will never again be able to disturb the peace of the world. We are determined to disarm and disband all German armed forces; break up

[1]Department of State, *Bulletin,* XII (1945), pp. 213-216.

for all time the German General Staff that has repeatedly contrived the resurgence of German militarism; remove or destroy all German military equipment; eliminate or control all German industry that could be used for military
production; bring all war criminals to just and swift punishment and exact
reparation in kind for the destruction wrought by the Germans; wipe out the
Nazi Party, Nazi laws, organizations and institutions, remove all Nazi and
militarist influences from public office and from the cultural and economic life
of the German people; and take in harmony such other measures in Germany
as may be necessary to the future peace and safety of the world. It is not our
purpose to destroy the people of Germany, but only when Nazism and militarism have been extirpated will there be hope for a decent life for Germans,
and a place for them in the comity of nations.

Reparation by Germany

We have considered the question of the damage caused by Germany to the
Allied nations in this war and recognized it as just that Germany be obliged
to make compensation for this damage in kind to the greatest extent possible.
A commission for the compensation of damage will be established. The commission will be instructed to consider the question of the extent and methods
for compensating damage caused by Germany to the Allied countries. The
commission will work in Moscow. . . .[2]

Declaration on Liberated Europe

The Premier of the Union of Soviet Socialist Republics, the Prime Minister
of the United Kingdom, and the President of the United States of America
have consulted with each other in the common interests of the peoples of their
countries and those of liberated Europe. They jointly declare their mutual
agreement to concert during the temporary period of instability in liberated
Europe the policies of their three governments in assisting the peoples liberated
from the domination of Nazi Germany and the peoples of the former Axis
satellite states of Europe to solve by democratic means their pressing political
and economic problems.

The establishment of order in Europe and the rebuilding of national economic
life must be achieved by processes which will enable the liberated peoples to
destroy the last vestiges of Nazism and Fascism and to create democratic institutions of their own choice. This is a principle of the Atlantic Charter—the right
of all peoples to choose the form of government under which they will live—
the restoration of sovereign rights and self-government to those peoples who
have been forcibly deprived of them by the aggressor nations.

To foster the conditions in which the liberated peoples may exercise these
rights, the three governments will jointly assist the people in any European
liberated state or former Axis satellite state in Europe where in their judgment
conditions require (A) to establish conditions of internal peace; (B) to carry
out emergency measures for the relief of distressed peoples; (C) to form
interim governmental authorities broadly representative of all democratic elements in the population and pledged to the earliest possible establishment
through free elections of governments responsive to the will of the people; and
(D) to facilitate where necessary the holding of such elections.

The three governments will consult the other United Nations and pro-

---

[2]Here follows in the original a section dealing with the Dumbarton Oaks Conference
and the calling of the United Nations Conference at San Francisco.

visional authorities or other governments in Europe when matters of direct interest to them are under consideration.

When, in the opinion of the three governments, conditions in any European liberated state or any former Axis satellite state in Europe make such action necessary, they will immediately consult together on the measures necessary to discharge the joint responsibilities set forth in this declaration.

By this declaration we reaffirm our faith in the principles of the Atlantic Charter, our pledge in the declaration by the United Nations, and our determination to build in cooperation with other peace-loving nations world order under law, dedicated to peace, security, freedom and general well-being of all mankind.

In issuing this declaration, the three powers express the hope that the Provisional Government of the French Republic may be associated with them in the procedure suggested.

Poland

A new situation has been created in Poland as a result of her complete liberation by the Red Army. This calls for the establishment of a Polish provisional government which can be more broadly based than was possible before the recent liberation of Western Poland. The provisional government which is now functioning in Poland should therefore be reorganized on a broader democratic basis with the inclusion of democratic leaders from Poland itself and from Poles abroad. This new government should then be called the Polish Provisional Government of National Unity.

Mr. Molotov, Mr. Harriman and Sir A. Clark Kerr are authorized as a commission to consult in the first instance in Moscow with members of the present provisional government and with other Polish democratic leaders from within Poland and from abroad, with a view to the reorganization of the present government along the above lines. This Polish Provisional Government of National Unity shall be pledged to the holding of free and unfettered elections as soon as possible on the basis of universal suffrage and secret ballot. In these elections all democratic and anti-Nazi parties shall have the right to take part and to put forward candidates.

When a Polish Provisional Government of National Unity has been properly formed in conformity with the above, the government of the USSR, which now maintains diplomatic relations with the present provisional government of Poland, and the government of the United Kingdom and the government of the U.S.A. will establish diplomatic relations with the new Polish Provisional Government of National Unity, and will exchange ambassadors by whose reports the respective governments will be kept informed about the situation in Poland.

The three heads of government consider that the Eastern frontier of Poland should follow the Curzon line with digressions from it in some regions of five to eight kilometers in favor of Poland. They recognize that Poland must receive substantial accessions of territory in the North and West. They feel that the opinion of the new Polish Provisional Government of National Unity should be sought in due course on the extent of these accessions and that the final delimitation of the western frontier of Poland should thereafter await the peace conference. . . . .[3]

[3]The final sections of the Report dealt with Yugoslavia, the meeting of foreign ministers to be held in future, and the maintenance of unity among the Allies beyond the War.

VIII

DIRECTIVE TO COMMANDER-IN-CHIEF OF UNITED STATES FORCES OF OCCUPATION REGARDING MILITARY GOVERNMENT OF GERMANY

April 28, 1945[1]

It is considered appropriate, at the time of the release to the American public of the following directive setting forth United States policy with reference to the military government of Germany, to preface the directive with a short statement of the circumstances surrounding the issuance of the directive to General Eisenhower.

The directive was issued originally in April, 1945, and was intended to serve two purposes. It was to guide General Eisenhower in the military government of that portion of Germany occupied by United States forces. At the same time he was directed to urge the Control Council to adopt these policies for enforcement throughout Germany.

Before this directive was discussed in the Control Council, President Truman, Prime Minister Attlee, and Generalissimo Stalin met at Potsdam and issued a communiqué setting forth agreed policies for the control of Germany. This communiqué was made public on 2 August 1945. The directive, therefore, should be read in the light of the policies enumerated at Potsdam. In particular, its provisions regarding disarmament, economic and financial matters, and reparations should be read together with the similar provisions set out in the Potsdam Agreement on the treatment of Germany in the initial control period and in the agreement on reparations contained in the Potsdam communiqué. Many of the policy statements contained in the directive have been in substance adopted by the Potsdam Agreement. Some policy statements in the Potsdam Agreement differ from the policy statements on the same subjects in the directive. In such cases, the policies of the Potsdam Agreement are controlling. Where the Potsdam Agreement is silent on matters of policy dealt with in the directive, the latter continues to guide General Eisenhower in his administration of the United States zone in Germany.

DIRECTIVE TO COMMANDER-IN-CHIEF OF UNITED STATES FORCES OF OCCUPATION REGARDING THE MILITARY GOVERNMENT OF GERMANY

1. The Purpose and Scope of this Directive:

This directive is issued to you as Commanding General of the United States Forces of Occupation in Germany. As such you will serve as United States member of the Control Council and will also be responsible for the administration of military government in the zone or zones assigned to the United States for purposes of occupation and administration. It outlines the basic policies which will guide you in those two capacities after the termination of the combined command of the Supreme Commander, Allied Expeditionary Force.

This directive sets forth policies relating to Germany in the initial post-defeat period. As such it is not intended to be an ultimate statement of policies of this Government concerning the treatment of Germany in the postwar world.

---

[1]The document, known as JCS-1067, was sent by the Joint Chiefs of Staff to General Eisenhower on April 28, 1945. The Department of State released it to the press on October 17 adding the introductory statement. Department of State, *Bulletin*, Vol. XIII (1945), pp. 596-607.

It is therefore essential that, during the period covered by this directive, you assure that surveys are constantly maintained of economic, industrial, financial, social and political conditions within your zone and that the results of such surveys and such other surveys as may be made in other zones are made available to your Government, through the Joint Chiefs of Staff. These surveys should be developed in such manner as to serve as a basis for determining changes in the measures of control set forth herein as well as for the progressive formulation and development of policies to promote the basic objectives of the United States. Supplemental directives will be issued to you by the Joint Chiefs of Staff as may be required.

As a member of the Control Council you will urge the adoption by the other occupying powers of the principles and policies set forth in this directive and, pending Control Council agreement, you will follow them in your zone. It is anticipated that substantially similar directives will be issued to the Commanders-in-Chief of the UK, USSR and French forces of occupation.

PART I

GENERAL AND POLITICAL

2. The Basis of Military Government

a. The rights, power and status of the military government in Germany are based upon the unconditional surrender or total defeat of Germany.

b. Subject to the provisions of paragraph 3 below, you are, by virtue of your position, clothed with supreme legislative, executive, and judicial authority in the areas occupied by forces under your command. This authority will be broadly construed and includes authority to take all measures deemed by you necessary, appropriate or desirable in relation to military exigencies and the objectives of a firm military government.

c. You will issue a proclamation continuing in force such proclamations, orders and instructions as may have heretofore been issued by Allied Commanders in your zone, subject to such changes as you may determine. Authorizations of action by the Supreme Commander, Allied Expeditionary Force, may be considered as applicable to you unless inconsistent with this or later directives.

3. The Control Council and Zones of Occupation:

a. The Four Commanders-in-Chief, acting jointly, will constitute the Control Council in Germany, which will be the supreme organ of control over Germany in accordance with the agreement on Control Machinery in Germany. For purposes of administration of military government, Germany has been divided into four zones of occupation.

b. The authority of the Control Council to formulate policy and procedures and administrative relationships with respect to matters affecting Germany as a whole will be paramount throughout Germany. You will carry out and support in your zone the policies agreed upon in the Control Council. In the absence of such agreed policies you will act in accordance with this and other directives of the Joint Chiefs of Staff.

c. The administration of affairs in Germany shall be directed toward the decentralization of the political and administrative structure and the development of local responsibility. To this end you will encourage autonomy in regional, local and municipal agencies of German administration. The German economic structure shall also be decentralized. The Control Council may, however, to the minimum extent required for the fulfillment of purposes set forth herein, permit centralized administration or establish central control of (a) essential national public services, such as railroads, communications and power, (b) finance and foreign affairs and (c) production and distribution of essential commodities.

d. The Control Council should adopt procedures to effectuate, and you will facilitate in your zone, the equitable distribution of essential commodities between the zones. In the absence of a conflicting policy of the Control Council, you may deal directly with one or more zone commanders on matters of special concern to such zones.

e. Pending the formulation in the Control Council of uniform policies and procedures with respect to interzonal travel and movement of civilians, no civilians shall be permitted to leave or enter your zone without your authority, and no Germans within your zone shall be permitted to leave Germany except for specific purposes approved by you.

f. The military government personnel in each zone, including those dealing with regional and local branches of the departments of any central German administrative machinery, shall be selected by authority of the commander of that zone except that liaison officers may be furnished by the Commanders of the other three zones. The respective Commanders-in-Chief shall have exclusive jurisdiction throughout the whole of Germany over the members of the armed forces under their command and over the civilians who accompany them.

g. The Control Council should be responsible for facilitating the severance of all governmental and administrative connections between Austria and Germany and the elimination of German economic influences in Austria. Every assistance should be given to the Allied Administration in Austria in its efforts to effectuate these purposes.

4. Basic Objectives of Military Government in Germany:

a. It should be brought home to the Germans that Germany's ruthless warfare and the fanatical Nazi resistance have destroyed the German economy and made chaos and suffering inevitable and that the Germans cannot escape responsibility for what they have brought upon themselves.

b. Germany will not be occupied for the purpose of liberation but as a defeated enemy nation. Your aim is not oppression but to occupy Germany for the purpose of realizing certain important Allied objectives. In the conduct of your occupation and administration you should be just but firm and aloof. You will strongly discourage fraternization with the German officials and population.

c. The principal Allied objective is to prevent Germany from ever again becoming a threat to the peace of the world. Essential steps in the accomplishment of this objective are the elimination of Nazism and militarism in all their forms, the immediate apprehension of war criminals for punishment, the industrial disarmament and demilitarization of Germany, with continuing control over Germany's capacity to make war, and the preparation for an eventual reconstruction of German political life on a democratic basis.

d. Other Allied objectives are to enforce the program of reparations and restitution, to provide relief for the benefit of countries devastated by Nazi aggression, and to ensure that prisoners of war and displaced persons of the United Nations are cared for and repatriated.

5. Economic Controls:

a. As a member of the Control Council and as zone commander, you will be guided by the principle that controls upon the German economy may be imposed to the extent that such controls may be necessary to achieve the objectives enumerated in paragraph 4 above, and also as they may be essential to protect the safety and meet the needs of the occupying forces and assume the production and maintenance of goods and services required to prevent starvation or such disease and unrest as would endanger these forces. No action will be taken in execution of the reparations program or otherwise which would tend to support basic living conditions in Germany or in your zone on a higher level than that existing in any one of the neighboring United Nations.

b. In the imposition and maintenance of such controls as may be prescribed by you or the Control Council, German authorities will to the fullest extent practicable be ordered to proclaim and assume administration of such controls. Thus it should be brought home to the German people that the responsibility for the administration of such controls and for any breakdowns in those controls will rest with themselves and German authorities.

6. Denazification:

a. A Proclamation, dissolving the Nazi party, its formations, affiliated associations and supervised organizations, and all Nazi public institutions which were set up as instruments of Party domination, and prohibiting their revival in any form, should be promulgated by the Control Council. You will assure the prompt effectuation of that policy in your zone and will make every effort to prevent the reconstitution of any such organization in underground, disguised or secret form. Responsibility for continuing desirable non-political social services of dissolved Party organizations may be transferred by the Control Council to appropriate central agencies and by you to appropriate local agencies.

b. The laws purporting to establish the political structure of National Socialism and the basis of the Hitler regime and all laws, decrees and regulations which establish discriminations on grounds of race, nationality, creed or political opinions should be abrogated by the Control Council. You will render them inoperative in your zone.

c. All members of the Nazi party who have been more than nominal participants in its activities, all active supporters of Nazism or militarism and all other persons hostile to Allied purposes will be removed and excluded from public office and from positions of importance in quasi-public and private enterprises such as (1) civic, economic and labor organizations, (2) corporations and other organizations in which the German Government or subdivisions have a major financial interest, (3) industry, commerce, agriculture and finance, (4) education, and (5) the press, publishing houses and other agencies disseminating news and propaganda. Persons are to be treated as more than nominal participants in party activities and as active supporters of Nazism or militarism when they have (1) held office or otherwise been active at any level from local to national in the party and its subordinate organizations, or in organizations which further militaristic doctrines, (2) authorized or participated affirmatively in any Nazi crimes, racial persecutions or discriminations, (3) been avowed believers in Nazism or racial and militaristic creeds, or (4) voluntarily given substantial moral or material support or political assistance of any kind to the Nazi Party or Nazi officials and leaders. No such persons shall be retained in any of the categories of employment listed above because of administrative necessity, convenience or expediency.

d. Property, real and personal, owned or controlled by the Nazi party, its formations, affiliated associations and supervised organizations, and by all persons subject to arrest under the provisions of paragraph 8, and found within your zone, will be taken under your control pending a decision by the Control Council or higher authority as to its eventual disposition.

e. All archives, monuments and museums of Nazi inception, or which are devoted to the perpetuation of German militarism, will be taken under your control and their properties held pending decision as to their disposition by the Control Council.

f. You will make special efforts to preserve from destruction and take under your control records, plans, books, documents, papers, files, and scientific, industrial and other information and data belonging to or controlled by the following:

(1) The Central German Government and its subdivisions, German military organizations, organizations engaged in military research, and such other governmental agencies as may be deemed advisable;

(2) The Nazi Party, its formations, affiliated associations and supervised organizations;

(3) All police organizations, including security and political police;

(4) Important economic organizations and industrial establishments, including those controlled by the Nazi Party or its personnel;

(5) Institutes and special bureaus devoting themselves to racial, political, militaristic or similar research or propaganda.

7. *Demilitarization:*

a. In your zone you will assure that all units of the German armed forces, including para-military organizations, are dissolved as such, and that their personnel are promptly disarmed and controlled. Prior to their final disposition, you will arrest and hold all military personnel who are included under the provisions of paragraph 8.

b. The Control Council should proclaim, and in your zone you will effectuate, the total dissolution of all military and para-military organizations, including the General Staff, the German Officers' Corps, the Reserve Corps and military academies, together with all associations which might serve to keep alive the military tradition in Germany.

c. You will seize or destroy all arms, ammunition and implements of war and stop the production thereof.

d. You will take proper steps to destroy the German war potential, as set forth elsewhere in this directive.

8. *Suspected War Criminals and Security Arrests:*

a. You will search out, arrest and hold, pending receipt by you of further instructions as to their disposition, Adolf Hitler, his chief Nazi associates, other war criminals and all persons who have participated in planning or carrying out Nazi enterprises involving or resulting in atrocities or war crimes.

b. All persons who, if permitted to remain at large would endanger the accomplishment of your objectives will also be arrested and held in custody until trial by an appropriate semi-judicial body to be established by you. The following is a partial list of the categories of persons in order to carry out this policy.

[Note: There follows at this point in the directive a detailed list of categories of Nazi war criminals and others who are to be arrested. Some of these have not yet been found. It is considered that to publish the categories at this time would put the individuals concerned on notice and would interfere with their apprehension and punishment, where appropriate. The list of categories is, therefore, withheld from publication for the present.]

If in the light of conditions which you encounter in Germany, you believe that it is not immediately feasible to subject certain persons within these categories to this treatment, you should report your reasons and recommendations to your Government through the Joint Chiefs of Staff. If you believe it desirable, you may postpone the arrest of those whose cases you have reported, pending a decision communicated to you by the J.C.S. In no event shall any differentiation be made between or special consideration be accorded to persons arrested, either as to manner of arrest or conditions of detention, upon the basis of wealth or political, industrial, or other rank or position. In your discretion you may make such exceptions as you deem advisable for intelligence or other military reasons.

9. *Political Activities:*

a. No political activities of any kind shall be countenanced unless authorized by you. You will assure that your military government does not become committed to any political group.

b. You will prohibit the propagation in any form of Nazi militaristic or pan-German doctrines.

c. No German parades, military or political, civilian or sports, shall be permitted by you.

d. To the extent that military interests are not prejudiced and subject to the provisions of the three preceding subparagraphs and of paragraph 10, freedom of speech, press and religious worship will be permitted. Consistent with military necessity, all religious institutions will be respected.

10. *Public Relations and Control of Public Information:*

As a member of the Control Council, you will endeavor to obtain agreement for uniform and coordinated policies with respect to (a) control of public information media in Germany, (b) accrediting of foreign correspondents, (c) press censorship, and (d) issuance of official news communiqués dealing with Control Council matters. United States policies in these matters will be sent to you separately and you will be guided by these in your negotiations on the Control Council.

11. *German Courts:*

a. All extraordinary courts, including the *Volksgerichtshof* (People's Court) and the *Sondergerichte* (Special Courts), and all courts and tribunals of the Nazi Party and of its formations, affiliated associations and supervised organizations will be abolished immediately.

b. All ordinary criminal, civil and administrative courts, except those previously re-established by order of the military government, will be closed. After the elimination of all Nazi features and personnel you will permit those which are to exercise jurisdiction within the boundaries of your zone to resume operations under such regulations, supervision and control as you may consider appropriate. Courts which are to exercise jurisdiction over territory extending beyond the boundaries of your zone will be reopened only with the express authorization of the Control Council and under its regulation, supervision and control. The power to review and veto decisions of German courts shall be included within the power of supervision and control.

12. Police:

With the exception of the *Reichskriminalpolizei* (Criminal Police), all elements of the *Sicherheitspolizei* (Security Police), e.g., *Geheime Staatspolizei* (Gestapo), and the *Sicherheitsdienst der S.S.* will be abolished. Criminal and ordinary police will be purged of Nazi personnel and utilized under the control and supervision of the Military Government.

13. Political Prisoners:

Subject to military security and the interests of the individuals concerned, you will release all persons found within your zone who have been detained or placed in custody on grounds of race, nationality, creed or political opinions and treat them as displaced persons. You should make provision for the review of convictions of alleged criminal offenses about which there may be substantial suspicion of racial, religious or political persecution, and in which sentences of imprisonment have not been fully served by persons imprisoned within your zone.

14. Education:

a. All educational institutions within your zone, except those previously reestablished by Allied authority, will be closed. The closure of Nazi educational institutions, such as Adolf Hitler Schulen, Napolas and Ordensburgen, and of Nazi organizations within other educational institutions will be permanent.

b. A coordinated system of control over German education and an affirmative program of reorientation will be established, designed completely to eliminate Nazi and militaristic doctrines and to encourage the development of democratic ideas.

c. You will permit the reopening of elementary (*Volksschulen*), middle (*Mittelschulen*) and vocational (*Berufsschulen*) schools at the earliest possible date after Nazi personnel has been eliminated. Textbooks and curricula which are not free of Nazi and militaristic doctrine shall not be used. The Control Council should devise programs looking toward the reopening of secondary schools, universities and other institutions of higher learning. After Nazi features and personnel have been eliminated and pending the formulation of such programs by the Control Council, you may formulate and put into effect an interim program within your zone and in any case may permit the reopening of such institutions and departments which offer training which you consider immediately essential or useful in the administration of military government and the purpose of the occupation.

d. It is not intended that the military government will intervene in questions concerning denominational control of German schools, or in religious instruction in German schools, except insofar as may be necessary to insure that religious instruction and administration of such schools conform to such Allied regulations as are or may be established pertaining to purging of personnel and curricula.

15. Arts and Archives:

Subject to the provisions of paragraph 6 above, you will make all reasonable efforts to preserve historical archives, museums, libraries and works of art.

PART II

ECONOMIC

General Objectives and Methods of Control.

16. You will assure that the German economy is administered and controlled in such a way as to accomplish the basic objectives set forth in paragraphs 4 and 5 of this directive. Economic controls will be imposed only to the extent necessary to accomplish these objectives, provided that you will impose controls to the full extent necessary to achieve the industrial disarmament of Germany. Except as may be necessary to carry out these objectives, you will take no steps (a) looking toward the economic rehabilitation of Germany, or (b) designed to maintain or strengthen the German economy.

17. To the maximum extent possible without jeopardizing the successful execution of measures required to implement the objectives outlined in paragraphs 4 and 5 of this directive you will use German authorities and agencies and subject them to such supervision and punishment for non-compliance as is necessary to insure that they carry out their tasks.

For this purpose you will give appropriate authority to any German agencies and administrative services you consider essential; provided, however, that you will at all times adhere strictly to the provisions of this directive regarding denazification and dissolution or elimination of Nazi organizations, institutions, principles, features and practices.

To the extent necessary you will establish administrative machinery, not dependent upon German authorities and agencies, to execute or assure the execution of the provisions of paragraphs 19, 20, 30, 31, 32, 39 and 40 and any other measures necessary to an accomplishment of your industrial disarmament objectives.

18. In order to decentralize the structure and administration of the German economy to the maximum possible extent, you will:

a. Ensure that the action required to maintain or restore essential public utilities and industrial and agricultural activities is taken as far as possible on a local and regional basis;

b. on no account propose or approve in the Control Council the establishment of centralized administration of controls over the German economy except where such centralization of administration is clearly essential to the fulfillment of the objectives listed in paragraphs 4 and 5 of this directive. Decentralization in administration should not be permitted to interfere with attainment of the largest practicable measure of agreement on economic policies in the Control Council.

19. You will institute or assure the maintenance of such statistical records and reports as may be necessary in carrying out the objectives listed in paragraphs 4 and 5 of this directive.

20. You will initiate appropriate surveys which may assist you in achieving the objectives of the occupation. In particular you will promptly undertake surveys of supplies, equipment and resources in your zone. You will endeavor to obtain prompt agreement in the Control Council to the making of similar

surveys in the other zones of occupation, and you will urge appropriate steps to coordinate the methods and results of these and other future surveys conducted in the various zones. You will keep the Control Council, United States representative on the Reparation Commission and other appropriate authorities, currently apprised of the information obtained by means of intermediate reports or otherwise.

German Standards of Living

21. You will estimate requirements of supplies necessary to prevent starvation or widespread disease or such civil unrest as would endanger the occupying forces. Such estimates will be based upon a program whereby the Germans are made responsible for providing for themselves, out of their own work and resources. You will take all practicable economic and police measures to assure that German resources are fully utilized and consumption held to the minimum in order that imports may be strictly limited and that surpluses may be made available for the occupying forces and displaced persons and United Nations prisoners of war, and for reparation. You will take no action that would tend to support basic living standards in Germany on a higher level than that existing in any one of the neighboring United Nations and you will take appropriate measures to ensure that basic living standards of the German people are not higher than those existing in any one of the neighboring United Nations when such measures will contribute to raising the standards of any such nation.

22. You will urge upon the Control Council that uniform ration scales be applied throughout Germany, that essential items be distributed equitably among the zones, that net surpluses be made available for export to Allied countries, and that imports be limited to the net deficits of Germany as a whole.

Labor, Health and Social Insurance

23. You will permit the self-organization of employees along democratic lines, subject to such safeguards as may be necessary to prevent the perpetuation of Nazi or militarist influence under any guise or the continuation of any group hostile to the objectives and operations of the occupying forces.

24. You will permit free collective bargaining between employees and employers regarding wage, hour and working conditions and the establishment of machinery for the settlement of industrial disputes. Collective bargaining shall be subject to such wage, hour and other controls, if any, as may be instituted or revived by your direction.

25. Subject to the provisions of paragraph 48 of this directive you are authorized to direct German authorities to maintain or reestablish non-discriminatory systems of social insurance and poor relief.

26. You are authorized to direct the German authorities to maintain or reestablish such health services and facilities as may be available to them.

Agriculture, Industry and Internal Commerce

27. You will require the Germans to use all means at their disposal to maximize agricultural output and to establish as rapidly as possible effective machinery for the collection and distribution of agricultural output.

28. You will direct the German authorities to utilize large-landed estates and public lands in a manner which will facilitate the accommodation and settlement of Germans and others or increase agricultural output.

29. You will protect from destruction by the Germans, and maintain for such disposition as is determined by this and other directives or by the Control Coun-

cil, all plants, equipment, patents and other property, and all books and records of large German industrial companies and trade and research associations that have been essential to the German war effort or the German economy. You will pay particular attention to research and experimental establishments of such concerns.

30. In order to disarm Germany, the Control Council should

a. prevent the production, acquisition by importation or otherwise, and development of all arms, ammunition and implements of war, as well as all types of aircraft, and all parts, components and ingredients specially designed or produced for incorporation therein;

b. prevent the production of merchant ships, synthetic rubber and oil, aluminum and magnesium and any other products and equipment on which you will subsequently receive instructions;

c. Seize and safeguard all facilities used in the production of any of the items mentioned in this paragraph and dispose of them as follows:

(1) remove all those required for reparation;

(2) destroy all those not transferred for reparation if they are especially adapted to the production of the items specified in this paragraph and are not of a type generally used in industries permitted to the Germans (cases of doubt to be resolved in favor of destruction);

(3) hold the balance for disposal in accordance with instructions which will be sent to you.

Pending agreement in the Control Council you will take these measures in your zone. You will not postpone enforcement of the prohibitions contained in sub-paragraphs a and b and the instructions in sub-paragraphs c without specific approval of your Government through the Joint Chiefs of Staff except that, in your discretion, you may permit the production of synthetic rubber and oil, aluminum and magnesium, to the minimum extent necessary to meet the purposes stated in paragraphs 4 and 5 of the directive pending action by the Joint Chiefs of Staff upon such recommendation for postponement as you may make.

31. As an additional measure of disarmament, the Control Council should

a. prohibit initially all research activities and close all laboratories, research institutions and similar technical organizations except those considered necessary to the protection of public health;

b. abolish all those laboratories and related institutions whose work has been connected with the building of the German war machine, safeguard initially such laboratories and detain such personnel as are of interest to your technological investigations, and thereafter remove or destroy their equipment;

c. permit the resumption of scientific research in specific cases, only after careful investigation has established that the contemplated research will in no way contribute to Germany's future war potential and only under appropriate regulations which (1) define the specific types of research permitted, (2) exclude from further research activity any persons who previously held key positions in German war research, (3) provide for frequent inspection, (4) require free disclosure of the results of the research and (5) impose severe penalties, including permanent closing of the offending institution, whenever the regulations are violated.

Pending agreement in the Control Council you will adopt such measures in your own zone.

32. Pending final Allied agreements on reparation and on control or elimination of German industries that can be utilized for war production, the Control Council should

a. prohibit and prevent production of iron and steel, chemicals, non-ferrous metals (excluding aluminum and magnesium), machine tools, radio and electrical equipment, automotive vehicles, heavy machinery and important parts thereof, except for the purposes stated in paragraphs 4 and 5 of this directive;

b. prohibit and prevent rehabilitation of plant and equipment in such industries except for the purposes stated in paragraphs 4 and 5 of this directive; and

c. safeguard plant and equipment in such industries for transfer on reparation account.

Pending agreement in the Control Council, you will put such measures into effect in your own zone as soon as you have had an opportunity to review and determine production necessary for the purposes stated in paragraphs 4 and 5 of this directive.

33. The Control Council should adopt a policy permitting the conversion of facilities other than those mentioned in paragraphs 30 and 32 to the production of light consumer goods, provided that such conversion does not prejudice the subsequent removal of plant and equipment on reparation account and does not require any imports beyond those necessary for the purposes specified in paragraphs 4 and 5 of this directive. Pending agreement in the Control Council, you may permit such conversion in your zone.

34. Subject to the provisions of paragraphs 30 and 32, the Control Council should assure that all feasible measures are taken to facilitate, to the minimum extent necessary for the purposes outlined in paragraphs 4 and 5 of this directive:

a. repairs to and restoration of essential transportation services and public utilities;

b. emergency repair and construction of the minimum shelter required for the civilian population;

c. production of coal and any other goods and services (excluding goods specified in paragraphs 30 and 32, unless measures to facilitate production are specifically approved by this Government through the Joint Chiefs of Staff) required for the purposes outlined in paragraphs 4 and 5 of this directive.

You will assure that such measures are taken in your own zone pending agreement in the Control Council.

35. In your capacity as zone commander and as member of the Control Council you will take steps to provide for the equitable interzonal distribution and the movement of goods and services essential to the purposes set forth in paragraphs 4 and 5 of this directive.

36. You will prohibit all cartels or other private business arrangements and cartel-like organizations, including those of a public or quasi-public character, such as the *Wirtschaftsgruppen,* providing for the regulation of marketing conditions, including production, prices, exclusive exchange of technical information and processes, and allocation of sales territories. Such necessary public functions as have been discharged by these organizations shall be absorbed as rapidly as possible by approved public agencies.

37. It is the policy of your Government to effect a dispersion of the ownership and control of German industry. To assist in carrying out this policy you will make a survey of combines and pools, mergers, holding companies and interlocking directorates and communicate the results, together with recommen-

dations, to your Government through the Joint Chiefs of Staff. You will endeavor to obtain agreement in the Control Council to the making of this survey in the other zones of occupation and you will urge the coordination of the methods and results of this survey in the various zones.

38. With due regard to paragraph 4a, the Control Council should adopt such policies as are clearly necessary to prevent or restrain inflation of a character or dimension which would definitely endanger accomplishment of the objectives of the occupation. The Control Council, in particular, should direct and empower German authorities to maintain or establish controls over prices and wages and to take the fiscal and financial measures necessary to this end. Pending agreement in the Control Council you will assure that such measures as you consider necessary are taken in your own zone. Prevention or restraint of inflation shall not constitute an additional ground for the importation of supplies, nor shall it constitute an additional ground for limiting removal, destruction or curtailment of productive facilities in fulfillment of the program for reparation, demilitarization and industrial disarmament.

Power, Transportation and Communications

39. Both as a member of the Control Council and zone commander you will take appropriate steps to ensure that

a. power, transportation and communications facilities are directed in such a way as to carry out the objectives outlined in paragraphs 4 and 5 of this directive;

b. Germans are prohibited and prevented from producing, maintaining or operating all types of aircraft.

You will determine the degree to which centralized control and administration of power, transportation and communications is clearly necessary for the objectives stated in paragraphs 4 and 5 and urge the establishment of this degree of centralized control and administration by the Control Council.

Foreign Trade and Reparations

40. The Control Council should establish centralized control over all trades in goods and services with foreign countries. Pending agreement in the Control Council you will impose appropriate controls in your own zone.

41. Both as member of the Control Council and as zone commander you will take appropriate steps to ensure that

a. the foreign trade controls are designed to carry out the objectives stated in paragraphs 4 and 5 of this directive;

b. imports which are permitted and furnished to Germany are confined to those unavoidably necessary to the objectives stated in paragraphs 4 and 5;

c. exports to countries other than the United Nations are prohibited unless specifically authorized by the Allied Governments.

42. Both as member of the Control Council and as zone commander you will adopt a policy which would forbid German firms to participate in international cartels or other restrictive contracts and arrangements and order the prompt termination of all existing German participations in such cartels, contracts and arrangements.

43. You will carry out in your zone such programs of reparation and restitution as are embodied in Allied agreements and you will seek agreement in the Control Council on any policies and measures which it may be necessary to apply throughout Germany in order to ensure the execution of such programs.

PART III

FINANCIAL

44. You will make full application in the financial field of the principles stated elsewhere in this directive and you will endeavor to have the Control Council adopt uniform financial policies necessary to carry out the purposes stated in paragraphs 4 and 5 of this directive. You will take no steps designed to maintain, strengthen or operate the German financial structure except insofar as may be necessary for the purposes specified in this directive.

45. The Control Council should regulate and control to the extent required for the purposes set forth in paragraphs 4 and 5 the issue and volume of currency and the extension of credit in Germany and in accordance with the following principles:

a. United States and other Allied forces will use Allied Military marks and Reichsmark currency or coins in their possession. Allied Military marks and Reichsmark currency and coin now in circulation in Germany will be legal tender without distinction and will be interchangeable at the rate of 1 Allied Military mark for 1 Reichsmark. Reichskreditkassenscheine and other German military currency will not be legal tender in Germay.

b. The Reichsbank, the Rentenbank or any other bank or agency may be permitted or required to issue bank notes and currency which will be legal tender; without such authorization no German governmental or private bank or agency will be permitted to issue bank notes or currency.

c. The German authorities may be required to make available Reichsmark currency or credits free of cost and in amounts sufficient to meet all expenses of the forces of occupation, including the cost of Allied Military Government and including to the extent that compensation is made therefor, the cost of such private property as may be requisitioned, seized, or otherwise acquired, by Allied authorities for reparations or restitution purposes.

Pending agreement in the Control Council you will follow these policies in your own zone.

You will receive separate instructions relative to the currency which you will use in the event that for any reason adequate supplies of Allied Military marks and Reichsmarks are not available, or if the use of such currency is found undesirable.

You will not announce or establish in your zone, until receipt of further instructions, any general rate of exchange between the Reichsmark on the one hand and the U. S. dollar and other currencies on the other. However, a rate of exchange to be used exclusively for pay of troops and military accounting purposes in your zone will be communicated separately to you.

46. Subject to any agreed policies of the Control Council, you are authorized to take the following steps and to put into effect such further financial measures as you may deem necessary to accomplish the purposes of your occupation:

a. To prohibit, or to prescribe regulations regarding transfer or other dealings in private or public securities or real estate or other property.

b. To close banks, but only for a period long enough for you to introduce satisfactory control, to remove Nazi and other undesirable personnel and to issue instructions for the determination of accounts to be blocked under sub-paragraph 48e below.

c. To close stock exchanges, insurance companies and similar financial institutions for such periods of time as you deem appropriate.

d. To establish a general or limited moratorium or moratoria only to the extent clearly necessary to carry out the objectives stated in paragraphs 4 and 5 of this directive.

47. Resumption of partial or complete service on the internal public debt at the earliest feasible date is deemed desirable. The Control Council should decide the time and manner of such resumption.

48. Subject to any agreed policies of the Control Council,

a. You will prohibit:

(1) the payment of all military pensions, or emoluments or benefits, except compensation for physical disability limiting the recipient's ability to work, at rates which are no higher than the lowest of those for comparable physical disability arising from non-military causes.

(2) the payment of all public or private pensions or other emoluments or benefits granted or conferred:

(a) by reason of membership in or services to the former Nazi party, its formations, affiliated associations or supervised organizations;

(b) to any person who has been removed from an office or position in accordance with paragraph 6, and

(c) to any person arrested and detained in accordance with paragraph 8 during the term of his arrest, or permanently, in case of his subsequent conviction.

b. You will take such action as may be necessary to insure that all laws and practices relating to taxation or other fields of finance, which discriminate for or against any persons because of race, nationality, creed or political opinion, will be amended, suspended or abrogated to the extent necessary to eliminate such discrimination.

c. You will hold the German authorities responsible for taking such measures in the field of taxation and other fields of public finance, including restoration of the tax system and maintenance of tax revenues, as will further the accomplishment of the objectives stated in paragraphs 4 and 5.

d. You will exercise general supervision over German public expenditures in order to ensure that they are consistent with the objectives stated in paragraphs 4 and 5.

e. You will impound or block all gold, silver, currencies, securities, accounts in financial institutions, credits, valuable papers and all other assets falling within the following categories;

(1) Property owned or controlled directly or indirectly, in whole or in part, by any of the following:

(a) The German Reich, or any of the Laender, Gaue or provinces, any Kreis, municipality or other similar local subdivision; or any agency or instrumentality of any of them including all utilities, undertakings, public corporations or monopolies under the control of any of the above;

(b) Governments, nationals or residents of other nations, including those of territories occupied by them, at war with any of the United Nations at any time since September 1, 1939;

(c) The Nazi Party, its formations, affiliated associations and supervised organizations, its officials, leading members and supporters;

(d) All organizations, clubs or other associations prohibited or dissolved by military government;

(e) Absentee owners of non-German nationality including United Nations and neutral governments and Germans outside Germany;

(f) Any institution dedicated to public worship, charity, education or the arts and sciences which has been used by the Nazi Party to further its interests or to cloak its activities;

(g) Persons subject to arrest under provisions of paragraph 8, and all other persons specified by military government by inclusion in lists or otherwise.

(2) Property which has been the subject of transfer under duress or wrongful acts of confiscation, disposition or spoliation, whether pursuant to legislation or by procedure purporting to follow forms of laws or otherwise.

(3) Works of art or cultural material of value or importance, regardless of the ownership thereof.

You will take such action as will insure that any impounded or blocked assets will be dealt with only as permitted under licenses or other instructions which you may issue. In the case particularly of property blocked under (1) (a) above, you will proceed to adopt licensing measures which, while maintaining such property under surveillance, would permit its use in consonance with this directive. In the case of property blocked under (2) above, you will institute measures for prompt restitution, in conformity with the objectives stated in paragraphs 4 and 5 and subject to appropriate safeguards to prevent the cloaking of Nazi and militaristic influence.

49. All foreign exchange transactions, including those arising out of exports and imports, shall be controlled with the aim of preventing Germany from developing a war potential and of achieving the other objectives set forth in this directive. To effectuate these purposes the Control Council should

a. Seek out and reduce to the possession and control of a special agency all German (public and private) foreign exchange and external assets of every kind and description located within or outside Germany.

b. Prohibit, except as authorized by regulation or license, all dealings in gold, silver, foreign exchange, and all foreign exchange transactions of any kind. Make available any foreign exchange proceeds of exports for payment of imports directly necessary to the accomplishment of the objectives stated in paragraphs 4 and 5 of this directive, and authorize no other outlay of foreign exchange assets except for purposes approved by the Control Council or other appropriate authority.

c. Establish effective controls with respect to all foreign-exchange transactions, including:

(1) Transactions as to property between persons inside Germany and persons outside Germany;

(2) Transactions involving obligations owed by or to become due from any person in Germany to any person outside Germany; and

(3) Transactions involving the importation into or exportation from Germany of any foreign exchange asset or other form of property.

Pending agreement in the Control Council, you will take in your zone the action indicated in sub-paragraphs a, b and c above. Accordingly, you will in your zone reduce to the possession and control of a special agency established by you, within your Command, all German foreign exchange and external assets as provided in sub-paragraph a. You will endeavor to have similar agencies for the same purpose established in the other zones of occupation and to have them merged as soon as practicable in one agency for the entire occupied territory.

In addition, you will provide full reports to your government with respect to all German foreign exchange and external assets.

50. No extension of credit to Germany or Germans by any foreign person or Government shall be permitted except that the Control Council may in special emergencies grant permission for such extensions of credit.

51. It is not anticipated that you will make credits available to the Reichsbank or any other bank or to any public or private institution. If, in your opinion, such action becomes essential, you may take such emergency action as you may deem proper, but in any event, you will report the facts to the Control Council.

52. You will maintain such accounts and records as may be necessary to reflect the financial operations of the military government in your zone and you will provide the Control Council with such information as it may require, including information in connection with the use of currency by your forces, any governmental settlements, occupation costs, and other expenditures arising out of operations or activities involving participation of your forces.

IX

DOCUMENT OF MILITARY SURRENDER OF THE GERMAN ARMED FORCES

May 8, 1945[1]

1. We, the undersigned, acting by authority of the German High Command, hereby surrender unconditionally to the Supreme Commander, Allied Expeditionary Force, and simultaneously to the Supreme High Command of the Red Army all forces on land, at sea, and in the air who are at this date under German control.

2. The German High Command will at once issue orders to all German military, naval and air authorities and to all forces under German control to cease active operations at 2301 hours Central European time on 8th May 1945, to remain in the positions occupied at the time and to disarm completely, handing over their weapons and equipment to the local allied commanders or officers designated by Representatives of the Allied Supreme Commands. No ship, vessel, or aircraft is to be scuttled, or any damage done to their hull, machinery, or equipment, **and also to machines of all kinds, armament, apparatus, and all the technical means of prosecution of war in general.**

3. The German High Command will at once issue to the appropriate commanders, and ensure the carrying out of any further orders issued by the Supreme Commander, Allied Expeditionary Force and by the Supreme High Command of the Red Army.

4. This act of military surrender is without prejudice to, and will be superseded by any general instrument of surrender imposed by, or on behalf of the United Nations and applicable to GERMANY and the German armed forces as a whole.

5. In the event of the German High Command or any of the forces under

---

[1]This document signed at Berlin-Karlshorst by Admiral Friedeburg, General Keitel and General Stumpf on one side and by Marshals Tedder and Zhukov on the other is practically identical with the act of surrender signed at Rheims on May 7, 1945 by General Jodl and by Generals Smith, Susloparov, and Sevez. The Rheims document does not contain the statement which is marked by two asterisks. The texts were first officially published in Department of State, *Bulletin*, Vol. XIII (1945), p. 106.

their control failing to act in accordance with this Act of Surrender, the Supreme Commander, Allied Expeditionary Force and the Supreme Command of the Red Army will take such punitive or other action as they deem appropriate.

6. This Act is drawn up in the English, Russian and German languages. The English and Russian are the only authentic texts. Signed at Berlin on the 8th day of May, 1945.

X

DECLARATION REGARDING DEFEAT OF GERMANY AND ASSUMPTION OF SUPREME AUTHORITY BY ALLIED POWERS

June 5, 1945[1]

The German armed forces on land, at sea and in the air have been completely defeated and have surrendered unconditionally and Germany, which bears responsibility for the war, is no longer capable of resisting the will of the victorious powers. The unconditional surrender of Germany has thereby been effected, and Germany has become subject to such requirements as may now or hereafter be imposed upon her.

There is no central government or authority in Germany capable of accepting responsibility for the maintenance of order, the administration of the country and compliance with the requirements of the victorious Powers.

It is in these circumstances necessary, without prejudice to any subsequent decisions that may be taken respecting Germany, to make provision for the cessation of any further hostilities on the part of the German armed forces, for the maintenance of order in Germany and for the administration of the country, and to announce the immediate requirements with which Germany must comply.

The representatives of the Supreme Commands of the United States of America, the Union of Soviet Socialist Republics, the United Kingdom and the French Republic, hereinafter called the "Allied Representatives," acting by authority of their respective Governments and in the interests of the United Nations, accordingly make the following Declaration:

The Governments of the United States of America, the Union of Soviet Socialist Republics and the United Kingdom, and the Provisional Government of the French Republic, hereby assume supreme authority with respect to Germany, including all the powers possessed by the German Government, the High Command and any state, municipal or local government, or authority. The assumption, for the purposes stated above, of the said authority and powers does not effect the annexation of Germany.

The Governments of the United States of America, the Union of Soviet Socialist Republics and the United Kingdom, and the Provisional Government of the French Republic, will hereafter determine the boundaries of Germany or any part thereof and the status of Germany or of any area at present being part of German territory.

In virtue of the supreme authority and powers thus assumed by the four governments, the Allied representatives announce the following requirements arising from the complete defeat and unconditional surrender of Germany with which Germany must comply:

---

[1]The Declaration was signed in Berlin by General Eisenhower, Marshal Zhukov, Field Marshal Montgomery, General De Lattre de Tassigny. Department of State, *Bulletin*, Vol. XII (1945), pp. 1051-1055.

ARTICLE 1

Germany, and all German military, naval and air authorities and all forces under German control shall immediately cease hostilities in all theatres of war against the forces of the United Nations on land, at sea and in the air.

ARTICLE 2

(A) All armed forces of Germany or under German control, wherever they may be situated, including land, air, anti-aircraft and naval forces, the SS, SA and Gestapo, and all other forces or auxiliary organizations equipped with weapons, shall be completely disarmed, handing over their weapons and equipment to local Allied commanders or to officers designated by the Allied Representatives.

(B) The personnel of the formations and units of all forces referred to in paragraph (A) above shall, at the discretion of the Commander-in-Chief of the armed forces of the Allied state concerned, be declared to be prisoners of war, pending further decisions, and shall be subject to such conditions and directions as may be prescribed by the respective Allied Representatives.

(C) All forces referred to in paragraph (A) above, wherever they may be, will remain in their present positions pending instructions from the Allied Representatives.

(D) Evacuation by the said forces of all territories outside the frontiers of Germany as they existed on Dec. 31, 1937, will proceed according to instructions to be given by the Allied representatives.

(E) Detachments of civil police to be armed with small arms only, for the maintenance of order and for guard duties, will be designated by the Allied Representatives.

ARTICLE 3

(A) All aircraft of any kind or nationality in Germany or German-occupied or controlled territories or waters, military, naval or civil, other than aircraft in the service of the Allies, will remain on the ground, on the water or aboard ships pending further instructions.

(B) All German or German-controlled aircraft in or over territories or waters not occupied or controlled by Germany will proceed to Germany or to such other place or places as may be specified by the Allied Representatives.

ARTICLE 4

(A) All German or German-controlled naval vessels, surface and submarine, auxiliary naval craft, and merchant and other shipping, wherever such vessels may be at the time of this declaration, and all other merchant ships of whatever nationality in German ports, will remain in or proceed immediately to ports and bases as specified by the Allied Representatives. The crews of such vessels will remain on board pending further instructions.

(B) All ships and vessels of the United Nations, whether or not title has been transferred as the result of prize court or other proceedings, which are at the disposal of Germany or under German control at the time of this declaration, will proceed at the dates and to the ports or bases specified by the Allied Representatives.

ARTICLE 5

(A) All or any of the following articles in the possession of the German armed forces or under German control or at German disposal will be held intact and in good condition at the disposal of the Allied representatives, for such purposes and at such times and places as they may prescribe:

I. All arms, ammunition, explosives, military equipment, stores and supplies and other implements of war of all kinds and all other war material;

II. All naval vessels of all classes, both surface and submarine, auxiliary naval craft and all merchant shipping, whether afloat, under repair or construction, built or building;

III. All aircraft of all kinds, aviation and anti-aircraft equipment and devices;

IV. All transportation and communications facilities and equipment, by land, water or air;

V. All military installations and establishments, including airfields, seaplane bases, ports and naval bases, storage depots, permanent and temporary land and coast fortifications, fortresses and other fortified areas, together with plans and drawings of all such fortifications, installations and establishments;

VI. All factories, plants, shops, research institutions, laboratories, testing stations, technical data, patents, plans, drawings and inventions, designed or intended to produce or to facilitate the production or use of the articles, materials, and facilities referred to in sub-paragraphs I, II, III, IV and V above or otherwise to further the conduct of war.

(B) At the demand of the Allied Representatives the following will be furnished.

I. The labor, services and plant required for the maintenance or operation of any of the six categories mentioned in paragraph (A) above; and

II. Any information or records that may be required by the Allied representatives in connection with the same.

(C) At the demand of the Allied Representatives all facilities will be provided for the movement of Allied troops and agencies, their equipment and supplies, on the railways, roads and other land communications or by sea, river or air. All means of transportation will be maintained in good order and repair, and the labor, services and plant necessary therefor will be furnished.

ARTICLE 6

(A) The German authorities will release to the Allied Representatives, in accordance with the procedure to be laid down by them, all prisoners of war at present in their power, belonging to the forces of the United Nations, and will furnish full lists of these persons, indicating the places of their detention in Germany or territory occupied by Germany. Pending the release of such prisoners of war, the German authorities and people will protect them in their persons and property and provide them with adequate food, clothing, shelter, medical attention, and money in accordance with their rank or official position.

(B) The German authorities and people will in like manner provide for and release all other nationals of the United Nations who are confined, interned or otherwise under restraint, and all other persons who may be confined, interned or otherwise under restraint for political reasons or as a result of any Nazi action, law or regulation which discriminates on the ground of race, color, creed or political belief.

(C) The German authorities will, at the demand of the Allied Representatives, hand over control of places of detention to such officers as may be designated for the purpose by the Allied Representatives.

ARTICLE 7

The German authorities concerned will furnish to the Allied Representatives:

(A) Full information regarding the forces referred to in Article 2 (A), and in particular, will furnish forthwith all information which the Allied representatives may require concerning the numbers, locations and dispositions of such forces, whether located inside or outside Germany;

(B) Complete and detailed information concerning mines, minefields and other obstacles to movement by land, sea or air, and the safety lanes in connection therewith. All such safety lanes will be kept open and clearly marked; all mines, minefields and other dangerous obstacles will as far as possible be rendered safe, and all aids to navigation will be reinstated. Unarmed German military and civilian personnel with the necessary equipment will be made available and utilized for the above purpose and for the removal of mines, minefields and other obstacles as directed by the Allied Representatives.

ARTICLE 8

There shall be no destruction, removal, concealment, transfer or scuttling of, or damage to, any military, naval, air, shipping, port, industrial and other like property and facilities and all records and archives, wherever they may be situated, except as may be directed by the Allied Representatives.

ARTICLE 9

Pending the institution of control by the Allied Representatives over all means of communication, all radio and telecommunication installations and other forms of wire or wireless communications, whether ashore or afloat, under German control, will cease transmission except as directed by the Allied Representatives.

ARTICLE 10

The forces, nationals, ships, aircraft, military equipment and other property in Germany or in German control or service or at German disposal, of any other country at war with any of the Allies, will be subject to the provisions of this declaration and of any proclamations, orders, ordinances or instructions issued thereunder.

ARTICLE 11

(A) The principal Nazi leaders as specified by the Allied Representatives, and all persons from time to time named or designated by rank, office or employment by the Allied Representatives as being suspected of having committed, ordered or abetted war crimes or analogous offenses, will be apprehended and surrendered to the Allied Representatives.

(C) The German authorities and people will comply with any instructions given by the Allied Representatives for the apprehension and surrender of such persons.

ARTICLE 12

The Allied Representatives will station forces and civil agencies in any or all parts of Germany as they may determine.

ARTICLE 13

(A) In the exercise of the supreme authority with respect to Germany assumed by the Government of the United States of America, the Union of

Soviet Socialist Republics and the United Kingdom, and the Provisional Government of the French Republic, the four Allied Governments will take such steps, including the complete disarmament and demilitarization of Germany, as they deem requisite for future peace and security.

(B) The Allied Representatives will impose on Germany additional political, administrative, economic, financial, military and other requirements arising from the complete defeat of Germany. The Allied Representatives, or persons or agencies duly designated to act on their authority, will issue proclamations, orders, ordinances and instructions for the purpose of laying down such additional requirements, and of giving effect to the other provisions of this declaration. All German authorities and the German people shall carry out unconditionally the requirements of the Allied Representatives, and shall fully comply with all such proclamations, orders, ordinances and instructions.

ARTICLE 14

This declaration enters into force and effect at the date and hour set forth below. In the event of failure on the part of the German authorities or people promptly and completely to fulfill their obligations hereby or hereafter imposed, the Allied Representatives will take whatever action may be deemed by them to be appropriate under the circumstances.

ARTICLE 15

This declaration is drawn up in English, Russian, French and German languages. The English, Russian and French are the only authentic texts.

Berlin, June 5, 1945.

XI

AMERICAN DIRECTIVE ON THE MILITARY GOVERNMENT OF AUSTRIA

June 27, 1945[1]

1. The Purpose and Scope of this Directive:

a. This directive is issued to you as Commanding General of the United States forces of occupation in Austria. As such you will serve as United States member of the Allied Council of the Allied Commission for Austria and will also be responsible for the administration of military government in the zone or zones assigned to the United States for purposes of occupation and administration. It outlines the basic policies which will guide you in those two capacities after the termination of the combined command in Austria. Supplemental directives will be issued to you by the Joint Chiefs of Staff as may be required.

b. As a member of the Allied Council you will urge the adoption by the other occupying powers of the principles and policies set forth in this directive and, pending Allied Council agreement, you will follow them in your zone. It is anticipated that substantially similar directives will be issued to the Commanders in Chief of the United Kingdom, the Union of Soviet Socialist Republics, and French forces of occupation.

c. In the event that recognition is given by the four governments to a pro-

---

[1]The Directive was prepared by the State-War-Navy Coordinating Committee and transmitted to General Mark Clark by the Joint Chiefs of Staff on June 27, 1945. It was made public by the State Department on October 28, 1945. Department of State, *Bulletin*, Vol. XIII (1945), pp. 661-673.

visional national government of Austria, such government should be delegated authority in appropriate matters to conduct public affairs in accordance with the principles set forth in this directive or agreed upon by the occupying powers. Such delegation, however, shall be subject to the authority of the occupying powers and to their responsibility to see that their policies are in fact carried out.

d. Any provisional national government of Austria which is not recognized by all of the four Governments of the occupying powers shall not be treated by you as possessing any authority. Only individuals who recognize your supreme authority in your zone will be utilized by you in administration.

PART I
GENERAL AND POLITICAL

2. The Basis of Military Government:

a. The rights, power and status of the military government in Austria prior to the unconditional surrender and total defeat of Germany, were based upon the military occupation of Austria and the decision of the occupying powers to reestablish an independent Austrian state. Thereafter the rights, powers and status are based, in addition, upon such surrender or defeat. The Text of the Instrument of Unconditional Surrender of Germany published as a separate document has been made available to you.[2] You will assure that the policies set forth in that Instrument are carried out in your zone of occupation insofar as they are applicable in Austria even though the defeat of Germany is not followed by a formal signing of the Instrument.

b. Subject to the provisions of paragraph 3 below, you are, by virtue of your position, clothed with supreme legislative, executive, and judicial authority in the areas occupied by forces under your command. This authority will be broadly construed and includes authority to take all measures deemed by you necessary, appropriate or desirable in relation to military exigencies and the objectives set forth in this and other directives.

c. You will issue a proclamation continuing in force such proclamations, orders and instructions as may have heretofore been issued by Allied Commanders in your zone, subject to such changes as you may determine. Authorizations of action by the Supreme Allied Commander, Mediterranean, or by the Supreme Commander, Allied Expeditionary Force, may be considered as applicable to you unless inconsistent with this or other directives.

3. The Allied Council and Zones of Occupation:

a. The four Commanders in Chief, acting jointly, will constitute the Allied Council which will exercise supreme authority in Austria. The United States proposal for an agreement on the organization of the Control Machinery in Austria published as a separate document has been made available to you. When approved by the occupying powers, the text of the agreement on Control Machinery in Austria will be furnished you. For purposes of administration of military government, Austria will be divided into four zones of occupation. When the occupying powers have agreed upon the zones of occupation in Austria, the text of the protocol in that regard will be furnished you.

b. The authority of the Allied Council to formulate policy and procedures and administrative relationships with respect to matters affecting Austria as a

---
[2]Appendix IX.

whole will be paramount throughout Austria. This authority shall be broadly construed to the end that, through maximum uniformity of policy and procedures throughout Austria, the establishment of an independent Austrian Government may be accelerated. In your capacity as a member of the Allied Council, you will seek maximum agreement with respect to policy and maximum uniformity of action by the Commanders-in-Chief in their respective zones of occupation. You will carry out and support in your zone the policies agreed upon in the Allied Council. In the absence of such agreed policies you will act in accordance with this and other directives of the Joint Chiefs of Staff.

c. The Allied Council should cooperate with the Control Council in Germany in effecting the severance of all political and administrative connections between Austria and Germany, and the elimination of German economic and financial influences in Austria. You will in every way possible assist the accomplishment of this purpose.

d. The Allied Council should adopt procedures to effectuate, and you will facilitate in your zone, the equitable distribution of essential commodities between the zones. In the absence of a conflicting policy of the Allied Council, you may deal directly with one or more zone commanders on matters of special concern to such zones.

e. Pending the formulation in the Allied Council of uniform policies and procedures with respect to travel and movement of persons to and from Austria, no persons shall be permitted to cross the Austrian frontier in your zone except for specific purposes approved by you.

f. The military government personnel in your zone, including those dealing with regional and local branches of the departments of any central Austrian administrative machinery, shall be selected by your authority except that liaison officers may be furnished by the Commanders of the other three zones. The respective Commanders-in-Chief shall have exclusive jurisdiction throughout the whole of Austria over the members of the armed forces under their command and over the civilians who accompany them.

4. Basic Objectives of Military Government in Austria:

a. You will be chiefly concerned in the initial stages of military government with the elimination of German domination and Nazi influences. Consistently with this purpose, you will be guided at every step by the necessity to ensure the reconstruction of Austria as a free, independent and democratic state. It will be essential therefore that every measure be undertaken from the early stages of occupation with this objective in mind.

b. The Allied Council should, as soon as it is established, proclaim the complete political and administrative separation of Austria from Germany, and the intention of the occupying powers to pave the way for the reestablishment of Austria as an independent democratic state. You will make it clear to the Austrian people that military occupation of Austria is intended principally (1) to aid Allied military operations and the strict enforcement of the applicable provisions of the German unconditional surrender instrument in Austria; (2) to eliminate Nazism, Pan-Germanism, militarism, and other forces opposed to the democratic reconstitution of Austria; (3) to cooperate with the Control Council for Germany in the application and enforcement of measures designed to prevent the recurrence of German aggression; (4) to establish Allied Control over the use and disposition of German property in Austria;

(5) to effect the complete political and administrative separation of Austria from Germany and free Austria from Nazi and German economic and financial influences; (6) to facilitate the development of a sound Austrian economy devoted to peaceful pursuits and not vitally dependent upon German supplies, markets and technical and financial assistance; and (7) to foster the restoration of local self-government and the establishment of an Austrian central government freely elected by the Austrian people themselves. Other objectives of the occupation will be to apprehend war criminals, to care for and repatriate displaced persons and prisoners-of-war who are members of the armed forces of the United Nations, and to carry out approved programs of reparation and restitution insofar as these are applicable to Austria.

c. You will assure that there is no fraternization by your troops with any German elements remaining in Austria. While in the initial period of occupation the relationship of the troops to the Austrian civil population will be distant and aloof but courteous, a progressively more friendly relationship may be permitted as experience justifies.

5. Denazification:

a. A Proclamation dissolving the Nazi Party, its formations, affiliated associations and supervised organizations, and all Nazi public institutions which were set up as instruments of Party domination, and prohibiting their revival in any form, should be promulgated by the Allied Council. You will assure the prompt effectuation of that policy in your zone and will make every effort to prevent the reconstitution of any such organization in underground, disguised or secret form. Responsibility for continuing desirable non-political social services of dissolved Party Organizations may be transferred by the Governing Body to appropriate central agencies and by you to appropriate local agencies.

b. All laws which extended the political structure of National Socialism to Austria or otherwise brought about the destruction of the Austrian state or which established discriminations on grounds of race, nationality, creed, or political opinion should be abrogated by the Allied Council. You will render them inoperative in your zone.

c. All members of the Nazi Party who were German nationals prior to March 13, 1938, Germans who entered Austria after that date, and other Germans directly connected with the Nazi exploitation of Austria will immediately be removed from government positions and all other categories of employment listed below, and will be expelled from Austria in accordance with paragraph 21. All Austrian members of the Nazi Party who have been more than nominal participants in its activities, all active supporters of Nazism and other persons hostile to Allied purposes will be removed and excluded from public office and from positions of importance in quasi-public and private enterprises such as (1) civic, economic, and labor organizations, (2) corporations and other organizations in which the German Government or subdivisions have a major financial interest, (3) industry, commerce, agriculture, and finance, (4) education, and (5) the press, publishing houses and other agencies disseminating news and propaganda. Persons are to be treated as more than nominal participants in Party activities and as active supporters of Nazism when they (1) held office or otherwise were active at any level from local to national in the Party and its subordinate organizations, (2) authorized or participated affirmatively in any Nazi crimes, racial persecutions or discriminations, (3) been avowed believers in Nazi doctrines, or (4) voluntarily given substantial moral or material support or political assistance of any kind to the Nazi Party or Nazi officials and leaders. No such persons shall be retained in any of the categories of employment listed above because of administrative necessity, convenience or expediency.

d. Property, real and personal, owned or controlled by the Nazi Party, its formations, affiliated associations and supervised organizations, and by all persons subject to arrest under the provisions of paragraph 7 below, and found within your zone will be taken under your control pending a decision by the Allied Council or higher authority as to its eventual disposition.

e. All archives, monuments and museums of Nazi inception, or which are devoted to the perpetuation of militarism, will be taken under your control and their properties held pending decision as to their disposition by the Allied Council.

f. You will make special efforts to preserve from destruction and take under your control records, plans, books, documents, papers, files, and scientific, industrial and other information and data belonging to or controlled by the following:

(1) The central German Government and its subdivisions, the offices of the Reichsstatthalter, the former Austrian state and its subdivisions, German and Austrian military organizations, organizations engaged in military research, and such other governmental agencies as may be deemed advisable;

(2) The Nazi Party, its formations, affiliated associations and supervised organizations;

(3) All police organizations, including security and political police;

(4) Important economic organizations and industrial establishments including those controlled by the Nazi Party or its personnel;

(5) Institutes and special bureaus devoting themselves to racial, political, militaristic or similar research or propaganda.

6. Elimination of pre-Nazi Influences:

a. You will remove and exclude from the positions enumerated in subparagraph 5 c above all persons who took an active and prominent part in the undemocratic measures of the pre-Nazi Fascist regime or in any of its paramilitary organizations such as the *Heimwehr* and the *Ostmaerkische Sturmscharen.*

b. You will prevent the revival of any organization seeking to restore the pre-Nazi Fascist regime.

7. Suspected War Criminals and Security Arrests:

a. You will search out, arrest, and hold, pending receipt by you of further instructions as to their disposition, Adolf Hitler, his chief Nazi associates, other war criminals, and all persons who have participated in planning or carrying out Nazi enterprises involving or resulting in atrocities or war crimes.

b. All persons who if permitted to remain at large would endanger the accomplishment of your objectives will also be arrested and held in custody until their disposition is otherwise determined by an appropriate semi-judicial body to be established by you.

[Note: There follows at this point in the directive a detailed list of categories of Nazi war criminals and others who are to be arrested. Some of these have not yet been found. It is considered that to publish the categories at this time would put the individuals concerned on notice and would interfere with their apprehension and punishment, where appropriate. The list of categories is, therefore, withheld from publication for the present.]

If in the light of conditions which you encounter in Austria you believe it is not immediately feasible to subject certain persons within these categories to this treatment, you should report your reasons and recommendations to your Government through the Joint Chiefs of Staff. If you believe it desirable, you may postpone the arrest of those whose cases you have reported, pending a decision communicated to you by the Joint Chiefs of Staff. In no event shall any differentiation be made between or special consideration be accorded to persons arrested, either as to manner of arrest, or conditions of detention, upon the basis of wealth or political, industrial, or other rank or position. In your discretion you may make such exception as you deem advisable for intelligence or other military reasons.

8. Demilitarization:

a. In your zone you will assure that all units of the German armed forces including para-military organizations are dissolved as such and that their personnel are promptly disarmed and controlled in accordance with the policies and procedures set forth in the Instrument of Unconditional Surrender of Germany or in other directives which may be issued to you. Prior to their final disposition you will arrest and hold all military personnel who are included under the provisions of paragraph 7. Subject to military considerations and priority to be accorded repatriation of United Nations nationals, the Allied Council should cooperate with the Control Council for Germany in arranging the early repatriation or other disposition of German members of the German armed forces, including para-military organizations, found within Austria. The two Allied agencies should likewise concert the prompt return to Austria of Austrian members of the German armed forces found within Germany, except those held as active Nazis, suspected war criminals, or for other reasons.

b. The Allied Council should proclaim, and in your zone you will effectuate, the total dissolution of all military and para-military organizations together with all associations which might serve to keep alive militarism in Austria.

c. All persons who have actively supported organizations promoting militarism or who have been active proponents of militaristic doctrines will be removed and excluded from any of the categories of employment listed in subparagraph 5 c.

d. You will seize or destroy all arms, ammunition and implements of war, including all aircraft, military and civil, and stop the production thereof.

9. Police:

With the exception of the *Kriminalpolizei* (Criminal Police), all elements of the *Sicherheitspolizei* (Security Police), e.g., *Geheime Staatspolizei* (Gestapo), and the *Sicherheitsdienst der S.S.* will be abolished. Criminal and ordinary police will be purged of Nazi personnel and utilized under the control and supervision of the military government.

10. Administration of Justice:

a. All extraordinary courts, including the *Volksgerichtshof* (People's Court) and the *Sondergerichte* (Special Courts), and all courts and tribunals of the

Nazi Party and of its formations, affiliated associations and supervised organizations will be abolished immediately.

b. All ordinary criminal, civil and administrative courts, except those previously re-established by Allied authority, will be closed. After the elimination of all Nazi or other objectionable features and personnel you will permit those which are to exercise jurisdiction within the boundaries of your zone to resume operations under such regulations, supervision and control as you may consider appropriate. Courts which are to exercise jurisdiction over territory extending beyond the boundaries of your zone will be reopened only with the express authorization of the Allied Council and under its regulation, supervision and control. The power to review and veto decisions of German and Austrian courts shall be included within the power of supervision and control.

11. Political Prisoners:

Subject to military security and to the interests of the individuals concerned, you will release all persons found within your zone who have been detained or placed in custody on grounds of race, nationality, creed or political opinion and treat them as displaced persons. You should make provision for the review of convictions of alleged criminal offenses about which there may be substantial suspicion of racial, religious or political persecution, and in which sentences of imprisonment have not been fully served by persons imprisoned within your zone.

12. Reconstitution of an Administrative System:

a. As soon as Nazi and Fascist influences have been eliminated from public offices in Austria, the reconstitution of Austrian administrative agencies shall be carried out in such a way as not to prejudice the political and constitutional future of Austria. The Allied Council should be responsible for the early establishment of such nation-wide administrative and judicial machinery as may be required to facilitate the uniform execution of its policy throughout Austria, to ensure freedom of transit and communication to and between the separate zones of occupation, and to lay the foundation for the restoration of an Austrian national administrative system. Administrative officials with powers extending throughout Austria should be appointed only by or under the authority of the Allied Council.

b. The formal abrogation of the Anschluss (Act of March 13, 1938) will not be considered as reestablishing the legal and constitutional system of Austria as it existed prior to that event. Such portions of earlier Austrian legislation or of Reich legislation relating to Austria may be retained or restored to force as is deemed appropriate for the purposes of military government and the reconstitution of Austria on a democratic basis. Insofar as it may prove desirable to utilize constitutional laws for Austrian administration, suitable provisions of the Austrian Constitution of 1920, as amended in 1925 and 1929, should be applied.

c. You will assure the severance of all connections between regional (Gau) and local agencies on the one hand and Reich administrative agencies on the other, and will reconstitute Austrian Provincial (Land) and local administration at the earliest possible moment. You may utilize such agencies of the present regional and local administrations as may be deemed useful.

13. Restoration of Regional and Local Self-Government:

As a member of the Allied Council, you will urge the restoration of regional and local self-government throughout Austria at the earliest possible moment. In the absence of agreement, you will facilitate the holding of elections to local and regional public offices within your zone. If prior to or during occupation, local and regional popular councils or similar organs appear, they may be granted temporary recognition pending approval by the Allied Council and be utilized in administration in the event that they possess popular support and are free from Nazi or Fascist sympathizers and affiliations.

14. Establishment of Independent Austrian Government:

The Allied Council should, and in your zone you will, make it clear to the Austrian people that the Allied Powers do not intend through military government to appoint or establish a national government for Austria but will aid the Austrian people themselves to prepare for the election of a national assembly by democratic means. The Austrian people will be free to determine their own form of government provided the new regime be democratic in character and assume appropriate internal and international responsibilities and obligations.

15. Political Activity and Civil Rights:

a. At the earliest possible moment you will permit such political activity and organization by democratic groups as neither threatens military security nor presents substantial danger of public disorder nor engender suspicion and disunity among the United Nations.

b. You will prohibit the propagation in any form of Nazi, Fascist, militaristic, and pan-German doctrines.

c. To the extent that military interests are not prejudiced and subject to the provisions of the two preceding subparagraphs and paragraph 16, you will permit freedom of speech, assembly, press, association, and religious worship.

d. For purposes of military government you may consider as Austrian citizens all persons who held Austrian citizenship on or before March 13, 1938, or who would have automatically acquired citizenship by operation of the law of Austria in force on March 13, 1938. The acts of July 30, 1925 and August 16, 1933 should not be considered as depriving of citizenship Austrians who have entered the service of foreign states or who have taken up arms against the Reich since 1938. German laws purporting to affect Austrian citizenship should be ignored.

16. Public Relations and Control of Public Information:

As a member of the Allied Council you will endeavor to obtain agreement for uniform or coordinated policies with respect to (a) control of public information media in Austria, (b) accrediting of foreign correspondents, (c) press censorship, and (d) issuance of official news communiques dealing with matters within the jurisdiction of the Allied Council. United States policies in these matters will be sent to you separately and you will be guided by these in your negotiations in the Allied Council.

17. Education:

a. You will initially close all schools and universities except those previously re-established by Allied authority. The closure of Nazi educational institutions, such as Adolf Hitler Schulen, Napolas and Ordensburgen, and of Nazi organizations within other educational institutions, will be permanent.

b. A coordinated system of control over Austrian education and an affirmative program of reorientation will be established designed completely to eliminate Nazi, Fascist and militaristic doctrines and to encourage the development of democratic ideas.

c. You will permit the reopening of elementary (Volksschulen), middle (Hauptschulen), and vocational (Berufsschulen) schools at the earliest possible date after Nazi and other objectionable personnel has been eliminated. Textbooks and curricula which are not free of Nazi, Fascist and militaristic doctrines shall not be used. The Allied Council should assure that programs are devised for the early reopening of secondary schools, universities and other institutions of higher learning. After Nazi and other objectionable personnel and features have been eliminated and pending the formulation of such programs by the Allied Council, you may formulate and put into effect an interim program within your zone and, in any case, you will encourage the reopening of such institutions and departments which offer training which you consider immediately essential or useful in the administration of military government and the purposes of the occupation.

d. It is not intended that the military government will intervene in questions concerning denominational control of Austrian schools, or in religious instruction in Austrian schools, except in so far as may be necessary to ensure that religious instruction and administration of such schools conform to such Allied regulations as are or may be established pertaining to purging of personnel and curricula.

18. *Religious Affairs:*

a. The Allied Council should leave to the Austrian churchmen of the respective faiths the revision of the constitutions, rituals or internal relationships of purely ecclesiastical bodies.

b. You will protect freedom of religious belief and worship.

c. You will refrain from intervening in matters concerning religious instruction in schools, the establishment or continuation of denominational schools and the re-establishment of ecclesiastical control of any publicly supported schools.

d. You will take necessary measures to protect churches, shrines, church schools, and other ecclesiastical property from damage and from any treatment which lacks respect for their religious character.

e. You may permit religious bodies to conduct appropriate youth, sport, and welfare activities and to receive contributions for such purposes.

f. Subject to the provisions of paragraph 15, you will permit the establishment or revival of religious periodicals and the publication of other religious literature.

19. *Treatment of Displaced Persons and Refugees in Austria:*

a. Subject to any international agreements and to the agreed policies of the Allied Council, you will undertake the repatriation, return to former residence or resettlement of displaced persons who are (1) nationals of the United Nations and of neutral states, (2) stateless persons, (3) nationals of enemy or former enemy countries who have been persecuted by the enemy for reasons of race, nationality, creed or political opinion, (4) nationals of Italy, as rapidly as military considerations and arrangements with their respective governments permit. Due consideration will be given to the wishes of the individuals involved, and preference will be accorded to nationals of the United Nations and persons freed from concentration camps or other places of detention.

b. You will establish or maintain centers for the assembly and repatriation, resettlement or return of the foregoing displaced persons. Subject to the general control and responsibility of military government, existing Austrian agencies will be required to maintain essential supply and other services for them, including adequate food, shelter, clothing and medical care.

c. Subject to your general control, you will hold existing Austrain agencies responsible for the care and disposition of refugees and those displaced persons who are nationals of Germany or former enemy countries not otherwise provided herein. You will facilitate their repatriation or return, subject to whatever control you may deem necessary, as rapidly as military considerations and appropriate arrangements with authorities in their respective home countries permit.

d. Subject to agreed policies of the Allied Council, you will determine the extent to which UNRRA, the Inter-Governmental Committee on Refugees, or other civilian agencies will participate in handling displaced persons and refugees.

e. You will accord liaison on matters connected with displaced persons to representatives of each of the other Occupying Powers accredited therefor by their respective Commander-in-Chief and to representatives of any of the United Nations and neutral states and of Italy accredited therefor by the Allied Council or other competent authority. You will arrange for such representatives to have access to displaced persons who are nationals of their countries and are authorized to permit them to use the facilities of their governments for purposes of repatriation.

f. The term "displaced persons" includes (1) non-Austrian civilian nationals who have been obliged to leave their own countries or to remain in Austria by reason of the war, (2) stateless persons, and (3) persons who have been persecuted by the enemy for reasons of race, nationality, creed or political opinion. The term "refugees" includes Austrian civilian nationals within Austria who are temporarily homeless because of military operations, or are residing at some distance from their homes for reasons related to the war.

20. *Return of Austrian Civilians to Austria:*

In accordance with military considerations and appropriate arrangements with authorities in sending countries, you will cooperate in rapid repatriation of Austrian civilian nationals outside Austria, exclusive of active Nazis and persons suspected of having committed war crimes or held for other reasons.

21. *The Removal of German Officials and Civilians from Austria:*

a. All German officials, members of the Nazi Party who were German nationals prior to March 13, 1938, Germans who entered Austria after that date and other Germans directly connected with the Nazi exploitation of Austria, except those whom it may be desirable to hold for security or other reasons, should be expelled from Austria. The Allied Council should consult with the Control Council in Germany regarding the removal to Germany of such persons. Removal will be effected at the earliest time consistent with the availability of transport facilities and with the prospect of orderly absorption into Germany.

b. Subject to instructions issued by the Allied Council in accordance with the provisions of the subparagraph a above, you will in your zone take all practicable measures to facilitate and expedite the removal to Germany of all German officials and of German citizens to be repatriated.

22. Diplomatic and Consular Officials and Properties:

All diplomatic and consular officials of countries with which any one of the United Nations has been at war since December 31, 1937 will be taken into protective custody and held for further disposition. The diplomatic and consular property and records belonging to such countries or governments and to their official personnel will be seized and secured if not found in the custody of a protecting power.

23. Arts and Archives:

Subject to the provisions of paragraph 5 above, you will make all reasonable efforts to preserve historical archives, museums, libraries and works of art.

PART II
ECONOMIC

General Economic Provisions

24. The Allied Council should ensure the direction of the Austrian economy in such a way as to carry out the objectives set forth in paragraph 4 b of this directive and should establish centralized control and administration of the Austrian economy to the extent necessary to achieve the maximum utilization of Austrian resources and equitable distribution of essential goods and services and to obtain uniformity of policies and operations throughout Austria.

You will urge the establishment of such centralized control and administration and, pending agreement in the Allied Council, you will take such measures in your own zone as are necessary to carry out the provisions of this directive.

25. To the maximum extent possible without jeopardizing the successful execution of measures required to implement the objectives outlined in paragraph 4 b of this directive, Austrian authorities and agencies should be used, subject to such supervision as is necessary to ensure that they carry out their task. For this purpose appropriate authority should be given to Austrian agencies and administrative services, subject to strict observance of the provisions of this directive regarding denazification and dissolution or prohibition of Nazi and Fascist organizations, institutions, principles, features and practices.

26. You will preserve all significant records pertaining to important economic, financial and research organizations and activities. You will institute or assure the maintenance of such statistical records and reports as may be necessary to carry out the objectives of this directive.

27. You will initiate appropriate surveys which may assist you in achieving the objectives of the occupation. In particular, you will promptly undertake surveys, equipment and resources in your zone. You will endeavor to obtain prompt agreement in the Allied Council to similar surveys in the other zones of occupation and urge appropriate steps to coordinate the methods and results

of these and other future surveys undertaken in the various zones. You will keep the Allied Council and your government currently apprised of the information obtained by means of intermediate reports or otherwise.

Responsibility for Supplies from U.S. Military Sources

28. Imports of supplies from U.S. Military supply sources, for which you will assume responsibility, will be limited to the basic essentials necessary in your zone (a) to avoid disease and unrest which might endanger the occupying forces and (b) for the care of displaced persons. Imports will be undertaken only after maximum utilization of indigenous supplies.

Agriculture, Industry and Internal Commerce

29. You will make maximum use of supplies and resources available within Austria and you will require the Austrians to use all means at their disposal to maximize the production of foodstuffs and other essential goods and to establish as rapidly as possible effective rationing and other machinery for the distribution thereof. You will urge upon the Allied Council that uniform ration scales be applied throughout Austria.

30. The Allied Council should assure to the maximum possible extent the free movement and equitable distribution of goods and services throughout Austria.

31. The Allied Council should facilitate emergency repair and construction for the minimum housing needs of the civil population and restoration of transportation and communications services and public utilities essential to the objectives outlined in paragraph 4 b.

32. In order to supplement the measures taken by the Control Council in Germany for the industrial disarmament of Germany and pending final decision as to the steps necessary in Austria to eliminate Germany's war potential, you should, in cooperation with the other zone commanders, take steps to

a. prevent the production, acquisition and development of all arms, ammunition and implements of war, including all types of aircraft, and all parts, components and ingredients specially designed or produced for incorporation therein;

b. seize and safeguard, pending instructions as to disposal, all facilities which are specially designed or adapted to the production of the items mentioned in *a* and cannot be converted to non-military production, using in such conversion only materials and equipment readily available and not emanating from Germany;

c. take an inventory of all German-owned plant and equipment in Austria, and all plant and equipment regardless of ownership erected or expanded in Austria subsequent to Anschluss, in the following industries: iron mining; steel and ferro-alloys; armaments (including aircraft); machinery (including automotive vehicles, agricultural machinery, locomotives and rolling stock, bearings and other special components, electrical machinery, and general industrial equipment); electronic equipment; electric power; non-ferrous metals, including light metals; rubber and oil, including synthetic rubber and oil; wood pulp; synthetic fibers; instruments; optical glass; chemicals (including pharmaceuticals and plastics) and photographic equipment; in order that the Allied Council may determine what portion of it is redundant to the development of a sound peacetime Austrian economy and make recommendations to the governments of the occupying powers regarding the treatment of these industries:

d. prevent large-scale exportation of light metals pending subsequent instructions on the policy to be followed regarding the Austrian light metals industry;

e. prevent the construction of plant capacity for the production of synthetic oil and rubber; and establish procedures, in consultation with the Control Council for Germany, for reviewing any projected construction of new or expanded capacity for materials the production of which is prohibited or limited in Germany as a measure of industrial disarmament, in order to ensure that such expansion is not for the purpose of evading controls in Germany;

f. close initially all laboratories, research institutions and similar technical organizations except those considered necessary for the protection of public health and safety, and provide for the maintenance and security of physical facilities where deemed necessary and for the detention of such personnel as are of interest to technological and counter-intelligence investigations. After the provisions of paragraphs 5, 6, 7 and 8 (c) have been applied, the reopening of laboratories, research institutions and similar organizations should be permitted under license and periodic supervision, in accordance with policies which will be communicated to you.

33. Without prejudice to the possible eventual transfer of equipment or production on reparation account in accordance with any Allied agreements which may be reached, the Allied Council should facilitate the conversion of industrial facilities to non-military production. In such conversion it will be your policy to give priority to the production of essential goods and equipment in short supply.

34. The Allied Council should assure that all semi-official or quasi-public business and trade organizations of an authoritarian character are abolished and that any organizations of commerce, industry, agriculture and handicrafts which the Austrians may wish to establish are based on democratic principles.

35. The Allied Council should adopt a policy prohibiting cartels or other private business arrangements and cartel-like organizations including those of public or quasi-public character, such as the Wirtschaftsgruppen, which provide for the regulation of marketing conditions, including production, prices, exclusive exchange of technical information and processes, and allocation of sales territories. Such necessary public functions as have been discharged by these organizations should be absorbed as rapidly as possible by approved public agencies. Pending agreement in the Allied Council, you should take no action in your own zone with regard to this paragraph.

36. The Allied Council should adopt policies designed to prevent or restrain inflation of a character or dimension which would endanger accomplishment of the objectives of the occupation. The Allied Council in particular, should direct and empower Austrian authorities to maintain or establish controls over prices and wages and to take the fiscal and financial measures necessary to this end.

Labor, Health and Social Insurance

37. The Allied Council should permit the self-organization of employees along democratic lines, subject to such safeguards as may be necessary to prevent the perpetuation or revival of Nazi, Fascist or militarist influence under any guise or the continuation of any group hostile to the objectives and operations of the occupying forces. The Allied Council should permit free collective bar-

gaining between employees and employers regarding wages, hours, and working conditions and the establishment of machinery for the settlement of industrial disputes. Collective bargaining shall be within the framework of such wage, hour and other controls as may be instituted or revived.

38. The Allied Council should permit the retention or re-establishment of health services and facilities and non-discriminatory systems of social insurance and poor relief.

Reparation and Restitution

39. As a member of the Allied Council and as zone commander you will ensure that the programs of reparation and restitution embodied in Allied agreements are carried out in so far as they are applicable in Austria. The Allied Council should cooperate with the Control Council in Germany for this purpose. You should urge the Allied Council to an agreement that, until appropriate Allied authorities formulate reparation and restitution program for application in Austria,

a. no removals should be permitted on reparation account; and

b. restitution to other countries should be confined to identifiable looted works of art, books, archives and other cultural property.

Foreign Trade

40. The Allied Council should take prompt steps to re-establish Austrian customs autonomy subject to the provisions of paragraph 51 and establish centralized control over all trade in goods and services with foreign countries.

41. In the control of foreign trade the objectives of the Allied Council should be (a) to obtain as much as possible of Austria's essential imports through regular trade; (b) encourage the development by Austrians as rapidly as possible of foreign markets and sources of supply; and (c) to promote the orientation of Austrian trade away from Germany.

The Allied Council should seek to obtain from sources other than military supply sources any imports essential to the achievement of the objectives set forth in this directive. Arrangements may be made with appropriate authorities in Germany for the importation of essential supplies from Germany, whenever in your judgment such supplies cannot be readily obtained from other sources.

The Allied Council should favor the conclusion of such arrangements for the exchange of Austrian goods and services with those of foreign countries including the development of entrepot trade, as will aid in the revival of the Austrian economy on a sound basis and will not prejudice the eventual development of trade on a multilateral basis.

The Allied Council in cooperation with the Austrian authorities, should make a survey of Austrian foreign exchange resources and of the possibilities for foreign markets and sources of supply for Austrian industry and trade to serve as the basis of a program for the development of a sound economy. You will communicate to your government through the Joint Chiefs of Staff the results of such a survey, together with such recommendations as you may deem appropriate.

42. The Allied Council should adopt a policy which would forbid participation of Austrian firms in international cartels or other restrictive contracts and arrangements, and should order the prompt termination of all existing Austrian participation in such cartels, contracts and arrangements. Pending agreement

in the Allied Council, you should take no action in your own zone with regard to this paragraph.

PART III

FINANCIAL

General Provisions

43. The Allied Council should adopt, for application throughout Austria, uniform financial measures which are necessary to the accomplishment of the objectives stated in paragraph 4 (b) of this directive and which are in conformity with the principles and policies set forth below. You will urge the establishment of centralized administration of such measures to the extent necessary to achieve these objectives and, pending agreement in the Allied Council, you will adopt such necessary measures in your own zone as are in conformity with the provisions of this directive.

44. In the administration of financial matters you will follow the principles set forth in paragraph 25 of this directive.

45. You will maintain such accounts and records as may be necessary to reflect the financial operations of the military government in your zone, and you will provide the Allied Council with such information as it may require, including information in connection with the use of currency by your forces, any governmental settlements, occupation costs, and other expenditures arising out of operations or activities involving participation of your forces.

46. You will take measures to safeguard books and records of all public and private banks and other financial institutions.

47. Subject to any agreed policies of the Allied Council, you are authorized to take the following steps:

a. to prohibit, or to prescribe regulations regarding transfers or other dealings in private or public securities or real estate or other property;

b. to close banks, insurance companies and other financial institutions for a period long enough for you to introduce satisfactory control, to ascertain their cash position, to apply the provisions of paragraphs 5, 6, 7 and 8 (c) of this directive, and to issue instructions for the determination of accounts and assets to be blocked under paragraph 55 below;

c. to close stock and commodity exchanges and similar institutions for such periods as you deem appropriate and apply the provisions of paragraphs 5, 6, 7 and 8 (c) of this directive;

d. to establish a general or limited moratorium, or moratoria, to the extent necessary to carry out the objectives stated in this directive. In particular, it may prove desirable to prevent foreclosures of mortgages and the exercise of similar remedies by creditors against individuals and small business enterprises;

e. to issue regulations prescribing the purposes for which credit may be extended and the terms and conditions governing the extension of credit;

f. to put into effect such further financial measures as you deem necessary to accomplish the purposes stated in this directive.

48. The Allied Council should designate a suitable bank, preferably the former Vienna Branch of the Reichsbank, to perform under its direction central banking functions. Simultaneously, all connections between such designated bank and institutions or persons in Germany should be severed in accordance

with paragraph 57 of this directive. When satisfied that this bank is under adequate control, the Allied Council may, by ensuring that credits are made available only in schillings through the zone commanders or authorized issuing banks or agencies, place such bank in a position to finance other banks or other financial institutions for the conduct of approved business.

Pending the designation of such a bank by the Allied Council, you may designate a bank in your zone to perform similar functions under your direct control and supervision and subject to the conditions specified above.

In an emergency you are also authorized to make direct advances, in schillings only, to other financial institutions.

Currency

49. The Allied Council should regulate and control the issue and volume of currency in Austria in accordance with the following provisions:

a. United States forces and other Allied forces within Austria will use only Allied military schillings for pay of troops and other military requirements. Allied military schillings will be declared legal tender in Austria. As long as Reichsmarks are legal tender in Austria, Allied military schillings will circulate interchangeably with Reichsmarks at a rate of one Allied military schilling for one Reichsmark. Reichskreditkassenscheine and other military currency issued by the Germans will not be legal tender in Austria;

b. without authorization by the Allied Council, no Austrian governmental or private banks or agencies will be permitted to issue banknotes or currency;

c. appropriate Austrian authorities should, to the maximum extent possible, be required by the Allied Council to make funds available free of cost in amounts sufficient to meet all expenses of the forces of occupation, including the cost of Allied military government, the pay of Allied military personnel, and to the extent that compensation is made therefor the cost of such private property as may be requisitioned, seized, or otherwise acquired by Allied authorities for reparation or restitution purposes;

d. as soon as administratively practicable, a general conversion into Allied Military schillings of the Reichsmark and Rentenmark currency circulated in Austria should be undertaken by the Allied Council or by you in coordination with the other zone commanders.

You will receive separate instructions relative to the currency which you will use in the event that for any reason adequate supplies of Allied Military schillings are not available.

You will not announce or establish, until receipt of further instructions, any general rate of exchange between the Allied Military schilling on the one hand and the U.S. dollar and other currencies on the other. However, the rate of exchange to be used exclusively for pay of troops and military accounting purposes will be ten Allied Military schillings for one U.S. dollar.

Public Finance

50. Subject to any agreed policies of the Allied Council, you will take such action as may be necessary to insure that all laws and practices relating to taxation or other fields of finance, which discriminate for or against any persons because of race, nationality, creed or political opinion, will be amended, suspended or abrogated to the extent necessary to eliminate such discrimination. Consistent with the foregoing purpose, the Austrian authorities should be re-

quired to take such action in the field of taxation as is necessary to assure an adequate inflow of revenues. Any public revenue in Austria previously collected by the German government may be used for approved public expenditures.

51. Pending the determination of the long-range Austrian customs and trade policy, the Austrian authorities may impose duties on imports for revenue purposes. Duties for other purposes should only be imposed with the approval of the Allied Council. No duties will be imposed on imports for military account or for the account of such relief agencies as may be designated.

52. Subject to any agreed policies of the Allied Council, you will prohibit:

a. the payment to ex-soldiers of all military pensions, or other emoluments or benefits, except compensation for physical disability limiting the recipient's ability to work at rates which are no higher than the lowest of those for comparable physical disability arising from non-military causes;

b. the payment of all public or private pensions or other emoluments or benefits granted or conferred

(1) by reason of membership in or services to the former Nazi party, its formations, affiliated associations or supervised organizations or any pre-Nazi Fascist organizations, such as the Heimwehr and the Ostmärkische Sturmscharen;

(2) to any person who has been removed from an office or position in accordance with paragraphs 5, 6 and 8 (c); and

(3) to any person arrested and detained in accordance with paragraph 7 during the term of his arrest, or permanently, in case of his subsequent conviction.

53. The Allied Council should exercise general control and supervision over the expenditures of public funds to the extent necessary to achieve the purposes of the occupation.

54. The Allied Council should promptly initiate a survey for the purpose of ascertaining (a) the amount of the German government debt held in Austria, (b) the amount of all outstanding internal public debts in Austria, and (c) the fiscal position of Austria. You will promptly submit recommendations concerning the treatment of these debts, taking into consideration the effect on Austrian public credit of policies on this matter.

Property Control

55. Subject to any agreed policies of the Allied Council, you will impound or block all gold, silver, currencies, securities accounts in financial institutions, credits, valuable papers, and all other assets falling within the following categories:

a. Property owned or controlled, directly or indirectly, in whole or in part, by any of the following:

(1) the governments, nationals or residents of the German Reich, Italy, Bulgaria, Rumania, Hungary, Finland and Japan, including those of territories occupied by them;

(2) the Austrian State, the municipal and provincial government and all governmental authorities within Austria, including their agencies and instrumentalities;

(3) the Nazi Party, its formations, affiliated associations and supervised organizations, its officials, leading members and supporters;

(4) all organizations, clubs or other associations prohibited or dissolved by military government;

(5) absentee owners, including United Nations and neutral governments;

(6) any institution dedicated to public worship, charity, education or the arts and sciences, which has been used by the Nazi party to further its interests or to cloak its activities;

(7) persons subject to arrest under the provisions of paragraph 7, and all other persons specified by military government by inclusion in lists or otherwise;

b. Property which has been the subject of transfer under duress, or wrongful acts of confiscation, disposition or spoliation, whether pursuant to legislation or by procedures purporting to follow forms of law or otherwise;

c. Works of art or cultural material of value or importance, regardless of the ownership thereof.

You will take such action as will ensure that any impounded or blocked assets will be dealt with only as permitted under licenses or other instructions which you may issue. In the case particularly of property blocked under *a* (2) above, you will proceed to adopt licensing measures which, while maintaining such property under surveillance, would permit its use in consonance with this directive. Property taken from Austrians under the conditions stated in b above should be restored as promptly as possible, subject to appropriate safeguards to prevent the cloaking of Nazi, German or militaristic influence.

The Allied Council should seek out and reduce to the possession and control of a special agency all property interests of any type and description owned either directly or indirectly by Germany or a national or a resident thereof.

External Financial and Property Relations

56. All foreign exchange transactions, including those arising out of exports and imports, shall be controlled for the purpose of achieving the objectives set forth in this directive. To effectuate such objectives the Allied Council should

a. seek out and reduce to the possession and control of a special agency all Austrian (public and private) foreign exchange and external assets of every kind and description located within or outside Austria;

b. prohibit, except as authorized by regulation or license, all dealings in gold, silver, foreign exchange, and all foreign exchange transactions of any kind;

c. make available any foreign exchange proceeds of exports for payment of imports necessary to the accomplishment of the objectives set forth in this directive and authorize no other outlay of foreign exchange assets for purposes approved by the Allied Council or other appropriate authority;

d. establish effective controls with respect to all foreign exchange transactions, including:

(1) transactions as to property between persons inside Austria and persons outside Austria;

(2) transactions involving obligations owed by or to become due from any person in Austria to any person outside Austria; and

(3) transactions involving the importation or exportation from Austria of any currency, foreign exchange asset or other form of property.

57. The Allied Council should, in cooperation with the Control Council in Germany, take steps necessary to sever all managerial and other organizational connections of banks, including postal banking offices, and all other business enterprises located in Austria with banks and business enterprises or persons located in Germany.

XII

REPORT ON THE TRIPARTITE CONFERENCE OF POTSDAM

August 2, 1945[1]

On July 17, 1945, the President of the United States of America, Harry S. Truman; the Chairman of the Council of People's Commissars of the Union of Soviet Socialist Republics, Generalissimo J. V. Stalin and the Prime Minister of Great Britain, Winston S. Churchill, together with Mr. Clement R. Attlee, met in the Tripartite Conference of Berlin. They were accompanied by the Foreign Secretaries of the three Governments, Mr. James F. Byrnes, Mr. V. M. Molotoff, and Mr. Anthony Eden, the Chiefs of Staff, and other advisers.

There were nine meetings between July 17 and July 25. The Conference was then interrupted for two days while the results of the British general election were being declared.

On July 28 Mr. Attlee returned to the Conference as Prime Minister, accompanied by the new Secretary of State for Foreign Affairs, Mr. Ernest Bevin. Four days of further discussion then took place. During the course of the Conference there were regular meetings of the heads of the three Governments accompanied by the Foreign Secretaries, and also of the Foreign Secretaries alone. Committees appointed by the Foreign Secretaries for preliminary consideration of questions before the Conference also met daily.

The meetings of the Conference were held at the Cecilienhof, near Potsdam. The Conference ended on August 2, 1945.

Important decisions and agreements were reached. Views exchanged on a number of other questions and considerations of these matters will be continued by the Council of Foreign Ministers established by the Conference.

President Truman, Generalissimo Stalin and Prime Minister Attlee leave this Conference, which has strengthened the ties between the three Governments and extended the scope of their collaboration and understanding, with renewed confidence that their Governments and peoples, together with the other United Nations, will insure the creation of a just and enduring peace.

ESTABLISHMENT OF A COUNCIL OF FOREIGN MINISTERS

The Conference reached an agreement for the establishment of a Council of Foreign Ministers representating the five principal powers to continue the necessary preparatory work for the peace settlements and to take up other matters which from time to time may be referred to the Council by agreement of the Governments participating in the Council.

The text of the agreement for the establishment of the Council of Foreign Ministers is as follows:

1. There shall be established a Council composed of the Foreign Ministers of the United Kingdom, the Union of the Soviet Socialist Republics, China, France and the United States.

2. (I) The Council shall normally meet in London, which shall be the permanent seat of the Joint Secretariat which the Council will form. Each of the Foreign Ministers will be accompanied by a high-ranking deputy, duly authorized to carry on the work of the Council in the absence of his Foreign Minister, and by a small staff of technical advisers.

---

[1]The Potsdam Declaration was released to the press on August 2, 1945. Department of State, *Bulletin*, Vol. XIII (1945), pp. 153-161.

(II) The first meeting of the Council shall be held in London not later than September 1, 1945. Meetings may be held by common agreement in other capitals as may be agreed from time to time.

3. (I) As its immediate important task the Council shall be authorized to draw up, with a view to their submission to the United Nations, treaties of peace with Italy, Rumania, Bulgaria, Hungary and Finland, and to propose settlements of territorial questions outstanding on the termination of the war in Europe. The Council shall be utilized for the preparation of a peace settlement for Germany to be accepted by the government of Germany when a government adequate for the purpose is established.

(II) For the discharge of each of these tasks the Council will be composed of the members representing those states which were signatory to the terms of surrender imposed upon the enemy state concerned. For the purpose of the peace settlement for Italy, France shall be regarded as a signatory to the terms of surrender for Italy. Other members will be invited to participate when matters directly concerning them are under discussion.

(III) Other matters may from time to time be referred to the Council by agreement between the member Governments.

4. (I) Whenever the Council is considering a question of direct interest to a State not represented thereon, such State should be invited to send representatives to participate in the discussion and study of that question.

(II) The Council may adapt its procedure to the particular problem under consideration. In some cases it may hold its own preliminary discussions prior to the participation of other interested states. In other cases, the Council may convoke a formal conference of the state chiefly interested in seeking a solution of the particular problem.

In accordance with the decision of the Conference the three Governments have each addressed an identical invitation to the Governments of China and France to adopt this text and to join in establishing the Council.

The establishment of the Council of Foreign Ministers for the specific purposes named in the text will be without prejudice to the agreement of the Crimea Conference that there should be periodic consultation among the Foreign Secretaries of the United States, the Union of Soviet Socialist Republics and the United Kingdom.

The Conference also considered the position of the European Advisory Commission in the light of the agreement to establish the Council of Foreign Ministers. It was noted with satisfaction that the Commission had ably discharged its principal task by the recommendations that it had furnished for the terms of Germany's unconditional surrender, for the zones of occupation in Germany and Austria and for the inter-Allied control machinery in those countries. It was felt that further work of a detailed character for the coordination of Allied policy for the control of Germany and Austria would in future fall within the competence of the Allied Control Council at Berlin and the Allied Commission at Vienna. Accordingly, it was agreed to recommend that the European Advisory Commission be dissolved.

GERMANY

The Allied armies are in occupation of the whole of Germany and the German people have begun to atone for the terrible crimes committed under the leadership of those whom in the hour of their success they openly approved and blindly obeyed.

Agreement has been reached at this conference on the political and economic principles of a coordinated Allied policy toward defeated Germany during the period of Allied control.

The purpose of this agreement is to carry out the Crimea Declaration on Germany. German militarism and Nazism will be extirpated and the Allies will take in agreement together, now and in the future, the other measures necessary to assure that Germany never again will threaten her neighbors or the peace of the world.

It is not the intention of the Allies to destroy or enslave the German people. It is the intention of the Allies that the German people be given the opportunity to prepare for the eventual reconstruction of their life on a democratic and peaceful basis. If their own efforts are steadily directed to this end, it will be possible for them in due course to take their place among the free and peaceful peoples of the world.

The text of the agreement is as follows:

THE POLITICAL AND ECONOMIC PRINCIPLES TO GOVERN THE TREATMENT OF GERMANY IN THE INITIAL CONTROL PERIOD

A. POLITICAL PRINCIPLES.

1. In accordance with the agreement on control machinery in Germany, supreme authority in Germany is exercised on instructions from their respective Governments, by the Commander in Chief of the Armed Forces of the United States of America, the United Kingdom, the Union of Soviet Socialist Republics, and the French Republic, each in his own zone of occupation, and also jointly, in matters affecting Germany as a whole, in their capacity as members of the Control Council.

2. So far as is practicable, there shall be uniformity of treatment of the German population throughout Germany.

3. The purposes of the occupation of Germany by which the Control Council shall be guided are:

(I) The complete disarmament and demilitarization of Germany and the elimination or control of all German industry that could be used for military production. To these ends:

(a) All German land, naval and air forces, the S.S., S.A., S.D., and Gestapo, with all their organizations, staffs and institutions, including the General Staff, the Officers' Corps, Reserve Corps, military schools, war veterans' organizations and all other military and quasi-military organizations, together with all clubs and associations which serve to keep alive the military tradition in Germany, shall be completely and finally abolished in such manner as permanently to prevent the revival or reorganization of German militarism and Nazism.

(b) All arms, ammunition and implements of war and all specialized facilities for their production shall be held at the disposal of the Allies or destroyed. The maintenance and production of all aircraft and all arms, ammunition and implements of war shall be prevented.

(II) To convince the German people that they have suffered a total military defeat and that they cannot escape responsibility for what they have brought upon themselves, since their own ruthless warfare and the fanatical Nazi resistance have destroyed German economy and made chaos and suffering inevitable.

(III) To destroy the National Socialist Party and its affiliated and supervised organizations, to dissolve all Nazi institutions, to insure that they are not revived in any form, and to prevent all Nazi and militarist activity or propaganda.

(IV) To prepare for the eventual reconstruction of German political life on a democratic basis and for eventual peaceful cooperation in international life by Germany.

(4) All Nazi laws which provided the basis of the Hitler regime or established discrimination on grounds of race, creed, or political opinion shall be abolished. No such discriminations, whether legal, administrative or otherwise, shall be tolerated.

5. War criminals and those who have participated in planning or carrying out Nazi enterprises involving or resulting in atrocities or war crimes shall be arrested and brought to judgment. Nazi leaders, influential Nazi supporters and high officials of Nazi organizations and institutions and any other persons dangerous to the occupation or its objectives shall be arrested and interned.

6. All members of the Nazi party who have been more than nominal participants in its activities and all other persons hostile to Allied purposes shall be removed from public and semi-public office and from positions of responsibility in important private undertakings. Such persons shall be replaced by persons who, by their political and moral qualities, are deemed capable of assisting in developing genuine democratic institutions in Germany.

7. German education shall be so controlled as completely to eliminate Nazi and militaristic doctrines and to make possible the successful development of democratic ideas.

8. The judicial system will be reorganized in accordance with the principles of democracy, of justice under law, and of equal rights for all citizens without distinction of race, nationality or religion.

9. The administration of affairs in Germany should be directed toward the decentralization of the political structure and the development of local responsibility. To this end:

(I) Local self-government shall be restored throughout Germany on democratic principles and in particular through elective councils as rapidly as is consistent with military security and the purposes of military occupation;

(II) All democratic political parties with rights of assembly and of public discussions shall be allowed and encouraged throughout Germany;

(III) Representatives and elective principles shall be introduced into regional, provincial and state (land) administration as rapidly as may be justified by the successful application of these principles in local self-government;

(IV) For the time being no central German Government shall be established. Notwithstanding this, however, certain essential central German administrative departments, headed by State Secretaries, shall be established, particularly in the fields of finance, transport, communications, foreign trade and industry. Such departments will act under the direction of the Control Council.

10. Subject to the necessity for maintaining military security, freedom of speech, press and religion shall be permitted, and religious institutions shall be respected. Subject likewise to the maintenance of military security, the formation of free trade unions shall be permitted.

B. ECONOMIC PRINCIPLES

11. In order to eliminate Germany's war potential, the production of arms,

ammunition and implements of war as well as all types of aircraft and sea-going ships shall be prohibited and prevented. Production of metals, chemicals, machinery and other items that are directly necessary to a war economy shall be rigidly controlled and restricted to Germany's approved postwar peacetime needs to meet the objectives stated in paragraph 15. Productive capacity not needed for permitted production shall be removed in accordance with the repa-rations plan recommended by the Allied Commission on reparations and ap-proved by the Governments concerned, or if not removed shall be destroyed.

12. At the earliest practicable date the German economy shall be decentral-ized for the purpose of eliminating the present excessive concentration of eco-nomic power as exemplified in particular by cartels, syndicates, trusts and other monopolistic arrangements.

13. In organizing the German economy, primary emphasis shall be given to the development of agriculture and peaceful domestic industries.

14. During the period of occupation Germany shall be treated as a single economic unit. To this end common policies shall be established in regard to:

(a) Mining and industrial production and allocations;
(b) Agriculture, forestry and fishing;
(c) Wages, prices and rationing;
(d) Import and export program for Germany as a whole;
(e) Currency and banking, central taxation and customs;
(f) Reparation and removal of industrial war potential;
(g) Transportation and communications.

In applying these policies account shall be taken, where appropriate, of vary-ing local conditions.

15. Allied controls shall be imposed upon the German economy, but only to the extent necessary:

(a) To carry out programs of industrial disarmament and demilitarization, of reparations, and of approved exports and imports.

(b) To assure the production and maintenance of goods and services re-quired to meet the needs of the occupying forces and displaced persons in Ger-many, and essential to maintain in Germany average living standards not ex-ceeding the average of the standards of living of European countries. (Euro-pean countries means all European countries, excluding the United Kingdom and the Union of Soviet Socialist Republics.)

(c) To ensure in the manner determined by the Control Council the equi-table distribution of essential commodities between the several zones so as to produce a balanced economy throughout Germany and reduce the need for imports.

(d) To control German industry and all economic and financial international transactions, including exports and imports, with the aim of preventing Ger-many from developing a war potential and of achieving the other objectives named herein.

(e) To control all German public or private scientific bodies, research and experimental institutions, laboratories, etc., connected with economic activities.

16. In the imposition and maintenance of economic controls established by the Control Council German administrative machinery shall be created and the German authorities shall be required to the fullest extent practicable to proclaim and assume administration of such controls. Thus it should be brought home to the German people that the responsibility for the administration of such

controls and any breakdown in these controls will rest with themselves. Any German controls which may run counter to the objectives of occupation will be prohibited.

17. Measures shall be promptly taken:

(a) To effect essential repair of transport;

(b) To enlarge coal production;

(c) To maximize agricultural output; and

(d) To effect emergency repair of housing and essential utilities.

18. Appropriate steps shall be taken by the Control Council to exercise control and the power of disposition over German-owned external assets not already under the control of United Nations which have taken part in the war against Germany.

19. Payment of reparations should leave enough resources to enable the German people to subsist without external assistance. In working out the economic balance of Germany the necessary means must be provided to pay for imports approved by the Control Council in Germany. The proceeds of exports from current production and stocks shall be available in the first place for payment for such imports.

The above clause will not apply to the equipment and products referred to in paragraphs 4 (a) and 4 (b) of the reparations agreement.

REPARATIONS FROM GERMANY

In accordance with the Crimea decision that Germany be compelled to compensate to the greatest possible extent for the loss and suffering that she has caused to the United Nations and for which the German people cannot escape responsibility, the following agreement on reparations was reached:

1. Reparation claims of the USSR shall be met by removals from the zone of Germany occupied by the USSR and from appropriate German external assets.

2. The USSR undertakes to settle the reparation claims of Poland from its own share of reparations.

3. The reparation claims of the United States, the United Kingdom and other countries entitled to reparations shall be met from the western zones and from appropriate German external assets.

4. In addition to the reparations to be taken by the USSR from its own zone of occupation, the USSR shall receive additionally from the western zones:

(a) Fifteen per cent of such usable and complete industrial capital equipment, in the first place from the metallurgical, chemical and machine manufacturing industries, as is unnecessary for the German peace economy should be removed from the western zones of Germany, in exchange for an equivalent value of food, coal, potash, zinc, timber, clay products, petroleum products and such other commodities as may be agreed upon.

(b) Ten per cent of such industrial capital equipment as is unnecessary for the German peace economy and should be removed from the western zones, to be transferred to the Soviet Government on reparations account without payment or exchange of any kind in return.

Removals of equipment as provided in (a) and (b) above shall be made simultaneously.

5. The amount of equipment to be removed from the western zones on account of reparations must be determined within six months from now at the latest.

6. Removals of industrial capital equipment shall begin as soon as possible

and shall be completed within two years from the determination specified in paragraph 5. The delivery of products covered by 4 (a) above shall begin as soon as possible and shall be made by the USSR in agreed installments within five years of the date hereof. The determination of the amount and character of the industrial capital equipment unnecessary for the German peace economy and therefore available for reparations shall be made by the Control Council under policies fixed by the Allied Commission on Reparations, with the participation of France, subject to the final approval of the Zone Commander in the Zone from which the equipment is to be removed.

7. Prior to the fixing of the total amount of equipment subject to removal, advance deliveries shall be made in respect of such equipment as will be determined to be eligible for delivery in accordance with the procedure set forth in the last sentence of paragraph 6.

8. The Soviet Government renounces all claims in respect of reparations to shares of German enterprises which are located in the western zones of occupation in Germany, as well as to German foreign assets in all countries, except those specified in paragraph 9 below.

The Governments of the United Kingdom and the United States of America renounce their claims in respect of reparations to shares of German enterprises which are located in the eastern zone of occupation in Germany, as well as to German foreign assets in Bulgaria, Finland, Hungary, Rumania and eastern Austria.

10. The Soviet Government makes no claims to gold captured by the Allied troops in Germany.

DISPOSAL OF THE GERMAN NAVY AND MERCHANT MARINE

The Conference agreed in principle upon arrangements for the use and disposal of the surrendered German fleet and merchant ships. It was decided that the three governments would appoint experts to work out together detailed plans to give effect to the agreed principles. A further joint statement will be published simultaneously by the three governments in due course.

CITY OF KOENIGSBERG AND THE ADJACENT AREA

The Conference examined a proposal by the Soviet Government that pending the final determination of territorial questions at the peace settlement the section of the western frontier of the Union of Soviet Socialist Republics which is adjacent to the Baltic Sea should pass from a point on the eastern shore of the Bay of Danzig to the east, north of Braunsberg-Goldap, to the meeting point of the frontiers of Lithuania, the Polish Republic and East Prussia.

The Conference has agreed in principle to the proposal of the Soviet Government concerning the ultimate transfer to the Soviet Union of the city of Koenigsberg and the area adjacent to it as described above, subject to expert examination of the actual frontier.

The President of the United States and the British Prime Minister have declared that they will support the proposal of the Conference at the forthcoming peace settlement.

WAR CRIMINALS

The three governments have taken note of the discussions which have been proceeding in recent weeks in London between British, United States, Soviet and French representatives with a view to reaching agreement on the methods of trial of those major war criminals whose crimes under the Moscow Declarations of October 1943, have no particular geographical localization.

The three Governments reaffirm their intention to bring those criminals to swift and sure justice. They hope that the negotiations in London will result in speedy agreement being reached for this purpose, and they regard it as a matter of great importance that the trial of those major criminals should begin at the earliest possible date. The first list of defendants will be published before September 1.

AUSTRIA

The conference examined a proposal by the Soviet Government on the extension of the authority of the Austrian Provisional Government to all of Austria.

The three Governments agreed that they were prepared to examine this question after the entry of the British and American forces into the city of Vienna.

POLAND

The conference considered questions relating to the Polish Provisional Government and the western boundary of Poland.

On the Polish Provisional Government of National Unity they defined their attitude in the following statement:

A. We have taken note with pleasure of the agreement reached among representative Poles from Poland and abroad which has made possible the formation, in accordance with the decisions reached at the Crimea Conference, of a Polish Provisional Government of National Unity recognized by the three Powers. The establishment by the British and United States Governments of diplomatic relations with the Polish Provisional Government has resulted in the withdrawal of their recognition from the former Polish Government in London, which no longer exists.

The British and United States Governments have taken measures to protect the interest of the Polish Provisional Government, as the recognized Government of the Polish State, in the property belonging to the Polish State located in their territories and under their control, whatever the form of this property may be. They have further taken measures to prevent alienation to third parties of such property. All proper facilities will be given to the Polish Provisional Government for the exercise of the ordinary legal remedies for the recovery of any property belonging to the Polish State which may have been wrongfully alienated.

The three Powers are anxious to assist the Polish Provisional Government in facilitating the return to Poland as soon as practicable of all Poles abroad who wish to go, including members of the Polish armed forces and the merchant marine. They expect that those Poles who return home shall be accorded personal and property rights on the same basis as all Polish citizens.

The three Powers note that the Polish Provisional Government, in accordance with the decisions of the Crimea Conference, has agreed to the holding of free and unfettered elections as soon as possible on the basis of universal suffrage and secret ballot in which all democratic and anti-Nazi parties shall have the right to take part and to put forward candidates, and that representatives of the Allied press shall enjoy full freedom to report to the world upon developments in Poland before and during the elections.

B. The following agreement was reached on the western frontier of Poland:

In conformity with the agreement on Poland reached at the Crimea Conference the three heads of Government have sought the opinion of the Polish Provisional Government of National Unity in regard to the accession of territory in the north and west which Poland should receive. The president of the National Council of Poland and members of the Polish Provisional Government of National Unity have been received at the conference and have fully presented their views. The three heads of Government reaffirm their opinion that the final de-limitation of the western frontier of Poland should await the peace settlement.

The three heads of Government agree that, pending the final determination of Poland's western frontier, the former German territories east of a line running from the Baltic Sea immediately west of Swinemünde, and thence along the Oder River to the confluence of the western Neisse River and along the western Neisse to the Czechoslovak frontier, including that portion of East Prussia not placed under the administration of the Union of Soviet Socialist Republics in accordance with the understanding reached at this Conference and including the area of the former free city of Danzig, shall be under the administration of the Polish State and for such purposes should not be considered as part of the Soviet zone of occupation in Germany.

CONCLUSION OF PEACE TREATIES AND ADMISSION TO THE UNITED NATIONS ORGANIZATION

The Conference agreed upon the following statement of common policy for establishing, as soon as possible, the conditions of lasting peace after victory in Europe:

The three Governments consider it desirable that the present anomalous position of Italy, Bulgaria, Finland, Hungary and Rumania should be terminated by the conclusion of peace treaties. They trust that the other interested Allied Governments will share these views.

For their part, the three Governments have included the preparation of a peace treaty for Italy as the first among the immediate important tasks to be undertaken by the new Council of Foreign Ministers. Italy was the first of the Axis powers to break with Germany, to whose defeat she has made a material contribution, and has now joined with the Allies in the struggle against Japan.

Italy has freed herself from the Fascist regime and is making good progress toward the re-establishment of a democratic government and institutions. The conclusion of such a peace treaty with a recognized and democratic Italian Government will make it possible for the three Governments to fulfill their desire to support an application from Italy for membership of the United Nations.

The three Governments have also charged the Council of Foreign Ministers with the task of preparing peace treaties for Bulgaria, Finland, Hungary and Rumania.

The conclusion of peace treaties with recognized democratic governments in these states will also enable the three Governments to support applications from them for membership of the United Nations. The three Governments agree to examine, each separately in the near future, in the light of the conditions then prevailing, the establishment of diplomatic relations with Finland, Rumania, Bulgaria and Hungary to the extent possible prior to the conclusion of peace treaties with those countries.

The three Governments have no doubt that in view of the changed conditions resulting from the termination of the war in Europe, representatives of the Allied press will enjoy full freedom to report to the world upon developments in Rumania, Bulgaria, Hungary and Finland.

As regards the admission of other States into the United Nations organization, Article 4 of the Charter of the United Nations declared that:

"1. Membership in the United Nations is open to all other peace-loving States who accept the obligations contained in the present Charter and, in the judgment of the organization, are able and willing to carry out these obligations;

"2. The admission of any such state to membership in the United Nations will be effected by a decision of the General Assembly upon the recommendation of the Security Council."

The three Governments, so far as they are concerned, will support applications for membership from those States which have remained neutral during the war and which fulfill the qualifications set out above.

The three Governments feel bound however to make it clear that they for their part would not favor any application for membership put forward by the present Spanish Government, which, having been founded with the support of the Axis Powers, does not, in view of its origins, its nature, its record and its close association with the aggressor States, possess the qualifications necessary to justify such membership.

TERRITORIAL TRUSTEESHIPS

The conference examined a proposal by the Soviet Government concerning trusteeship territories as defined in the decision of the Crimea Conference and in the Charter of the United Nations Organization.

After an exchange of views on this question it was decided that the disposition of any former Italian territories was one to be decided in connection with the preparation of a peace treaty for Italy and that the question of Italian territory would be considered by the September council of Ministers of Foreign Affairs.

REVISED ALLIED CONTROL COMMISSION PROCEDURE IN RUMANIA, BULGARIA, AND HUNGARY

The three Governments took note that the Soviet representatives on the Allied Control Commissions in Rumania, Bulgaria and Hungary have communicated to their United Kingdom and United States colleagues proposals for improving the work of the control commission, now that hostilities in Europe have ceased.

The three Governments agreed that the revision of the procedures of the Allied Control Commissions in these countries would now be undertaken, taking into account the interests and responsibilities of the three Governments which together presented the terms of armistice to the respective countries, and accepting as a basis the agreed proposals.

ORDERLY TRANSFERS OF GERMAN POPULATIONS

The conference reached the following agreement on the removal of Germans from Poland, Czechoslovakia and Hungary:

The three Governments having considered the question in all its aspects, recognize that the transfer to Germany of German populations, or elements thereof, remaining in Poland, Czechoslovakia and Hungary will have to be undertaken. They agree that any transfers that take place should be effected in an orderly and humane manner.

Since the influx of a large number of Germans into Germany would increase the burden already resting on the occupying authorities, they consider that the Allied Control Council in Germany should in the first instance examine the problem with special regard to the question of the equitable distribution of these Germans among the several zones of occupation. They are accordingly instructing their respective representatives on the control council to report to their Governments as soon as possible the extent to which such persons have already entered Germany from Poland, Czechoslovakia and Hungary, and to submit an estimate of the time and rate at which further transfers could be carried out, having regard to the present situation in Germany.

The Czechoslovak Government, the Polish Provisional Government and the Control Council in Hungary are at the same time being informed of the above and are being requested meanwhile to suspend further expulsions pending the examination by the Governments concerned of the report from their representatives on the control council.

MILITARY TALKS

During the conference there were meetings between the Chiefs of Staff of of the three Governments on military matters of common interest.

Approved:

> J. V. Stalin,
> Harry S. Truman,
> C. R. Attlee.

XIII
DECLARATION DEFINING TERMS FOR JAPANESE SURRENDER
July 26, 1945[1]

(1) We—the President of the United States, the President of the National Government of the Republic of China, and the Prime Minister of Great Britain—representing the hundreds of millions of our countrymen, have conferred and agree that Japan shall be given an opportunity to end this war.

(2) The prodigious land, sea and air forces of the United States, the British Empire and of China, many times reinforced by their armies and air fleets from the west, are poised to strike the final blows upon Japan. This military power is sustained and inspired by the determination of all the Allied Nations to prosecute the war against Japan until she ceases to resist.

(3). The result of the futile and senseless German resistance to the might of the aroused free peoples of the world stands forth in awful clarity as an example to the people of Japan. The might that now converges on Japan is immeasurably greater than that which, when applied to the resisting Nazis, necessarily laid waste to the lands, the industry and the method of life of the whole German people. The full application of our military power, backed by our resolve, *will* mean the inevitable and complete destruction of the Japanese homeland.

---

[1]This Potsdam Declaration was issued by the heads of governments of the United States, Great Britain, and China, the President of the National Government of China communicating with President Truman by dispatch. Department of State, *Bulletin,* Vol. XIII (1945) pp. 137-138.

(4) The time has come for Japan to decide whether she will continue to be controlled by those self-willed militaristic advisers whose unintelligent calculations have brought the Empire of Japan to the threshold of annihilation, or whether she will follow the path of reason.

(5) Following are our terms. We will not deviate from them. There are no alternatives. We shall brook no delay.

(6) There must be eliminated for all time the authority and influence of those who have deceived and misled the people of Japan into embarking on world conquest, for we insist that a new order of peace, security and justice will be impossible until irresponsible militarism is driven from the world.

(7) Until such a new order is established *and* until there is convincing proof that Japan's war-making power is destroyed, points in Japanese territory to be designated by the Allies shall be occupied to secure the achievement of the basic objectives we are here setting forth.

(8) The terms of the Cairo Declaration shall be carried out and Japanese sovereignty shall be limited to the islands of Honshu, Hokkaido, Kyushu, Shikoku and such minor islands as we determine.

(9) The Japanese military forces, after being completely disarmed, shall be permitted to return to their homes with the opportunity to lead peaceful and productive lives.

(10) We do not intend that the Japanese shall be enslaved as a race or destroyed as a nation, but stern justice shall be meted out to all war criminals, including those who have visited cruelties upon our prisoners. The Japanese Government shall remove all obstacles to the revival and strengthening of democratic tendencies among the Japanese people. Freedom of speech, of religion, and of thought, as well as respect for the fundamental human rights shall be established.

(11) Japan shall be permitted to maintain such industries as will sustain her economy and permit the exaction of just reparations in kind, but not those which would enable her to re-arm for war. To this end, access to, as distinguished from control of, raw materials shall be permitted. Eventual Japanese participation in world trade relations shall be permitted.

(12) The occupying forces of the Allies shall be withdrawn from Japan as soon as these objectives have been accomplished and there has been established in accordance with the freely expressd will of the Japanese people a peacefully inclined and responsible government.

(13) We call upon the government of Japan to proclaim now the unconditional surrender of all Japanese armed forces, and to provide proper and adequate assurances of their good faith in such action. The alternative for Japan is prompt and utter destruction.

XIV

DOCUMENTS CONCERNING JAPANESE SURRENDER

A. EXCHANGE OF NOTES BETWEEN SWISS CHARGE AND SECRETARY OF STATE

August 10/11, 1945[1]

Sir: August 10, 1945

I have the honor to inform you that the Japanese Minister to Switzerland,

---

[1] Department of State, *Bulletin*, Vol. XIII (1945), pp. 205-206. 255-256.

upon instructions received from his Government, has requested the Swiss Political Department to advise the Government of the United States of America of the following:

"In obedience to the gracious command of His Majesty the Emperor who, ever anxious to enhance the cause of world peace, desires earnestly to bring about a speedy termination of hostilities with a view to saving mankind from the calamities to be imposed upon them by further continuation of the war, the Japanese Government several weeks ago asked the Soviet Government, with which neutral relations then prevailed, to render good offices in restoring peace vis a vis the enemy powers. Unfortunately, these efforts in the interest of peace having failed, the Japanese Government in conformity with the august wish of His Majesty to restore the general peace and desiring to put an end to the untold sufferings entailed by war as quickly as possible, have decided upon the following.

"The Japanese Government are ready to accept the terms enumerated in the joint declaration which was issued at Potsdam on July 26th, 1945, by the heads of the Governments of the United States, Great Britain and China, and later subscribed by the Soviet Government, with the understanding that the said declaration does not comprise any demand which prejudices the prerogatives of His Majesty as a Sovereign Ruler.

"The Japanese Government sincerely hope that this understanding is warranted and desire keenly that an explicit indication to that effect will be speedily forthcoming."

In transmitting the above message the Japanese Minister added that his Government begs the Government of the United States to forward its answer through the intermediary of Switzerland. Similar requests are being transmitted to the Governments of Great Britain and the Union of Soviet Socialist Republics through the intermediary of Sweden, as well as to the Government of China through the intermediary of Switzerland. The Chinese Minister at Berne has already been informed of the foregoing through the channel of the Swiss Political Department.

Please be assured that I am at your disposal at any time to accept for and forward to my Government the reply of the Government of the United States.

Accept [etc.]

Grässli

August 11, 1945

Sir:

I have the honor to acknowledge receipt of your note of August 10, and in reply to inform you that the President of the United States has directed me to send to you for transmission by your Government to the Japanese Government the following message on behalf of the Governments of the United States, the United Kingdom, the Union of Soviet Socialist Republics, and China:

"With regard to the Japanese Government's message accepting the terms of the Potsdam proclamation but containing the statement, 'with the understanding that the said declaration does not comprise any demand which prejudices the prerogatives of His Majesty as a sovereign ruler,' our position is as follows:

"From the moment of surrender the authority of the Emperor and the Japanese Government to rule the state shall be subject to the Supreme Commander of the Allied powers who will take such steps as he deems proper to effectuate the surrender terms.

"The Emperor will be required to authorize and ensure the signature by the Government of Japan and the Japanese Imperial General Headquarters of the surrender terms necessary to carry out the provisions of the Potsdam Declaration, and shall issue his commands to all the Japanese military, naval and air authorities and to all the forces under their control wherever located to cease active operations and to surrender their arms, and to issue such other orders as the Supreme Commander may require to give effect to the surrender terms.

"Immediately upon the surrender the Japanese Government shall transport prisoners of war and civilian internees to places of safety, as directed, where they can quickly be placed aboard Allied transports.

"The ultimate form of government of Japan shall, in accordance with the Potsdam Declaration, be established by the freely expressed will of the Japanese people.

"The armed forces of the Allied Powers will remain in Japan until the purposes set forth in the Potsdam Declaration are achieved."

Accept [etc.]

James F. Byrnes

B. JAPANESE ACCEPTANCE OF POTSDAM DECLARATION
August 14, 1945[2]

"Communication of the Japanese Government of August 14, 1945, addressed to the Governments of the United States, Great Britain, the Soviet Union, and China:

"With reference to the Japanese Government's note of August 10 regarding their acceptance of the provisions of the Potsdam Declaration and the reply of the Governments of the United States, Great Britain, the Soviet Union, and China sent by American Secretary of State Byrnes under the date of August 11, the Japanese Government have the honor to communicate to the Governments of the four powers as follows:

"1. His Majesty the Emperor has issued an Imperial rescript regarding Japan's acceptance of the provisions of the Potsdam declaration.

"2. His Majesty the Emperor is prepared to authorize and ensure the signature by his Government and the Imperial General Headquarters of the necessary terms for carrying out the provisions of the Potsdam declaration. His Majesty is also prepared to issue his commands to all the military, naval, and air au thorities of Japan and all the forces under their control wherever located to cease active operations, to surrender arms and to issue such other orders as may be required by the Supreme Commander of the Allied Forces for the execution of the above-mentioned terms."

C. INSTRUMENT OF JAPANESE SURRENDER
September 2, 1945[3]

We, acting by command of and in behalf of the Emperor of Japan, the Japanese Government and the Japanese Imperial General Headquarters, hereby

---

[2]The communication, which was received through Swiss channels, was made public by President Truman. Department of State, *Bulletin*, Vol. XIII (1945), p. 255.

[3]The instrument was signed at Tokyo Bay by the Japanese Foreign Minister, Shigemitsu, and Chief of Staff, Umezu, and accepted by General MacArthur, Supreme Commander for the Allied Powers, and representatives of the United States, China, Britain, USSR, Australia, Canada, France, Netherlands, New Zealand. Department of State, *Bulletin*, Vol. XIII (1945), pp. 362-365.

accept the provisions set forth in the declaration issued by the heads of the Governments of the United States, China and Great Britain on 26 July 1945, at Potsdam, and subsequently adhered to by the Union of Soviet Socialist Republics, which four powers are hereafter referred to as the Allied Powers.

We hereby proclaim the unconditional surrender to the Allied Powers of the Japanese Imperial General Headquarters and of all Japanese armed forces and all armed forces under Japanese control wherever situated.

We hereby command all Japanese forces wherever situated and the Japanese people to cease hostilities forthwith, to preserve and save from damage all ships, aircraft, and military and civil property and to comply with all requirements which may be imposed by the Supreme Commander for the Allied Powers or by agencies of the Japanese Government at his direction.

We hereby command the Japanese Imperial General Headquarters to issue at once orders to the Commanders of all Japanese forces and all forces under Japanese control wherever situated to surrender unconditionally themselves and all forces under their control.

We hereby command all civil, military and naval officials to obey and enforce all proclamations, orders and directives deemed by the Supreme Commander for the Allied Powers to be proper to effectuate this surrender and issued by him or under his authority and we direct all such officials to remain at their posts and to continue to perform their non-combatant duties unless specifically relieved by him or under his authority.

We hereby undertake for the Emperor, the Japanese Government and their successors to carry out the provisions of the Potsdam Declaration in good faith, and to issue whatever orders and take whatever action may be required by the Supreme Commander for the Allied Powers or by any other designated representative of the Allied Powers for the purpose of giving effect to that Declaration.

We hereby command the Japanese Imperial Government and the Japanese Imperial General Headquarters at once to liberate all Allied prisoners of war and civilian internees now under Japanese control and to provide for their protection, care, maintenance and immediate transportation to places as directed.

The authority of the Emperor and the Japanese Government to rule the state ⌐hall be subject to the Supreme Commander for the Allied Powers who will ⌐ke such steps as he deems proper to effectuate these terms of surrender.

XV

STATEMENT ON UNITED STATES INITIAL POST-SURRENDER POLICY FOR JAPAN

August 29, 1945[1]

This document is intended as a statement of general initial policies relating to Japan after surrender. Following Presidential approval, it will be distributed to appropriate United States departments and agencies for their guidance. It is recognized that this document does not deal with all matters relating to the occupation of Japan requiring policy determinations. Policies upon such matters as are not included or not fully covered herein will be dealt with in subsequent papers.

---

[1]The statement was issued to the press by the White House on September 6, 1945. Department of State, *Bulletin*, Vol. XIII (1945), pp. 423-427.

The ultimate objectives of the United States in regard to Japan, to which policies in the initial period must conform, are:

a. To insure that Japan will not again become a menace to the United States or to the peace and security of the world.

b. To bring about the eventual establishment of a peaceful and responsible government which will respect the rights of other states and will support the objectives of the United States as reflected in the ideals and principles of the Charter of the United Nations. The United States desires that this government should conform as closely as may be to principles of democratic self-government but it is not the responsibility of the Allied Powers to impose upon Japan any form of government not supported by the freely expressed will of the people.

These objectives will be achieved by the following principal means:

a. Japan's sovereignty will be limited to the islands of Honshu, Hokkaido, Kyushu, Shikoku and such minor outlying islands as may be determined, in accordance with the Cairo Declaration and other agreements to which the United States is or may be a party.

b. Japan will be completely disarmed and demilitarized. The authority of the militarists and the influence of militarism will be totally eliminated from her political, economic, and social life. Institutions expressive of the spirit of militarism and aggression will be vigorously suppressed.

c. The Japanese people shall be encouraged to develop a desire for individual liberties and respect for fundamental human rights, particularly the freedoms of religion, assembly, speech, and the press. They shall also be encouraged to form democratic and representative organizations.

d. The Japanese people shall be afforded opportunity to develop for themselves an economy which will permit the peacetime requirements of the population to be met.

PART II—ALLIED AUTHORITY

1. *Military Occupation*—There will be a military occupation of the Japanese home islands to carry into effect the surrender terms and further the achievements of the ultimate objectives stated above. The occupation shall have the character of an operation in behalf of the principal Allied powers acting in the interests of the United Nations at war with Japan. For that reason, participation of the forces of other nations that have taken a leading part in the war against Japan will be welcomed and expected. The occupation forces will be under the command of a Supreme Commander designated by the United States.

Although every effort will be made, by consultation and by constitution of appropriate advisory bodies, to establish policies for the conduct of the occupation and the control of Japan which will satisfy the principal Allied powers, in the event of any differences of opinion among them, the policies of the United States will govern.

2. *Relationship to Japanese Government*—The authority of the Emperor and the Japanese Government will be subject to the Supreme Commander, who will possess all powers necessary to effectuate the surrender terms and to carry out the policies established for the conduct of the occupation and the control of Japan.

In view of the present character of Japanese society and the desire of the

United States to attain its objectives with a minimum commitment of its forces and resources, the Supreme Commander will exercise his authority through Japanese governmental machinery and agencies, including the Emperor, to the extent that this satisfactorily furthers United States objectives. The Japanese Government will be permitted, under his instructions, to exercise the normal powers of government in matters of domestic administration. This policy, however, will be subject to the right and duty of the Supreme Commander to require changes in governmental machinery or personnel or to act directly if the Emperor or other Japanese authority does not satisfactorily meet the requirements of the Supreme Commander in effectuating the surrender terms. This policy, moreover, does not commit the Supreme Commander to support the Emperor or any other Japanese governmental authority in opposition to evolutionary changes looking toward the attainment of United States objectives. The policy is to use the existing form of Government in Japan, not to support it. Changes in the form of Government initiated by the Japanese people or government in the direction of modifying its feudal and authoritarian tendencies are to be permitted and favored. In the event that the effectuation of such changes involves the use of force by the Japanese people or government against persons opposed thereto, the Supreme Commander should intervene only where necessary to ensure the security of his forces and the attainment of all other objectives of the occupation.

3. *Publicity as to Policies*—The Japanese people, and the world at large, shall be kept fully informed of the objectives and policies of the occupation, and of progress made in their fulfillment.

PART III—POLITICAL

1. *Disarmament and Demilitarization*—Disarmament and demilitarization are the primary tasks of the military occupation and shall be carried out promptly and with determination. Every effort shall be made to bring home to the Japanese people the part played by the military and naval leaders, and those who collaborated with them, in bringing about the existing and future distress of the people.

Japan is not to have an army, navy, air force, secret police organization, or any civil aviation. Japan's ground, air and naval forces shall be disarmed and disbanded and the Japanese Imperial General Headquarters, the General Staff and all secret police organizations shall be dissolved. Military and naval materiel, military and naval vessels and military and naval installations, and military, naval and civilian aircraft shall be surrendered and shall be disposed of as required by the Supreme Commander.

High officials of the Japanese Imperial General Headquarters, and General Staff, other high military and naval officials of the Japanese Government, leaders of ultra-nationalist and militarist organizations and other important exponents of militarism and aggression will be taken into custody and held for future disposition. Persons who have been active exponents of militarism and militant nationalism will be removed and excluded from public office and from any other position of public or substantial private responsibility. Ultra-nationalistic or militaristic social, political, professional and commercial societies and institutions will be dissolved and prohibited.

Militarism and ultra-nationalism, in doctrine and practice, including paramilitary training, shall be eliminated from the educational system. Former career military and naval officers, both commissioned and non-commissioned, and all other exponents of militarism and ultra-nationalism shall be excluded from supervisory and teaching positions.

2. War Criminals—Persons charged by the Supreme Commander or appropriate United Nations Agencies with being war criminals, including those charged with having visited cruelties upon United Nations prisoners or other nationals, shall be arrested, tried and, if convicted, punished. Those wanted by another of the United Nations for offenses against its nationals, shall, if not wanted for trial or as witnesses or otherwise by the Supreme Commander, be turned over to the custody of such other nation.

3. Encouragement of Desire for Individual Liberties and Democratic Processes—Freedom of religious worship shall be proclaimed promptly on occupation. At the same time it should be made plain to the Japanese that ultra-nationalistic and militaristic organizations and movements will not be permitted to hide behind the cloak of religion.

The Japanese people shall be afforded opportunity and encouraged to become familiar with the history, institutions, culture, and the accomplishments of the United States and the other democracies. Association of personnel of the occupation forces with the Japanese population should be controlled, only to the extent necessary, to further the policies and objectives of the occupation.

Democratic political parties, with rights of assembly and public discussion, shall be encouraged, subject to the necessity for maintaining the security of the occupying forces.

Laws, decrees and regulations which establish discriminations on grounds of race, nationality, creed or political opinion shall be abrogated; those which conflict with the objectives and policies outlined in this document shall be repealed, suspended or amended as required; and agencies charged specifically with their enforcement shall be abolished or appropriately modified. Persons unjustly confined by Japanese authority on political grounds shall be released. The judicial, legal and police systems shall be reformed as soon as practicable to conform to the policies set forth in Articles 1 and 3 of this Part III and thereafter shall be progressively influenced, to protect individual liberties and civil rights.

PART IV—ECONOMIC

1. Economic Demilitarization—The existing economic basis of Japanese military strength must be destroyed and not be permitted to revive.

Therefore, a program will be enforced containing the following elements, among others; the immediate cessation and future prohibition of production of all goods designed for the equipment, maintenance, or use of any military force or establishment; the imposition of a ban upon any specialized facilities for the production or repair of implements of war, including naval vessels and all forms of aircraft; the institution of a system of inspection and control over selected elements in Japanese economic activity to prevent concealed or disguised military preparation; the elimination in Japan of those selected industries of branches of production whose chief value to Japan is in preparing for war; the prohibition of specialized research and instruction directed to the development of warmaking power; and the limitation of the size and character of Japan's heavy industries to its future peaceful requirements, and restriction of Japanese merchant shipping to the extent required to accomplish the objectives of demilitarization.

The eventual disposition of those existing production facilities within Japan which are to be eliminated in accord with this program, as between conversion to other uses, transfer abroad, and scrapping will be determined after inventory. Pending decision, facilities readily convertible for civilian production should not be destroyed, except in emergency situations.

2. Promotion of Democratic Forces—Encouragement shall be given and favor shown to the development of organizations in labor, industry, and agriculture, organized on a democratic basis. Policies shall be favored which permit a wide distribution of income and of the ownership of the means of production and trade.

Those forms of economic activity, organization and leadership shall be favored that are deemed likely to strengthen the peaceful disposition of the Japanese people, and to make it difficult to command or direct economic activity in support of military ends.

To this end it shall be the policy of the Supreme Commander:

a. To prohibit the retention in or selection for places of importance in the economic field of individuals who do not direct future Japanese economic effort solely towards peaceful ends; and

b. To favor a program for the dissolution of the large industrial and banking combinations which have exercised control of a great part of Japan's trade and industry.

3. Resumption of Peaceful Economic Activity—The policies of Japan have brought down upon the people great economic destruction and confronted them with the prospect of economic difficulty and suffering. The plight of Japan is the direct outcome of its own behavior and the Allies will not undertake the burden of repairing the damage. It can be repaired only if the Japanese people renounce all military aims and apply themselves diligently and with single purpose to the ways of peaceful living. It will be necessary for them to undertake physical reconstruction, deeply to reform the nature and direction of their economic activities and institutions, and to find useful employment for their people along lines adapted to and devoted to peace. The Allies have no intention of imposing conditions which would prevent the accomplishment of these tasks in due time.

Japan will be expected to provide goods and services to meet the needs of the occupying forces to the extent that this can be effected without causing starvation, widespread disease and acute physical distress.

The Japanese authorities will be expected, and if necessary directed, to maintain, develop and enforce programs that serve the following purposes:

a. To avoid acute economic distress.

b. To assure just and impartial distribution of available supplies.

c. To meet the requirements for reparations deliveries agreed upon by the Allied Governments.

d. To facilitate the restoration of Japanese economy so that the reasonable peaceful requirements of the population can be satisfied.

In this connection, the Japanese authorities on their own responsibility shall be permitted to establish and administer controls over economic activities, including essential national public services, finance, banking, and production and distribution of essential commodities, subject to the approval and review of the Supreme Commander in order to assure their conformity with the objectives of the occupation.

4. *Reparations and Restitution*—a. Reparations—Reparations for Japanese aggression shall be made:

(1) Through the transfer—as may be determined by the appropriate Allied authorities—of Japanese property located outside of the territories to be retained by Japan.

(2) Through the transfer of such goods or existing capital equipment and facilities as are not necessary for a peaceful Japanese economy or the supplying of the occupying forces. Exports other than those directed to be shipped on reparation account or as restitution may be made only to those recipients who agree to provide necessary imports in exchange or agree to pay for such exports in foreign exchange. No form of reparation shall be exacted which will interfere with or prejudice the program for Japan's demilitarization.

b. Restitution—Full and prompt restitution will be required of all identifiable looted property.

5. *Fiscal, Monetary, and Banking Policies*—The Japanese authorities will remain responsible for the management and direction of the domestic fiscal, monetary, and credit policies subject to the approval and review of the Supreme Commander.

6. *International Trade and Financial Relations*—Japan shall be permitted eventually to resume normal trade relations with the rest of the world. During occupation and under suitable controls, Japan will be permitted to purchase from foreign countries raw materials and other goods that it may need for peaceful purposes, and to export goods to pay for approved imports.

Control is to be maintained over all imports and exports of goods, and foreign exchange and financial transactions. Both the policies followed in the exercise of these controls and their actual administration shall be subject to the approval and supervision of the Supreme Commander in order to make sure that they are not contrary to the policies of the occupying authorities, and in particular that all foreign purchasing power that Japan may acquire is utilized only for essential needs.

7. *Japanese Property Located Abroad*—Existing Japanese external assets and existing Japanese assets located in territories detached from Japan under the terms of surrender, including assets owned in whole or part by the Imperial Household and Government, shall be revealed to the occupying authorities and held for disposition according to the decision of the Allied authorities.

8. *Equality of Opportunity for Foreign Enterprise within Japan*—The Japanese authorities shall not give, or permit any Japanese business organization to give, exclusive or preferential opportunity or terms to the enterprise of any foreign country, or cede to such enterprise control of any important branch of economic activity.

9. *Imperial Household Property*—Imperial Household property shall not be exempted from any action necessary to carry out the objectives of the occupation.

XVI
STATEMENT ON AMERICAN ECONOMIC POLICY
TOWARD GERMANY

December 12, 1945.[1]

A. STATEMENT BY THE SECRETARY OF STATE

The Department of State has formulated a statement of its economic policy toward Germany for the guidance of the United States occupying authorities and has transmitted that statement to the War Department and to the Governments of the other occupying powers. The fundamenal policy was, of course, laid down at Potsdam. The purpose of this statement is to make clear the American conception of the meaning of the Potsdam Declaration as it bears on present and impending economic issues in Germany.

The position of Germany in the present world picture must be looked at broadly against the whole background of recent history. For six years Germany has ruthlessly imposed war and destruction on Europe and the world. The Nazis who ruled there for more than a decade are now defeated, discredited and have been or are being rooted from positions of power. The final stages of war caused vast movements of Germans within their own country, and peace has permitted the return to their homes of millions of foreign laborers who had been enslaved in German mines and factories. The insistence of the Nazis on continuing the war to the bitter end caused enormous destruction to German cities, transport facilities and other capital of the country. These are the basic reasons for the present position of Germany, a position for which the Germans themselves are primarily responsible. German industrial production will for some time be low and her people ill-fed even if there were no occupation and no reparations program.

The Potsdam Declaration involves three stages in the return of Germany to normal economic conditions. The first covers the German economy from the surrender of the armed forces, last May, to at least the end of the present winter. In this interval our broad purposes are to ensure that our policy in Germany makes the maximum possible contribution to recovery in areas recently liberated from Germany and, positively, to set up a structure that will provide for the future recovery of Germany in conformity with the principles agreed to at Potsdam.

Within these broad objectives four principal immediate aims are these:

First, to increase to the greatest possible extent the export of coal from Germany to liberated areas. The rate of economic recovery in Europe depends upon the coal supplies available over this winter; and it is our intention to maintain the policy of hastening the recovery of liberated areas, even at the cost of delaying recovery in Germany.

Second, to use the months before spring to set up and to set into motion, in conjunction with our Allies, the machinery necessary to execute the reparations and disarmament programs laid down and agreed at Potsdam. A considerable part of the statement just issued is directed to making clear the technical basis on which we believe the reparations calculation should be made. This calculation, which requires definition of the initial postwar German economy, must be completed before February 2, 1946.

---

[1] Released to the press December 12. Department of State, *Bulletin,* Vol. XIII (1945), pp. 960-965.

Third, to set up German administrative agencies which would operate under close policy control of the occupying authorities in the fields of finance, transport, communications, foreign trade, and industry. Such agencies, explicitly required by the terms of the Potsdam agreement, must operate if Germany is to be treated as an economic unit and if we are to move forward to German recovery and to the eventual termination of military occupation.

Fourth, to prevent mass starvation in Germany. Throughout Europe there are many areas where the level of diet is at or close to starvation. In terms of world supply and of food shipments from the United States, liberated areas must enjoy a higher priority than Germany throughout this first post-war winter. The United States policy, in collaboration with its Allies, is to see that sufficient food is available in Germany to avoid mass starvation. At the moment the calory level for the normal German consumer has been established at 1,550 per day. This requires substantial imports of foodstuffs into Germany, especially of wheat; and for its own zones of Germany and Berlin the United States is now importing wheat to achieve this level. The bulk of the German population has been eating more than 1,550 calories daily, either because they can supplement the ration from foodstuffs available in the countryside, or because their work justifies a ration level higher than that of the normal consumer, as in the case of coal miners. In the major cities, and especially Berlin, however, a food problem exists and is particularly severe during the winter months. One thousand, five hundred and fifty calories is not sufficient to sustain in health a population over a long period of time, but as a basic level for the normal consumer it should prevent mass starvation in Germany this winter. If a higher level for the normal consumer is judged to be required and if it is justified by food standards in liberated areas, the ration level in Germany may be raised by agreement among the four occupying powers.

In short, this will be an exceedingly hard winter for Germany, although only slightly more difficult than for certain of the liberated areas. A softening of American policy toward the feeding of German civilians and toward the allocation of coal exports from Germany, while it would ease the difficult task of the four occupying authorities, could largely be at the expense of the liberated areas. We are, however, constructively preparing for the second stage in German economic policy, which should begin some time next spring.

In this second stage, it is envisaged that Germany will gradually recover. Simultaneously with the removal of plants under reparation, plants will be earmarked for retention; and as fuel and raw materials become available, German industry which is permitted to remain will be gradually reactivated and the broken transport system revived. Although coal exports from Germany will continue, the probable expansion in coal output should permit larger allocations in coal to the German economy, after the end of the winter. German industrial production will then increase and German exports should begin to approach a level where they can finance necessary imports and gradually repay the occupying forces for their outlays in the present emergency period.

The third stage of economic development will follow after the period of reparation removals, which under the terms of the Potsdam Declaration must be completed by February 2, 1948. The resources left to Germany at that time will be available to promote improvement of the German standard of living to a level equal to that of the rest of continental Europe other than the Soviet Union and the United Kingdom. Housing and transport will recover more rapidly than

in the previous stages of economic development. In general, the German people will during this period recover control over their economy subject to such residual limitations as the occupying powers decide to impose. These limitations, which will be determined by agreement among the occupying powers, should, in the opinion of this Government, be designed solely to prevent German rearmament and not to restrict or reduce the German standard of living.

In all these stages it must be borne in mind that the present occupying powers, as well as many other nations, have suffered severely from German aggression, have played a large role in the German defeat and have an enduring interest in the postwar settlement of Germany. The settlement agreed at Potsdam requires the shifting of boundaries in the East and the movement of several million Germans from other countries. That settlement also requires, in the interests of European rehabilitation and security, the removal from Germany of a large part of the industrial warmaking capacity which never served the German civilian, but which, from 1933 on, served to prepare for war and to make war. In the words of the Potsdam Declaration:

"It is not the intention of the Allies to destroy or enslave the German people. It is the intention of the Allies that the German people be given the opportunity to prepare for the eventual reconstruction of their life on a democratic and peaceful basis. If their own efforts are steadily directed to this end, it will be possible for them in due course to take their place among the free and peaceful peoples of the world."

B. STATE DEPARTMENT STATEMENT ON REPARATIONS SETTLEMENT AND PEACETIME ECONOMY OF GERMANY

(1) The determination of the amount and character of industrial capital equipment unnecessary for the German peacetime economy which is to be made by the Allied Control Council prior to February 2, 1946, has the limited purposes of eliminating the existing German war potential and deciding the volume of available reparation from the three western zones of occupation.

(a) The task of the Allied Control Council is to eliminate German industrial capacity to produce finished arms, ammunition, implements of war, aircraft and sea-going ships, either by removing such capacity as reparation or by destroying it, and to effectuate a drastic reduction in the capacities of the metallurgical, machinery and chemical[2] industries. The present determination, however, is not designed to impose permanent limitations on the German economy. The volume of permitted industrial production of a peacetime character will be subject to constant review after February 2, 1946; and final Allied decisions regarding restrictions to be maintained on German industrial capacity and production will not be made until the framing of the peace settlement with Germany.

(b) While reparation removals will undoubtedly retard Germany's economic recovery, the United States intends, ultimately, in cooperation with its Allies, to permit the German people under a peaceful democratic government of their

---

[2]The phrases "machine industry" and "machine manufacturing industry" in the Berlin Declaration should be interpreted broadly. The parallel language from J.C.S. 1067 covers machine-tool, automotive, and radio and electrical industries. It is suggested that the phrases should be interpreted to cover "metal-working industry," or, in British terminology, heavy and light engineering. The words "chemical industry" should be interpreted to include particularly that part of the industry which is devoted, or can be readily converted, to war production, and to exclude potash and salt industries, which should be included with extractive industries.

own choice to develop their own resources and to work toward a higher standard of living subject only to such restrictions designed to prevent production of armaments as may be laid down in the peace settlement.

(2) It is in the interest of the United States to abide strictly by the terms of the Berlin Declaration which imposes a severe reparation obligation on Germany in order to:

(a) weaken effectively the economic base from which war industry could be derived until a peaceful democratic Government is firmly established in Germany;

(b) provide material assistance to United Nations countries which have suffered from Nazi aggression and which now face tasks of rehabilitation and reconstruction from the damage of war;

(c) insure that, in the recovery from economic chaos left by war in Europe, the aggressor nation, Germany, shall not reconstitute a peacetime standard of living at an earlier date than the countries ravaged by German arms.

(3) The security interest of the United States and its Allies requires the destruction in Germany of such industrial capital equipment as cannot be removed as reparation and as can only be used for the production of armaments or of metallurgical, machinery or chemical products in excess of the peacetime needs of the German economy. It is not, however, the intention of the United States wantonly to destroy German structures and installations which can readily be used for permitted peacetime industrial activities or for temporary shelter. It will evidently be necessary to destroy specialized installations and structures used in shipbuilding, aircraft, armaments, explosives and certain chemicals which cannot be removed as reparation. Non-specialized installations and structures in the same fields may have to be destroyed in substantial part, if not desired as reparation, in cases of integrated industrial complexes the layout of which is such as substantially to facilitate reconversion from peacetime to war purposes at some later date. Finally, in removing equipment from plants declared available for reparation, no consideration should be given to withholding portions of the equipment desired by a reparation recipient in order to retain remaining installations and structures in more effective condition for peacetime uses. Within these limits, however, the reparation and security policies of the United States are not designed to result in punitive destruction of capital equipment of value to the German peacetime economy.

(4) For the purpose of determining the industrial capacity of the peacetime German economy, thus eliminating its war potential—the real basis on which the amount and character of reparation removals are to be calculated—it should be assumed that the geographical limits of Germany are those in conformity with provisions of the Berlin Declaration, i.e., those of the Altreich less the territory east of the Oder-Neisse line.

(5) The Berlin Declaration furnishes as a guide to removals of industrial equipment as reparation the concept of a balanced peacetime German economy capable of providing the German people with a standard of living not in excess of the European average (excluding the United Kingdom and the Union of Soviet Socialist Republics). In the view of the Department of State the Berlin Declaration is not intended to force a reduction in German living standards except as such reduction is required to enable Germany to meet her reparation payments. In effect, the Berlin Declaration merely provides that Germany's obligation to make reparation for the war damage which her aggression caused

to other countries should not be reduced in order to enable Germany to maintain a standard of living above the European average. The Department of State further interprets the standard-of-living criterion to refer to the year immediately following the two-year period of reparation removals. For the purpose of meeting this requirement, German industrial capacity after reparation removals should be physically capable of producing a standard of living equivalent to the European average in, say, 1948. Given the difficult problems of administration and economic organization which the German peacetime economy will still face in 1948, it may be doubted that industrial equipment remaining in Germany at that time will in fact produce at full capacity, so that the standard of living realized in Germany is likely for some time to fall short of the European average.

(6) It may be assumed that the European standard of living in 1948 would approximate the average standard of living over the period 1930-38. If this assumption be adopted, the German standard of living chosen as a basis for estimating the industrial capital equipment to remain in Germany could be arrived at by use of German consumption data in a year in which the German standard of living, as measured by national income indices, most closely approximated the 1930-38 average in Europe. The German consumption standard in the year selected should be subject to adjustments upwards or downwards to compensate for any over-all difference between the German standard in the year selected and the European average. Past consumption records defined as suggested above are meant only as a general guide. They would require the following further adjustments:

(a) Provision for change in population between year selected and 1948.

(b) Adjustment to allow for notable deviations in pattern of German consumption in selected year from normal pattern.

(c) Allowance to enable the German people to make good, at reasonable rates of reconstruction, the wide-spread damage to buildings in Germany, and to the transport system as scaled down to meet the requirements of the German peacetime economy. It is suggested that sufficient additional resources beyond those required to provide the adjusted output of the selected year should be left to overcome the building shortage in twenty years and to effect repairs to structures on rail and road transport systems over five years.

(d) Sufficient resources should be left to Germany to enable that country, after completion of industrial removals and reactivation of remaining resources, to exist without external assistance. This topic is more fully treated below.

(7) In planning the peacetime German economy, the interests of the United States are confined to the industrial disarmament of Germany and to the provision of a balanced economic position at the standard of living indicated. The United States does not seek to eliminate or weaken German industries of a peaceful character, in which Germany has produced effectively for world markets, for the purpose of protecting American markets from German goods, aiding American exports, or for any other selfish advantage. Similarly the United States is opposed to the attempt of any other country to use the industrial disarmament plan of the Berlin Declaration to its own commercial ends at the expense of a peacetime German economy. It is our desire to see Germany's economy geared to a world system and not an autarchical system.

(8) In determining the volume of removals for reparation purposes, the United States should not approve removals on such a scale that Germany would

be unable, owing to a shortage of capital equipment, to export goods in sufficient quantities to pay for essential imports. Thus capacity should be left to enable Germany to produce for export goods which yield enough foreign exchange to pay for the imports required for a standard of living equal to the average in Europe, excluding the United Kingdom and the Union of Soviet Socialist Republics. In this connection, the following points should be stressed:

(a) In determining the amount of capital equipment to be retained in Germany, provision need be made for capacity to produce exports sufficient to pay for estimated current imports. No allowance should be made in German export industry to provide capacity to pay for externally incurred occupation costs, including imports of goods consumed by forces of occupation, and troop pay not expended in Germany.

(b) The provision in the Berlin Declaration which stipulates that in organizing the German economy "primary emphasis shall be given to the development of agricultural and peaceful domestic industries" requires that the maximum possible provision be made for exports from sources other than the metal, machinery, and chemical industries.

(c) It is implicitly recognized in the Berlin Declaration that the policy of industrial capital equipment removals and the restriction of exports in the fields of metals, machinery and chemicals will require countries which have previously depended on Germany as a source of these products to obtain them elsewhere. Since capacity in the metal, machinery and chemical industries in excess of German peacetime needs is to be transferred to countries entitled to receive reparation from Germany, it is expected that the industrial capacity lost in Germany will after an interval be recovered in large part elsewhere in the world, and for the most part in Europe. But it should be borne in mind that the industry removed from Germany will in the main replace industry destroyed by the Germans and will not be sufficient to meet the prewar demand. It should be emphasized, however, that any effort toward industrial recovery in Germany must not be permitted to retard reconstruction in European countries which have suffered from German aggression.

(d) In determining the amount of capacity required to strike an export-import balance, the United States and other occupying powers cannot in fact guarantee that the export-import balance will be achieved. Their responsibility is only to provide reasonable opportunity for the attainment of balance at the agreed minimum level of standard of living. In fixing the amount of industrial capacity necessary for export, the provision of margins of safety is unnecessary if Germany's export potential is estimated on a reasonable basis. It should be noted that, if resources are left to enable Germany to make good her war damage and depreciation in housing and transport over certain numbers of years as suggested in paragraph 5 (d), extension of the period in which such deficits are liquidated would in case of need make some additional capacity available for production of export goods.

(9) The necessity which devolves upon the United States and other occupying powers to finance imports into Germany and possibly to pay for such imports in the next few years does not arise in the first instance from the policy of reparation removals agreed upon at Potsdam. The German economy was brought virtually to a standstill by Germany's defeat, which produced an almost complete breakdown of transport, economic organization, administration, and direction. If no removals of industrial capital equipment were attempted, Ger-

many would still require United Nations aid in financing and possibly in paying for minimum imports necessary to prevent disease and unrest. Even after substantial capital removals have been completed, it is doubtful that the German economy can operate for some time up to the limits of remaining industrial capacity, due to the limited availability of fuel, food, raw materials, and the slow progress which can be made in filling the gap left by the Nazis in the economic and political organization of Germany. It is possible, and even likely, that the physical transport of reparation removals will limit transport capacity available for recovery of the German economy and for the expansion of exports. It is in this respect only, however, that the reparation policy laid down in the Berlin Declaration may require the United Nations to finance German imports for a longer period, or to pay for them in greater degree, than if no provision for reparation from Germany had been made.

(10) During the next two years the United States and other occupying powers must finance minimum essential imports into Germany to the extent that exports from stocks and current production do not suffice to cover the cost of such imports. Since the Berlin Declaration makes no provision with respect to the German standard of living in the period of occupation, the occupying powers are not obliged to provide imports sufficient for the attainment in Germany of a standard of living equal to the European average. The present standard of supply in Germany, so far as the United States is concerned, is still governed by the "disease and unrest" formula. Under the conditions set forth in paragraph 9, it will prove desirable to extend the type and volume of imports into Germany not only because of our interest in avoiding disease and unrest endangering our occupying forces but also because of our interest in reactivating selected German export industries which would yield a volume of foreign exchange, and as far as possible to repay the past outlays of the occupying powers on imports. If, when the time comes for the conclusion of a peace treaty with Germany, there remains a backlog of unpaid imports, the occupying powers will have to decide whether or not to impose on Germany an obligation to pay off the accumulated deficit.

(11) For the immediate future, and certainly until next spring, military government authorities should concentrate on the repair of transport, emergency repair of housing and essential utilities, and the maximization of coal and agricultural production. Some coal will of course be required in Germany to effect the minimum repairs of transport, housing, and utilities called for in existing directives. As long as coal and raw materials remain in short supply in Europe, however, it is United States policy to make them available in maximum quantities for the revival of industrial output in liberated areas.

The maximization of coal exports in accordance with existing directives will make it impossible to allocate within Germany coal sufficient to attain a significant volume of industrial production and over the coming winter it will limit activity even in fields directly related to repair of transport, housing and utilities and to agriculture.

If and when the coal crisis in Europe is surmounted—perhaps by next spring —it will be possible to review the situation and ascertain whether larger amounts of German coal can be allocated for essential industrial production in Germany, and in particular for the selective reactivation of German export industries. The possibilities in this direction will depend not only on the satisfaction of coal requirements in liberated areas, but also on the success of military government authorities in raising German coal output and restoring the German transport system.

Meanwhile, military government authorities should survey the fuel and raw material requirements of German industries capable of supplying essential civilian goods and of manufacturing for export so that, as soon as coal and raw materials can be made available, a program for selective reactivation of remaining industrial capacity in Germany can get underway. In formulating this program, attempt must be made to give priority to industries which in relation to expenditures of fuel and raw materials will contribute most toward striking an ultimate export-import balance in Germany, as well as to the satisfaction of the most pressing internal requirements of the German economy.

(12) The role of the occupying authorities in the process of German revival should, in general, be that of providing and setting the conditions within which the Germans themselves assume responsibility for the performance of the German economy. To this end, the occupying authorities should devote primary attention in planning revival to the development of German administrative machinery, not only in the fields of intrazonal production and trade but in interzonal and international trade, and in the application of common policies in transport, agriculture, banking, currency, taxation, etc.

As one aspect of this process, denazification should be satisfactorily completed during the present period. For the rest, great importance attaches to the conclusion within the Allied Control Council of agreements governing policies to be followed in various aspects of the German economy enumerated and devising interzonal German machinery for their application.

XVII
MOSCOW COMMUNIQUÉ OF DECEMBER 27, 1945[1]

At the meeting which took place in Moscow from December 16 to December 26, 1945 of the Ministers of Foreign Affairs of the Union of Soviet Socialist Republics, the United States of America and the United Kingdom, agreement was reached on the following questions:

II
FAR EASTERN COMMISSION AND ALLIED COUNCIL FOR JAPAN

A. FAR EASTERN COMMISSION

Agreement was reached, with the concurrence of China, for the establishment of a Far Eastern Commission to take the place of the Far Eastern Advisory Commission. The Terms of Reference for the Far Eastern Commission are as follows:

I. *Establishment of the Commission*

A Far Eastern Commission is hereby established composed of the representatives of the Union of Soviet Socialist Republics, United Kingdom, United States, China, France, the Netherlands, Canada, Australia, New Zealand, India, and the Philippine Commonwealth.

---

[1]Only Sections II and III are reprinted here. For full text see Department of State, *Bulletin*, Vol. XIII (1945), pp. 1027-32.

II. *Functions*

A. The functions of the Far Eastern Commission shall be:

1. To formulate the policies, principles, and standards in conformity with which the fulfillment by Japan of its obligations under the Terms of Surrender may be accomplished.

2. To review, on the request of any member, any directive issued to the Supreme Commander for the Allied Powers or any action taken by the Supreme Commander involving policy decisions within the jurisdiction of the Commission.

3. To consider such other matters as may be assigned to it by agreement among the participating Governments reached in accordance with the voting procedure provided for in Article V-2 hereunder.

B. The Commission shall not make recommendations with regard to the conduct of military operations nor with regard to territorial adjustments.

C. The Commission in its activities will proceed from the fact that there has been formed an Allied Council for Japan and will respect existing control machinery in Japan, including the chain of command from the United States Government to the Supreme Commander and the Supreme Commander's command of occupation forces.

III. *Functions of the United States Government*

1. The United States Government shall prepare directives in accordance with policy decisions of the Commission and shall transmit them to the Supreme Commander through the appropriate United States Government agency. The Supreme Commander shall be charged with the implementation of the directives which express the policy decisions of the Commission.

2. If the Commission decides that any directive or action reviewed in accordance with Article II-A-2 should be modified, its decision shall be regarded as a policy decision.

3. The United States Government may issue interim directives to the Supreme Commander pending action by the Commission whenever urgent matters arise not covered by policies already formulated by the Commission; provided that any directives dealing with fundamental changes in the Japanese constitutional structure or in the regime of control, or dealing with a change in the Japanese Government as a whole will be issued only following consultation and following the attainment of agreement in the Far Eastern Commission.

4. All directives issued shall be filed with the Commission.

IV. *Other Methods of Consultation*

The establishment of the Commission shall not preclude the use of other methods of consultation on Far Eastern issues by the participating Governments.

V. *Composition*

1. The Far Eastern Commission shall consist of one representative of each of the States party to this agreement. The membership of the Commission may be increased by agreement among the participating Powers as conditions warrant by the addition of representatives of other United Nations in the Far East or having territories therein. The Commission shall provide for full and adequate consultations, as occasion may require, with representatives of the United Nations

not members of the Commission in regard to matters before the Commission which are are of particular concern to such nations.

2. The Commission may take action by less than unanimous vote provided that action shall have the concurrence of at least a majority of all the representatives of the four following Powers: United States, United Kingdom, Union of Soviet Socialist Republics and China.

VI. *Location and Organization*

1. The Far Eastern Commission shall have its headquarters in Washington. It may meet at other places as occasion requires, including Tokyo, if and when it deems it desirable to do so. It may make such arrangements through the Chairman as may be practicable for consultation with the Supreme Commander for the Allied Powers.

2. Each representative on the Commission may be accompanied by an appropriate staff comprising both civilian and military representation.

3. The Commission shall organize its secretariat, appoint such committtees as may be deemed advisable, and otherwise perfect its organization and procedure.

VII. *Termination*

The Far Eastern Commission shall cease to function when a decision to that effect is taken by the concurrence of at least a majority of all the representatives including the representatives of the four following Powers: United States, United Kingdom, Union of Soviet Socialist Republics and China. Prior to the termination of its functions the Commission shall transfer to any interim or permanent security organization of which the participating governments are members those functions which may appropriately be transferred.

It was agreed that the Government of the United States on behalf of the four Powers should present the Terms of Reference to the other Governments specified in Article I and invite them to participate in the Commission on the revised basis.

B. ALLIED COUNCIL FOR JAPAN

The following agreement was also reached, with the concurrence of China, for the establishment of an Allied Council for Japan:

1. There shall be established an Allied Council with its seat in Tokyo under the chairmanship of the Supreme Commander for the Allied Powers (or his Deputy) for the purpose of consulting with and advising the Supreme Commander in regard to the implementation of the Terms of Surrender, the occupation and control of Japan, and of directives supplementary thereto; and for the purpose of exercising the control authority herein granted.

2. The membership of the Allied Council shall consist of the Supreme Commander (or his Deputy) who shall be Chairman and United States member; a Union of Soviet Socialist Republics member; a Chinese member; and a member representing jointly the United Kingdom, Australia, New Zealand, and India.

3. Each member shall be entitled to have an appropriate staff consisting of military and civilian advisers.

4. The Allied Council shall meet not less often than once every two weeks.

5. The Supreme Commander shall issue all orders for the implementation

of the Terms of Surrender, the occupation and control of Japan, and directives supplementary thereto. In all cases action will be carried out under and through the Supreme Commander who is the sole executive authority for the Allied Powers in Japan. He will consult and advise with the Council in advance of the issuance of orders on matters of substance, the exigencies of the situation permitting. His decisions upon these matters shall be controlling.

6. If, regarding the implementation of policy decisions of the Far Eastern Commission on questions concerning a change in the regime of control, fundamental changes in the Japanese constitutional structure, and a change in the Japanese Government as a whole, a member of the Council disagrees with the Supreme Commander (or his Deputy), the Supreme Commander will withhold the issuance of orders on these questions pending agreement thereon in the Far Eastern Commission.

7. In cases of necessity the Supreme Commander may take decisions concerning the change of individual Ministers of the Japanese Government, or concerning the filling of vacancies created by the resignation of individual cabinet members, after appropriate preliminary consultation with the representatives of the other Allied Powers on the Allied Council.

III

KOREA

1. With a view to the re-establishment of Korea as an independent state, the creation of conditions for developing the country on democratic principles and the earliest possible liquidation of the disastrous results of the protracted Japanese domination in Korea, there shall be set up a provisional Korean democratic government which shall take all the necessary steps for developing the industry, transport and agriculture of Korea and the national culture of the Korean people.

2. In order to assist the formation of a provisional Korean government and with a view to the preliminary elaboration of the appropriate measures, there shall be established a Joint Commission consisting of representatives of the United States command in southern Korea and the Soviet command in northern Korea. In preparing their proposals the Commission shall consult with the Korean democratic parties and social organizations. The recommendations worked out by the Commission shall be presented for the consideration of the Governments of the Union of Soviet Socialist Republics, China, the United Kingdom and the United States prior to final decision by the two Governments represented on the Joint Commission.

3. It shall be the task of the Joint Commission, with the participation of the provisional Korean government and of the Korean democratic organizations to work out measures also for helping and assisting (trusteeship) the political, economic and social progress of the Korean people, the development of democratic self-government and the establishment of the national independence of Korea.

The proposals of the Joint Commission shall be submitted, following consultation with the provisional Korean Government for the joint consideration of the Governments of the United States, Union of Soviet Socialist Republics, United Kingdom and China for the working out of an agreement concerning a four-power trusteeship of Korea for a period of up to five years.

4. For the consideration of urgent problems affecting both southern and northern Korea and for the elaboration of measures establishing permanent coordination in administrative-economic matters between the United States command in southern Korea and the Soviet command in northern Korea, a conference of the representatives of the United States and Soviet commands in Korea shall be convened within a period of two weeks.

XVIII
PLAN OF THE ALLIED CONTROL COUNCIL FOR REPARATIONS AND THE LEVEL OF POST-WAR GERMAN ECONOMY
March 26, 1946[2]

The plan for reparations and the level of postwar German economy in accordance with the Berlin protocol:

1. In accordance with the Berlin protocol the Allied Control Council is to determine the amount and character of the industrial capital equipment unnecessary for the German peace economy and therefore available for reparations. The guiding principles regarding the plan for reparations and the level of the post-war German economy, in accordance with the Berlin protocol, are:

(a) Elimination of the German war potential and the industrial disarmament of Germany.

(b) Payment of reparations to the countries which had suffered from German aggression.

(c) Development of agriculture and peaceful industries.

(d) Maintenance in Germany of average living standards not exceeding the average standard of living of European countries (excluding the United Kingdom and the Union of Soviet Socialist Republics).

(e) Retention in Germany, after payment of reparations, of sufficient resources to enable her to maintain herself without external assistance.

2. In accordance with these principles, the basic elements of the plan have been accepted. The assumptions of the plan are:

(a) That the population of postwar Germany will be 66.5 millions.

(b) That Germany will be treated as a single economic unit.

(c) That exports from Germany will be acceptable in the international markets.

Prohibited Industries

1. In order to eliminate Germany's war potential, the production of arms, ammunition, and implements of war as well as all types of aircraft and sea-going ships is prohibited and will be prevented.

2. All industrial capital equipment for the production of the following items is to be eliminated:

(a) Synthetic gasoline and oil.

(b) Synthetic rubber.

(c) Synthetic ammonia.

(d) Ball and taper-roller bearings.

(e) Heavy machine tools of certain types.

---

[2]The Plan was adopted by the Allied Control Council in Berlin on March 26, 1946 and released to the press in Berlin March 28, in Washington April 1, 1946. Department of State, *Bulletin,* Vol. XIV (1946), pp. 636-639.

(f) Heavy tractors.
(g) Primary aluminum.
(h) Magnesium.
(i) Beryllium.
(j) Vanadium produced from Thomas Slags.
(k) Radioactive materials.
(l) Hydrogen peroxide above 50 percent strength.
(m) Specific war chemicals and gases.
(n) Radio transmitting equipment.

Facilities for the production of synthetic gasoline and oil, synthetic ammonia and synthetic rubber, and ball and taper-roller bearings will be temporarily retained to meet domestic requirements until the necessary imports are available and can be paid for.

Restricted Industries, Metallurgical Industries

1. Steel

(a) The production capacity of the steel industry to be left in Germany should be 7,500,000 ingot tons. This figure to be subject to review for further reduction should this appear necessary.

(b) The allowable production of steel in Germany should not exceed 5,800,-000 ingot tons in any future year without the specific approval of the Allied Control Council, but this figure will be subject to annual review by the Control Council.

(c) The steel plants to be left in Germany under the above program should, as far as practicable, be the older ones.

2. Non-ferrous metals. The annual consumption of non-ferrous metals (including exports of products containing these metals) is fixed at the following quantities:

Copper	140,000	tons
Zinc	135,000	tons
Lead	120,000	tons
Tin	8,000	tons
Nickel	1,750	tons

Chemical Industries

1. Basic chemicals. In the basic-chemical industries there will be retained 40 percent of the 1936 production capacity (measured by sales in 1936 values). This group includes the following basic chemicals: nitrogen, phosphate, calcium carbide, sulphuric acid, alkalies, and chlorine. In addition, to obtain the required quantities of fertilizer for agriculture, existing capacity for the production of nitrogen through the synthetic-ammonia process will be retained until the necessary imports of nitrogen are available and can be paid for.

2. Other chemicals. Capacity will be retained for the group of other chemical production in the amount of 70 percent of the 1936 production capacity (measured by sales in 1936 values). This group includes chemicals for building supplies, consumer-goods items, plastics, industrial supplies, and other miscellaneous chemical products.

3. Dyestuffs, pharmaceuticals, and synthetic fibers. In the pharmaceutical industry there will be retained capacity for the annual production of 80 percent

of the 1936 production (measured by sales in 1936 values). Capacity will be retained to produce annually 36,000 tons of dyestuffs and 185,000 tons of synthetic fibers.

Machine Manufacturing and Engineering

1. Machine tools. For the machine-tool industry there will be retained 11.4 percent of 1938 capacity, with additional restrictions on the type and size of machine tools which may be produced.

2. Heavy engineering. In the heavy-engineering industries there will be retained 31 percent of 1938 capacity. These industries produce metallurgical equipment, heavy mining machinery, material-handling plants, heavy power equipment (boilers and turbines, prime movers, heavy compressors, and turbo-blowers and turbopumps).

3. Other mechanical engineering. In other mechanical-engineering industries there will be retained 50 percent of 1938 capacity. This group produces constructional equipment, textile machinery, consumer-goods equipment, engineering small tools, food-processing equipment, woodworking machines, and other machines and apparatus.

4. Electroengineering. In the electroengineering industries there will be retained 50 percent of 1938 production capacity (based on sales in 1936 values). Capacity to produce heavy electrical equipment is to be reduced to 30 percent of 1938 production or 40,000,000 reichsmarks (1936 value). Heavy electrical equipment is defined as generators and converters, 6,000 kw. and over; high-tension switch gear; and large transformers, 1,500 kva and over. Electroengineering, other than heavy electrical equipment, includes electric lamps and light fittings, installation materials, electric heating and domestic appliances, cables and wires, telephone and telegraph apparatus, domestic radios, and other electrical equipment. Export of specified types of radio receiving sets is forbidden.

Transport Engineering

1. Transportation industry.

(a) In the automotive industry capacity will be retained to produce annually 80,000 automobiles, including 40,000 passenger cars, 40,000 trucks, and 4,000 light road tractors.

(b) Capacity will be retained to produce annually 10,000 motorcycles with cylinder sizes between 60 and 250 cc. Production of motorcycles with cylinder sizes of more than 250 cc. is prohibited.

(c) In the locomotive industry available capacity will be used exclusively for the repair of the existing stock of locomotives in order to build up a pool of 15,000 locomotives in 1949. A decision will be made later as to the production of new locomotives after 1949.

(d) Sufficient capacity will be retained to produce annually 30,000 freight cars, 1,350 passenger coaches, and 400 luggage vans.

2. Agricultural machinery. To permit maximization of agriculture, capacity will be retained for an annual production of 10,000 light agricultural tractors. Existing capacity for the production of other agricultural equipment, estimated at 80 percent of 1938 levels, is to be retained, subject to restrictions on the type and power of the equipment which may be produced.

3. Spare parts. In estimating capacities there will be taken into account the production of normal quantities of spare parts for transport and agricultural machinery.

4. Optics and precision instruments. Capacity will be retained to produce precision instruments in the value of 340,000,000 reichsmarks (1936 value), of which 220,000,000 reichsmarks is estimated as required for domestic use and 120,000,000 reichsmarks for export. A further limitation for this industry is possible, subject to the recommendation of the Committee for the Liquidation of German War Potential.

Mining Industries

1. Coal. Until the Control Council otherwise decides, coal production will be maximized as far as mining supplies and transport will allow. The minimum production is estimated at 155,000,000 tons (hard coal equivalent), including at least 45,000,000 tons for export. The necessary supplies and services to this end will be arranged to give the maximum production of coal.

2. Potash. The production of potash is estimated at over 100 percent of the 1938 level.

Electric Power

There will be retained an installed capacity of 9,000,000 kw.

Cement

Capacity will be retained to produce 8,000,000 tons of cement annually.

Other Industries

1. The estimated levels of the following industries have been calculated as shown as necessary for the German economy in 1949:

(a) Rubber. 50,000 tons, including 20,000 tons from reclaimed rubber and 30,000 tons from imports.

(b) Pulp, paper, and printing. 2,129,000 tons, based on 26 kg. per head per annum in 1949 plus 400,000 tons for export.

(c) Textiles and clothing industries. 665,000 tons of fiber, based on 10 kg. per head for 1949 and including 2 kg. for export.

(d) Boots and shoes. 113,000,000 pairs, based on 1.7 pairs per head in 1949 (figure excludes needs of occupying forces).
Production may exceed the above estimates in this paragraph (other industries) unless otherwise determined by the Control Council.

2. Building. No level will be determined for 1949. The industry will be free to develop within the limits of available resources and the licensing system.

3. Building-materials industries (including cement). Existing capacity will be retained. Production will be in accordance with building licensing and export requirements.

4. Other unrestricted industries. For the following industries no levels have been determined for 1949. These industries are free to develop within the limitations of available resources. These industries are as follows:

(a) Furniture and woodwork.
(b) Flat glass, bottle glass, and domestic glass.
(c) Ceramics.
(d) Bicycles.
(e) Motorbicycles under 60 cc.
(f) Potash.

General Level of Industry

It is estimated that the general effect of the plan is a reduction in the level of industry as a whole to a figure about 50 or 55 percent of the prewar level in 1938 (excluding building and building-materials industries).

Exports and Imports

The following agreement has been reached with respect to exports and imports:

(a) That the value of exports from Germany shall be planned as 3,000,-000,000 reichsmarks (1936 value) for 1949, and that sufficient industrial capacity shall be retained to produce goods to this value and to cover the internal requirements in Germany in accordance with the Potsdam Declaration.

(b) That approved imports will not exceed 3,000,000,000 reichsmarks (1936 value), as compared with 4,200,000,000 reichsmarks in 1936.

(c) That of the total proceeds from exports it is estimated that nòt more than 1,500,000,000 reichsmarks can be utilized to pay for imports of food and fodder if this will be required, with the understanding that, after all imports approved by the Control Council are paid for, any portion of that sum not needed for food and fodder will be used to pay for costs of occupation, and services such as transport insurance, etc.

Determination of Capacities Available for Reparations

1. After the approval of this plan, the existing capacities of the separate branches of production shall be determined, and a list of enterprises available for reparations shall be compiled.

2. After decisions have been given on the matters now referred to the co-ordinating committee, the Economic Directorate would propose to prepare the final plan embodying these decisions and including a description of the various features of the plan, such as: disarmament, reparations, postwar German economy, and the German balance of trade.

XIX

ALLIED AGREEMENT ON CONTROL MACHINERY FOR AUSTRIA

June 28, 1946[1]

Preamble

The Governments of the United Kingdom of Great Britain and Northern Ireland, the United States of America, the Union of Soviet Socialist Republics and the Government of the French Republic (hereinafter called the four powers):

In view of the declaration issued at Moscow on November 1, 1943, in the name of the Governments of the United Kingdom, the United States of America and the Union of Soviet Socialist Republics, whereby the three governments announced their agreement that Austria should be liberated from German domination, and declared that they wished to see reestablished a free and independent Austria, and in view of the subsequent declaration issued at Algiers on November 16, 1943, by the French Committee of National Liberation concerning the independence of Austria;

Considering it necessary, in view of the establishment, as a result of free elec-

---

[1]The agreement was approved by the Allied Commission May 24, 1946 for reference to the four governments for final approval. It was officially signed by the four members of the Commission on June 28, 1946. Department of State, *Bulletin,* Vol. XV (1946), pp. 175-178.

tions held in Austria on November 25, 1945, of an Austrian Government recognized by the Four Powers, to redefine the nature and extent of the authority of the Austrian Government and of the functions of the Allied Organization and Forces in Austria and thereby to give effect to Article 14 of the agreement signed in the European Advisory Commission on July 4, 1945.

Have agreed as follows:

Article One

The authority of the Austrian Government shall extend fully throughout Austria, subject only to the following reservations:

(A) The Austrian Government and all subordinate Austrian authorities shall carry out such directions as they may receive from the Allied Commission.

(B) In regard to the matters specified in Article 5 below neither the Austrian Government nor any subordinate Austrian authority shall take action without the prior written consent of the Allied Commission.

Article Two

(A) The Allied Organization in Austria shall consist of: 1. An Allied Council, consisting of four high commissioners, one appointed by each of the Four Powers;

2. An Executive Committee, consisting of one high ranking representative of each of the high commissioners;

3. Staffs appointed respectively by the Four Powers, the whole organization being known as the Allied Commission for Austria.

(B) 1. The authority of the Allied Commission in matters affecting Austria as a whole shall be exercised by the Allied Council of the executive committee or the staffs appointed by the Four Powers when acting jointly.

2. The high commissioners shall within their respective zones ensure the execution of the decisions of the Allied Commission and supervise the execution of the directions of the central Austrian authorities.

3. The high commissioners shall also ensure within their respective zones that the actions of the Austrian Provincial authorities deriving from their autonomous functions do not conflict with the policy of the Allied Commission.

(C) The Allied Commission shall act only through the Austrian Government or other appropriate Austrian authorities except:

1. To maintain law and order if the Austrian authorities are unable to do so;

2. If the Austrian Government or other appropriate Austrian authorities do not carry out directions received from the Allied Commission;

3. Where, in the case of any of the subjects detailed in Article Five below, the Allied Commission acts directly.

(D) In the absence of action by the Allied Council, the four several high commissioners may act independently in their respective zones in any matter covered by subparagraphs 1 and 2 of subparagraph C of this article and by Article 5, and in any matter in respect of which power is conferred on them by the agreement to be made under Article 8 subparagraph A of this agreement.

(E) Forces of occupation furnished by the Four Powers will be stationed in the respective zones of occupation in Austria and Vienna as defined in the agreement on zones of occupation in Austria and the administration of the City of Vienna, signed in the European Advisory Commission on July 9, 1945.

Decisions of the Allied Council which requires implementation by the forces of occupation will be implemented by the latter in accordance with instructions from their respective high commissioners.

Article Three

The primary tasks of the Allied Commission for Austria shall be:

(A) To ensure the enforcement in Austria of the provisions of the Declaration on the Defeat of Germany signed at Berlin on June 5, 1945.

(B) To complete the separation of Austria from Germany, and to maintain the independent existence and integrity of the Austrian State, and pending the final definition of its frontiers to ensure respect for them as they were on December 31, 1937;

(C) To assist the Austrian Government to recreate a sound and democratic national life based on an efficient administration, stable economic and financial conditions and respect for law and order;

(D) To assist the freely elected government of Austria to assume as quickly as possible full control of the affairs of state in Austria.

(E) To ensure the institution of a progressive long-term educational program designed to eradicate all traces of Nazi ideology and to instill into Austrian youth democratic principles.

Article Four

(A) In order to facilitate the full exercises of the Austrian Government's authority equally in all zones and to promote the economic unity of Austria, the Allied Council will from the date of signature of this agreement ensure the removal of all remaining restrictions on the movement within Austria of persons, goods, or other traffic, except such as may be specifically prescribed by the Allied Council or required in frontier areas for the maintenance of effective control of international movements. The zonal boundaries will then have no other effect than as boundaries of the spheres of authority and responsibility of the respective high commissioners and the location of occupation troops.

(B) The Austrian Government may organize a customs and frontier administration, and the Allied Commission will take steps as soon as practicable to transfer to it customs and travel control functions concerning Austria which do not interfere with the military needs of the occupation forces.

Article Five

The following are the matters in regard to which the Allied Commission may act directly as provided in Article 2 (C) 3 above: 1. Demilitarization and disarmament (military, economic, industrial, technical and scientific).

2. The protection and security of the Allied Forces in Austria, and the fulfillment of their military needs in accordance with the agreement to be negotiated under Article 8 (A).

3. The protection, care and restitution of property belonging to the governments of any of the United Nations or their nationals.

4. The disposal of German property in accordance with the existing agreements between the Allies.

5. The early evacuation of, and exercise of judicial authority over prisoners of war and displaced persons.

6. The control of travel into and out of Austria until Austrian travel controls can be established.

7 (a). The tracing, arrest and handing over of any person wanted by one of the Four Powers or by the International Court for War Crimes and Crimes Against Humanity.

(b). The tracing, arrest and handing over of any person wanted by other United Nations for the crimes specified in the preceding paragraph and included in the lists of the United Nations Commission for War Crimes.

The Austrian Government will remain competent to try any other person accused of such crimes and coming within its jurisdiction subject to the Allied Council's right of control over prosecution and punishment for such crimes.

Article Six

(A) All legislative measures, as defined by the Allied Council, and international agreements which the Austrian Government wishes to make except agreements with one of the Four Powers, shall, before they take effect or are published in the State Gazette be submitted by the Austrian Government to the Allied Council. In the case of constitutional laws, the written approval of the Allied Council is required, before any such law may be published and put into effect. In the case of all other legislative measures and international agreements it may be assumed that the Allied Council has given its approval if within thirty-one days of the time of receipt by the Allied Commission it has not informed the Austrian Government that it objects to a legislative measure or an international agreement. Such legislative measure or international agreement may then be published and put into effect. The Austrian Government will inform the Allied Council of all international agreements entered into with one or more of the Four Powers.

(B) The Allied Council may at any time inform the Austrian Government or the appropriate Austrian authority of its disapproval of any of the legislative measures or administrative actions of the Government or of such authority, and may direct that the action in question shall be cancelled or amended.

Article Seven

The Austrian Government is free to establish diplomatic and consular relations with the Governments of the United Nations. The establishment of diplomatic and consular relations with other governments shall be subject to the prior approval of the Allied Council. Diplomatic missions in Vienna shall have the right to communicate directly with the Allied Council. Military missions accredited to the Allied Council shall be withdrawn as soon as their respective governments establish diplomatic relations with the Austrian Government, and in any case within two months of the signature of this agreement.

Article Eight

(A) A further agreement between the Four Powers shall be drawn up and communicated to the Austrian Government as soon as possible and within three months of this day's date defining the immunities of the members of the Allied Commission and of the forces in Austria of the Four Powers and the rights they shall enjoy to ensure their security and protection and the fulfillment of their military needs.

(B) Pending the conclusion of the further agreement required by Article 8(A) the existing rights and immunities of members of the Allied Commission and of the forces in Austria of the Four Powers, deriving either from the Declaration on the Defeat of Germany or from the powers of a Commander-in-Chief in the field, shall remain unimpaired.

Article Nine

(A) Members of the Allied Council, the Executive Committee and other staffs appointed by each of the Four Powers as part of the Allied Commission may either be civilian or military.

(B) Each of the Four Powers may appoint as its High Commissioner either the Commander-in-Chief of its forces in Austria or its diplomatic or political representative in Austria or such other official as it may care to nominate.

(C) Each High Commissioner may appoint a deputy to act for him in his absence.

(D) A High Commissioner may be assisted in the Allied Council by a political adviser and/or a military adviser who may be respectively the diplomatic or political representative of his government in Vienna or the Commander-in-Chief of the forces in Austria of his government.

(E) The Allied Council shall meet at least twice in each month or at the request of any member.

Article Ten

(A) Members of the Executive Committee, shall, when necessary, attend meetings of the Allied Council.

(B) The Executive Committee shall act on behalf of the Allied Council in matters delegated to it by the Council.

(C) The Executive Committee shall ensure that the decisions of the Allied Council and its own decisions are carried out.

(D) The Executive Committee shall coordinate the activities of the staffs of the Allied Commission.

Article Eleven

(A) The staffs of the Allied Commission in Vienna shall be organized in divisions matching one or more of the Austrian Ministries or departments with the addition of certain divisions not corresponding to any Austrian Ministry or department. The list of divisions is given in Annex 1 to this agreement; this organization may be changed at any time by the Allied Council.

(B) The divisions shall maintain contact with the appropriate departments of the Austrian Government and shall take such action and issue such directions as are within the policy approved by the Allied Council or the Executive Committee.

(C) The divisions shall report as necessary to the Executive Committee.

(D) At the head of each division there shall be four directors, one from each of the Four Powers, to be collectively known as the Directorate of that division. Directors of divisions or their representatives may attend meetings of the Allied Council or of the Executive Committee in which matters affecting the work of their divisions are being discussed. The four officials acting as the head of each division may appoint such temporary subcommittees as they deem desirable.

Article Twelve

The decisions of the Allied Council, Executive Committee, and other constituted bodies of the Allied Commission shall be unanimous.

The Chairmanship of the Allied Council, Executive Committee and directorates shall be held in rotation.

Article Thirteen

The existing Inter-Allied Command in Vienna, formerly known as the *Kommandatura*, shall continue to act as the instrument of the Allied Commission for affairs concerning Vienna as a whole until its functions in connection with civil administration can be handed over to the Vienna Municipality. These will be handed over progressively and as rapidly as possible. The form of supervision which will then be applied will be decided by the Allied Council. Meanwhile the Vienna Inter-Allied Command shall have the same relation to the municipal administration of Vienna as the Allied Commission has to the Austrian Government.

Article Fourteen

The present agreement shall come into operation as from this day's date and shall remain in force until it is revised or abrogated by agreement between the Four Powers. On the coming into effect of the present agreement the agreement signed in the European Advisory Commission on July 4, 1945, shall be abrogated. The Four Powers shall consult together not more than six months from this day's date with a view to its revision.

In witness whereof the present agreement has been signed on behalf of each of the Four Powers by its High Commissioner in Austria.

Done this 28th day of June 1946 at Vienna in quadruplicate in English, French, and in Russian, each text being equally authentic. A translation into German shall be agreed between the four High Commissioners and communicated by them as soon as possible to the Austrian Government.

XX

SHIPMENTS OF CIVILIAN SUPPLIES BY THE UNITED STATES ARMY[1]

[1]The tables on the following pages were obtained from the War Department. Table A shows cumulative U. S. shipments of civilian supplies to all areas through February 1946. Table B shows cumulative U. S. shipments of civilian supplies to European areas through 31 January 1946, broken down by commodities and by theaters of destination. And Table C shows U. S. civilian supply shipments to European areas, monthly, through 31 January 1946. Figures of shipments from the United States, of course, are not a completely reliable indication of overseas issues, since they do not reflect the occasional diversion of supplies upon arrival overseas, supplies shipped to theaters from other countries, or any indigenous supplies issued for relief purposes. Table D contains recent available figures on civilian supply issues in the European Theater from all sources and is cumulative through 30 September 1945.

A

U. S. CIVILIAN SUPPLY SHIPMENTS TO ALL AREAS COMBINED AND UNILATERAL RESPONSIBILITY CUMULATIVE THROUGH FEBRUARY 1946

Period	Long Tons			Landed Cost (Thousands)		
	All Areas	European Areas	Pacific Areas	All Areas	European Areas	Pacific Areas
ACTUAL—TOTAL	7,466,150	7,256,281	209,869	$1,073,593	$1,007,928	$65,665
1943—Total	161,086	161,086	0	28,429	28,429	0
1944—Total	1,393,321	1,376,910	16,411	196,378	191,555	4,823
1945—Total	5,742,389	5,548,936	193,453	816,355	755,541	60,814
Jan.	239,614	229,807	9,807	43,152	39,431	3,721
Feb.	296,967	289,121	7,846	48,822	46,119	2,703
Mar.	369,357	349,881	19,476	86,860	80,705	6,155
Apr.	489,915	470,786	19,129	101,339	96,057	5,282
May	873,271	837,063	36,208	142,338	130,992	11,346
June	841,123	822,016	19,107	99,833	92,187	7,646
July	1,205,583	1,186,399	19,184	110,079	102,878	7,201
Aug.	877,938	841,893	36,045	98,154	88,151	10,003
Sept.	283,579	258,330	25,249	51,615	45,864	5,751
Oct.	129,941	129,449	492	14,019	13,836	183
Nov.	61,302	60,846	456	10,322	10,040	282
Dec.	73,799	73,345	454	9,822	9,281	541
1946—Jan.	169,354	169,349	5	32,431	32,403	28

B

U. S. SHIPMENTS OF CIVILIAN SUPPLIES TO EUROPEAN AREAS[a] COMBINED AND UNILATERAL RESPONSIBILITY CUMULATIVE THROUGH 31 JANUARY 1946

(WEIGHT IN LONG TONS)

Commodity Group	Total	Mediterranean Theatre				European Theatre	
		Italy	French North Africa	Balkans	Austria	U.S. Zone	U.K. Zone
ALL COMMODITIES—TOTAL	7,256,281	2,851,905	355,963	370,777	132,840	2,001,828	1,542,968
Wheat and Flour	3,542,750	1,025,444	0	266,219	109,303	911,515	1,230,269
Other Foodstuffs	1,095,367	392,584	0	80,035	19,943	317,777	285,028
Medical & San. Supplies	17,709	10,278	0	1,017	11	2,022	4,381
Soap	26,085	8,080	0	223	584	12,535	4,663
Coal	2,403,051	1,329,876	355,963	0	0	717,212	0
Petroleum Products	a	a	a	a	a	a	a
Transportation Equip.	17,439	16,723	0	679	0	0	37
Communication Equip.	0	0	0	0	0	0	0
Other Utility Repair Equip. & Supplies	401	401	0	0	0	0	0
Clothing, Shoes & Text.	53,720	11,299	0	9,111	2,999	14,455	15,856
Agri. Supplies & Equip.	53,053	39,644	0	11,260	0	1,846	303
Ind. Repr. Equip. & Sup.	2,705	2,226	0	479	0	0	0
Other Equipment	0	0	0	0	0	0	0
Misc. Mf'd. End Products	42,254	13,767	0	1,643	0	24,413	2,431
Misc. Mat'ls. & Prods.	1,747	1,583	0	111	0	53	0

[a]Compiled from reports of Office, Fiscal Director and Technical Services. Covers ships sailing during this period. Excludes petroleum products and theatre transfers. Figures for French North Africa represent coal only; other shipments to Africa are included in Italy since they were reshipped to Italy or replaced previous loans to Italy. Data for Austria include shipments made through Mediterranean Theatre only.

C

U. S. CIVILIAN SUPPLY SHIPMENTS TO EUROPEAN AREAS[a] COMBINED AND UNILATERAL RESPONSIBILITY MONTHLY THROUGH 31 JANUARY 1946

(IN LONG TONS)

Month	Total	Mediterranean Theatre					European Theatre		
		Total	Italy	Balkans	Austria	French North Africa	Total	U. S. Zone	U. K. Zone
TOTAL	7,256,281	3,711,485	2,851,905	370,777	132,840	355,963	3,544,796	2,001,828	1,542,968
1943									
July	4,257	4,257	4,257	0	0	0	0	0	0
Aug.	3,338	3,338	3,338	0	0	0	0	0	0
Sept.	542	542	542	0	0	0	0	0	0
Oct.	12,918	12,918	12,918	0	0	0	0	0	0
Nov.	30,578	30,578	30,578	0	0	0	0	0	0
Dec.	109,461	109,461	109,461	0	0	0	0	0	0
1944									
Jan.	123,595	123,595	123,595	0	0	0	0	0	0
Feb.	127,207	127,207	127,207	0	0	0	0	0	0
Mar.	113,041	113,041	113,041	0	0	0	0	c	0
Apr.	87,794	87,794	80,628	0	0	7,166	0	0	0
May	76,844	76,839	27,802	0	0	49,037	5	5	0
June	85,123	84,401	28,916	0	0	55,485	722	592	130
July	111,276	91,061	7,038	0	0	84,023	20,215	20,208	7
Aug.	45,460	13,769	5,203	11	0	8,555	31,691	15,982	15,709
Sept.	170,755	133,518	7,019	0	0	126,499	37,237	16,273	20,964

U. S. CIVILIAN SUPPLY SHIPMENTS TO EUROPEAN AREAS[a] COMBINED AND UNILATERAL RESPONSIBILITY MONTHLY THROUGH 31 JANUARY 1946 (*Continued*)

(*IN LONG TONS*)

Month	Total	Mediterranean Theatre					European Theatre		
		Total	Italy	Balkans	Austria	French North Africa	Total	U.S. Zone	U.K. Zone
Oct.	65,133	59,563	34,365	0	0	25,198	5,570	5,466	104
Nov.	169,432	110,413	99,198	11,215	0	0	59,019	38,617	20,402
Dec.	201,250	168,893	141,440	27,453	0	0	32,357	8,179	24,178
1945									
Jan.	229,807	172,804	90,639	82,165	0	0	57,003	47,426	9,577
Feb.	289,121	137,917	59,049	78,868	0	0	151,204	99,643	51,561
Mar.	349,881	114,477	84,953	29,524	0	0	235,404	148,543	86,861
Apr.	470,786	142,583	102,937	39,646	0	0	328,203	149,415	178,788
May	837,063	403,049	329,438	73,611	0	0	434,014	269,791	164,223
June	822,016	328,677	294,907	28,284	5,486	0	493,339	373,748	119,591
July	1,186,399	385,096	384,539	0	557	0	801,303	373,489	427,814
Aug.	841,893	398,372	382,712	0	15,660	0	443,521	197,358	246,163
Sept.	258,330	155,757	129,838	0	25,919	0	102,573	14,717	87,856
Oct.	129,449	65,142	8,998	0	56,144	0	64,307	65	64,242
Nov.	60,846	30,246	8,513	0	21,733	0	30,600	25,246	5,354
Dec.	73,345	2,856	2,570	0	286	0	70,489	51,200	19,289
1946									
Jan.	169,349	23,329	16,274	0	7,055	0	146,020	145,865	155

[a]Compiled from reports of Office, Fiscal Director and Technical Services. Covers ships sailing during the calendar month. Excludes petroleum products and theatre transfers. Figures for French North Africa represent coal only; other shipments to Africa are included in Italy since they were reshipped to Italy or replaced previous loans to Italy. Data for Austria includes shipments made through Mediterranean Theatre only.

D

CIVILIAN SUPPLY ISSUES IN EUROPEAN THEATRE FROM ALL SOURCES OF SUPPLY CUMULATIVE THROUGH
30 SEPTEMBER 1945[a]

(IN NET LONG TONS)

Item	Total	France	Belgium	Nether-lands	Denmark	Luxem-bourg	Norway and Finmark	Germany and Austria[a]
ALL ITEMS	6,364,261	2,737,250	952,466	1,032,778	312,644	36,293	800,969	491,861
Wheat & Flour........	1,717,655	312,873	546,119	357,582	0	24,730	48,934	427,417
Other Foodstuffs	677,188	156,993	189,183	233,673	25,346	6,330	17,939	47,724
Med. & San. Supplies.....	5,289	1,646	811	1,460	10	59	352	951
Soap & Materials.........	29,159	12,491	4,131	10,223	0	382	904	1,028
Coal & Supplies..........	2,365,635	1,405,457	50,922	65,062	202,449	0	641,234	511
Petrol, Oil & Lub......	1,516,038	817,691	154,697	356,300	82,428	2,615	89,948	12,359
Clothing & Footwear......	10,752	2,304	2,309	3,402	0	235	1,392	1,110
Blankets & Comft's.	2,621	1,040	128	629	0	62	6	756
Agri. Equip. & Sup.......	33,703	23,776	2,370	3,107	2,411	1,784	250	5
Newsprint	6,170	2,972	1,796	1,306	0	96	0	0
Miscellaneous	51	7	0	34	0	0	10	0

[a]Source: CCALA report dated Nov. 1945. Excludes military and miscellaneous issues totaling 7,448 tons; also vehicles, tires and other items not reported by weight. Total for Germany and Austria includes 339,972 tons for Germany, 54,008 tons for Displaced Persons, 97,867 tons for U. S. Zone of Austria and 14 tons issued to Czechs. Food for France includes about 2,500 tons transferred by Fifteenth Army to French Zone for D. P.'s. Data for Norway are incomplete.

INDEX

83
88